GRANDAD BOATS
A FISHERMANS STORY
TREVOR JAMES POTTER

GRANDAD BOATS – A FISHERMANS STORY
Copyright © 2011 Trevor James Potter

ISBN: 978-1-907011-28-3

Published in the United Kingdom by
EsteemWorld Publications

British Library Cataloguing In Publication Data
A Record of this Publication is available from the British Library.

The right of Trevor James Potter to be identified as the Author of this Work has been asserted by him in accordance with the Copyright, Design and Patents Act 1988.

All rights reserved. Written permission must be secured from the publisher to use or reproduce any part of the book except for brief quotations in critical reviews, magazines or articles.

For further information or permission, address:
EsteemWorld Publications
United Kingdom.
E-mail: info@esteemworldpublications.com
www.esteemworldpublications.com

With thanks to Peter Fryer, from his photo album, Let Go found at amber online.com

Printed in Great Britain for EsteemWorld Publications

HI BEFORE I START THIS BOOK GOT TO TELL YOU.

It is not a book about fishing methods, nor is it a book on ships and boats, it is a fisherman's true tale of my life at sea and ashore, the up and the down side of life. It could be a miner or a postman or a welder.

But I was a fisherman, there are a lot of different types of boats and the way they catch fish.

My wife and brother and little sister Janice have told me I should explain the methods so the layman can understand what I am on about. (wish I knew), I have done TRAWLING/ ANCHOR BASHING/ PAIRE TRAWLING/ FLY SHOOTING/ GILL NETTING/ AND LINEING/

So here we go. If you are an x fisherman you can skip this bit. Trawling. The net is towed behind the boat and large otter boards (doors) are used to keep the net open, there are all sizes of doors depending on the boats horse power.

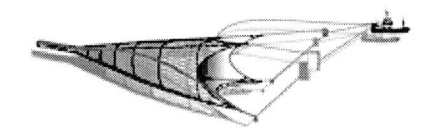

Next paire trawling now two boats are used to keep the net open, they can fish on bottom on hard ground, or mid water for herring or sprats & mackerel. Bottom for cod

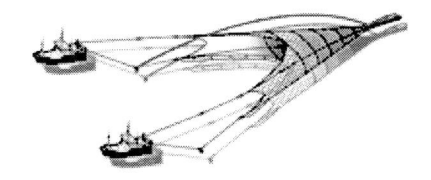

Next is anchor bashing and fly shooting

Seine netting ,setting of an anchored dhan from where first one drag line was set ,about one and a halve mile long then the net , and then another mile and a half of line , in a large triangular shape. Back at the dhan the boat then cliped up to the anchor. On hauling the winch that had three gears, hauled in the ropes ,slow at first then faster as the ropes closed together. The fish did not swim over the sandy cload the ropes made, as the gear was about closed third gear was then used and the net scooped up most of the fish.

Scottish fly shooting was almost the same except instead of an anchor they used the propeller to hold the boat still in the water, problem with that methord was you used a lot more diesel.

But the advantage was they can pull the net over very hard ground.

GILL NETTING.

Very straight forward, a curtin of net is anchored to the sea bed, normally about six feet high, as the fish hit the net they tried to turn away and the gills got tangled, the downfall of this type of fishing was if the nets were left on the sea bed to long the worms hould get to the fish so it was then unfit for sale.

    Glad that boring bit is over now on with the book.

PREFACE

Hi over the years when fishermen were sat in the pub, sharing yarns, funny and tragic, I was told by a lot of strangers that they had over heard us talking, and a few of them said that we could write a book.

I never thought anything about it; I am a fisherman, not a writer.

But in 2010, I buried my mother, she was 90, and I realised that I never knew my grand parents.

I was amazed to find out that my grand father had been killed by a horse, on a farm; this saddened me a bit, as I was never told about it.

When I told my wife Pat, she said," well Trev get it on paper, for your grand children, and their children".

Well this is the outcome. I started out trying to keep the book light hearted, but as in life the tragic and bad sides come out.

Any way this is dedicated to all the men I have sailed with, and to my children, and grand children.

Also to the many dockside workers that I got to know over the years.

The title of the book was given to me by my grandson Thomas Potter; he was born with autism, my son Barry used to bring him round to the flat a couple of times a week. It was full of pictures of fishing boats, also a couple of model boats.

Barry told me that one day when he arrived; Thomas said to him "Grand dad boats", so thank you Thomas for the title of my life.

I may have got some of the dates, and trips wrong, but to the best of my memory, and help from my old log books, everything you read is true.

Fishing is not a job, it is a way of life, and the boat, and the crew come first, the family second.

To lots of people that may sound hard, but the fact is that is fishing and I can turn into a seagull knowing that my children love me.

GRANDAD BOATS.   LOWESTOFT 1963

My life at sea

Wow we found a key! And it fitted every electricity meter in the street.so what
 Do you do?

Open them, small problem dad worked for eastern electricity board, so I said to Steven my mate? Get rid I don't want

To know, and he says I will trev {doh} so of I trot to school like a good lad, Try goon, Any way its mid-1963 and lots of ladies at work as well as husbands, and so lots of empty houses with doors left unlocked for the kids .

You can imagine when the meter man came; four houses had only used about £1.00 of electrickery in a month strange.

So next thing I know I was being interviewed by police, I kept stum then mother arrived noooo she said he will not lie to me and I did not.

Anyway Steve got two years in North Sea camp {borstal} and I got one year probation. What saved me was the fact I had signed up for a course at nautical training college, I wanted to be a fisherman and so I started July.

No way mother said I would rather he goes to prison, she did not like water, and the fact that Stevens father was lost at sea two years earlier on the m f v Susan m with all hands did not help. Good old dad stepped in and said he can go I give him one trip, And he will be begging to work ashore.

Wow dad confidence in your son? Or was he being crafty to calm mother, I think the latter,

Two weeks into training school thirty two lads from all over England, we were sent on an observation trip. Why waste money training no hopers? I was lucky my boat was only three years old, m f v Carlton Queen , some of the lads got older boats, up to twenty years old, well I thought I was that comes later.

The firm was very good they gave me new oil skins, thigh boots, and mattress, being fourteen they were all to big think I was four foot ten at the time, I say they gave me but if I stayed fishing it would come out of first years wages, a year to pay for protection gear how kind.

Any way sailing day arrives and off we go, I was a little bit shaky (shit scared) but I looked at the crew and they seemed relaxed, so everything must be ok. First three days I cannot remember was laid on the after deck being seasick, if I went into the galley or cabin up it came, apparently we were fishing now, I remember one of the crew telling me not to worry it was normal .NORMAL?

He says to me the first day or two you hope you won't die, the next two you will wish you had, (great help).

Any way I pulled round on day four or five, and the crew were kind enough to let me sort fish and shovel seaweed over the side, about one ton every four hours how kind. Not a lot to say about the trip because I cannot remember the drudgery of the next five days.

Two days to go and the big cleanup starts, after ten days of spilt co coa, and fag ash in the wheelhouse skipper kindly let me clean it .mostly brass and copper, it only took me seven or eight hours but you could see your face in it, then I was told to do the wireless cabin ,why do they call it that I sat looking at all the brass clamps that held the wires to the bulkhead, (wall) about three miles of it, and set about cleaning every brass clamp one at a time, (about three hundred) anyway after two days of cleaning brass

The skipper says son you done a great job, he then rewarded me with twenty fags, three shillings and six pence, not bad for two days work. Last day the mate asks me to clean his cabin, another five hours graft but he gave me ten shillings, fifty pence today!

Wow in two and a halve days of polishing I earned thirteen shillings and sixpence, (sixty five pence to you).

And I took the mick of the guys who sailed on the old boats, all their brass was painted over.

Anyway homeward bound, (thank you god) I do not know how much fish we had and to be honest I did not give a jot.

Down the fish room the mate was sorting out the crews Fry's, (fish to take home) all crew got the same twelve plaice, two small cod, Two haddock, and two lemon soles, not bad for twelve days work.

On docking the crew says come on titch, (small Trevor) were off for a pint? Me fourteen, o well I was a fisherman now.

Two drinks later I was thinking this job is great, but to be honest I never wanted to see another fishing boat as long as I lived.

Staggering to the bus stop ,I lived ten miles from the fish dock village called Beccles in Suffolk, with a kit bag full of smelly clothes, and an even smellier bag of fish ,it had been in a warm bar for two hours or so.

While waiting for the bus I made a solemn oath to myself never again, bus arrives and away home for a bath and two days sleep.

Walking into the kitchen mam was standing at the sink, dad was sat in his usual chair at the table, and well mother says "did you like it?" I looked at dad with a

Did he shit look on his face, so I had to tell the honest truth, yes ma it's a brilliant job, (doh) and the pride in dads face made me think, well I can finish the training course at least. And I did. Anyway I says to mam I got some fish but it has not been filleted, dad "did they not show you how"? No father on the boat we catch it not get it ready for the shop, "halve a job then?" No got to give the shore workers a job, dare not tell him his new fisherman could not fillet a fish to save his life, mam used to work at birds eye so she stood and done it all.

Brilliant forty fillets of fish and no fridge, never mind a freezer, closest thing mam had to a fridge to save fish was if it was snowing. So all heart, she tells my little sis to take some fish to Stevens ma, he is still in borstal by the way. Poor Janice, eight year old and she had to deliver fish to half the street, I never did ask her if anyone gave her anything for it, if I had her job I would have sold it to them, but in the sixty's everyone helped each other.

That came to be Jan's job every two weeks; if mother had sold the fish she could have bought a fridge.

Next day back to school, wondering how big the class would be after the other thirty five lads had finished their trips?

Twenty two, not bad at least there was thirteen sane lads left In England, for the next eight weeks we were taught basic seamanship, net mending, and navigation, I say navigate that was the skippers job, to get us from a to b. we had to learn how not to hit anything in between, and they taught us a short rime what was to be referred by me for the next thirty years, it goes'

   When both lights you see ahead starboard the wheel and show your red,

   When to your starboard red appear it is your duty to keep clear,

   So act with judgment says it proper, turn starboard, or port, or back, or stop her,

   But when upon your port is seen a steamers starboard light of green,

   There's not too much for you to do, for green to port keeps clear of you,

   Both in safety but in doubt get the f****** skipper out.

Not a lot to tell about the training, I enjoyed the net mending, and rigging all sorts of gear, but the classroom
Side of it was a bit boring, one thing it seemed strange to light up a cigarette in class, and I don't think it was the same as sneaking behind the bike shed.
As I am sat writing this bit, I look up at the picture of the lads in the class, forty seven years ago and wonder
How many are still with us, in my life ahead I was to fish from Lowestoft/Grimsby/and North Shields,
And you lose touch.

The boys of 1963.

Trevor middle right handsome or not? Well young and daft will do.
So end of school now to work on a real scale, October now and I am given my first real fisherman's berth.
Mfv Ormesby Queen compared to the Carlton she was a scrap heap, me thinks send them on a new boat at first,
Then give us the crap, o well it does the same job and a lot less brass to clean.
Starting wages for a decky learner was £5.00 per week and nine pence poundage .try to explain that well for every £100.00 the boat makes I get nine pence (old money). An average trip for a north sea trawler then was about £1500.00 so my bonus for two weeks worked out at around one hundred and forty pence,
Any way that's about sixty pence to you, drinks all round, I am earning £5.60 a week. O no forgot I still had to pay for oilskins and boots and mattress, be fair they only stopped five shillings a trip so I can still afford a night in.
I noticed the crew on the Ormesby were a lot younger than the Carlton, and mostly single lads, wonder if they only give the new boats to older married men. I remember I was only sea sick for two days this trip, or maybe they made me work hard and I never had time to think about it, after three or four days I was helping Nigel

the mate in the fish room, I say helping chopping ice as he called for it, but to be honest I enjoyed it.

Doing my bit made me feel one of the lads, after fish was stowed the mate and I, last off the deck, as I emerged from fish room I saw that the ton or more of weed still in the pound, (fish deck) I says to Nigel they (the three deck hands) have left the weed, laughing he says what do you think we carry you for. If you hurry there might be some grub left. So I hurried and there was cold fish and one slice of bread, to be fair it was about two inches thick and fresh baked.

By the way take a pot of tea up to the skipper before you turn in, we haul again in two hours, and don't forget to spit in it. Well I twigged on he was joking so I just made normal tea and took it up to the wheelhouse, thanks lad did you spit in it? No way I says I thought nige was joking, he smiled and said he was, and do not even think about it. Get to bed we haul in an hour so don't sleep in.

Trawling can get a bit boring at times hauling net every four hours, gutting washing and stowing fish, it can have its interesting times, like you never know what's coming up next like a treasure chest, or even a war time mine, or bomb, but when we hauled this time it was only a rip in the net. Two hours mending and no fish, so no money, one small up side is we get a full four hours sleep the next tow; yep Trev is way out again,

I told the lads it was my birthday, fourteen and a fisherman so initiation time, they tied me naked to the steering flat (a wooden cover over the rudder) covered me in grease then gave me a treacle shampoo, not nice, they go to bed and leave me for three hours thinking I must keep my gob shut, let them do the talking.

Wow my hero arrives, the mate Nigel cut me free and says get a shower lad, we haul in one hour and I need you fit for chopping ice, and dumping weed, what a thoughtful man, so half an hour in shower and got rid of all the grease and most of the treacle, the rest had to wait till I got home.

We never made a brilliant trip but it must have been ok, because on top of my wages and bonus five of the deck crew gave me £3.00 each, like wow more than my wages, and of Coarse my bag of fish, poor sister more deliveries I must treat her, cannot remember but she tells me I did.

I did two more trips on the Ormesby Queen and they went ok, but Christmas trip she developed engine trouble so all the crew had to look for new boats. Every man's wages stopped the day the engine did, that's fishing.

Dad was a keen carpenter as a hobby, so I decided to get him a very large tool kit for Christmas, not that rich got it out of mum's catalogue, very proud at last I can spend on them instead of them on the kids.

I think on the day he was very happy with it, but says to me I will not use a lot of these tools, if you had told me you were buying it I could have saved you some money by just buying the ones I need, ungrateful? No sensible, in years to come I would tell my sons the same.

We'll all that's the first year over, 1963 only twenty nine to go, promise it gets better (I hope) see you in 1964.

My first trawler mfv Carlton queen.

Nice boat too much brass, and I do not mean money.

Hi 1964

Christmas and New Year over, with a hangover at fourteen, what else sit in a café all day wasting money on slot machines, no thanks, any way time to find another skipper daft enough to take me to sea. And I did Joe Colson, (they called him cod eye Colson) do not know if that's because he caught lots of cod, or because he had bulging eyes the same as a cod. (Both I think) well he had a boat called Wilton Queen, sister ship to Carlton Queen, shit more brass, why me? But lucky me Joe was more interested in catching cod than cleaning brass. O he kept a very clean ship but not over the top, you must be getting bored with brass I know I am, so on to the fishing side of the tale.

There was about two hundred trawlers based in LT at the time, and Wilton was one of only two boats that went fishing for cod. LT was a flat fish market. Before I droan on I must explain LT, not cos I am too lazy to type Lowestoft, but all fishing boats have a registration letter and number. Example, first letter and then last
Letter of home port, so LT Lowestoft/ GY Grimsby/ PD Peterhead/ and so on all over, sometimes you get two ports the same, Hartlepool, HL/ also hull, so cannot have same, being tight (stingy) hull says ok we will just have H and you have HL/ anything to save paint, the one I cannot understand is north shields, their reg is SN/so back to front. Ah well they are Geordies so we will let that one go. (By the way best people I have ever worked with) any way got that explained, so save me a lot of typing for the rest of the tale.

I was very shocked at the net when we started fishing, it had big wheels on it, I ask why, the third hand laughs and says welcome to real fishing, the wheels (bobbins) are so we can tow over hard ground, lots of torn nets son so keep you're needles full, my needles??.

He then tells me yup as trainee it's my job to make sure all mending needles are full of twine, and that I have plenty of settings cut, what are settings? He looks at me and says did they not teach you anything at collage? They did but I had forgot that bit, a long setting is six foot of twine, and a short one is four foot, ok got it.

He then says you never want to hear skipper or mate to tell you to cut yourself a long one at the end of the trip, why? Because it is to tie your gear up with in other words sacked.

O another thing never ever leave the deck with an empty needle in the basket, not even one, ok got that is that after I have dumped the entire weed? Weed that's one thing you will never see on this boat, we never tow on soft ground, when we haul it is all clean fish. HALALULYA no weed I am never going to leave this boat, Trevs done it again mouth in operation brain not in gear.

Any way we hauled and the boson was spot on, NO WEED, all clean fish and mostly cod, and haddock, can't remember how many, it was a long time ago, well I done about eight month on the Wilton and learnt a lot. Hardly ever had a crew change, and the money was ok. Fishing can get boring so I will not go on about it, just a couple of amusing tales about the wilton and that's it, o and one very sad one which I will never forget, so let's start with the funny ones,

The crew on a LT trawler consists of skipper/mate/third hand (boson)/ three deck hands/ cook/chief engineer and second engineer/ships cat/ last of all trainee/ me.(we never had a cat it was their way of telling me how high I was rated.) The cook and two engineers did not go on deck, but still got a catch bonus, skipper came on deck if net was damaged (because he was fast with a mending needle).

Two short tales about cleaning the second engineer and I were having a chat one night in the mess deck, and I commented on how clean the cook was, clean he says I have been aboard three years and never has he touched this deck head, (ceiling to you) so I says why don't you say something to him, because he is a bad tempered old sod and tells me to look after my job and not his, (I can see the cooks point) the deck head was covered with white plastic, or something like it and made up of nine panels ,a two inch wooden beading covering the joins, looked smart, well to me it did, I don't know why but I had got the engineer wound up.

What does he do? Gets a brillo pad and cleans the middle section, wow what a difference must remember to stay out of the cook's way tomorrow. The next amusing tale is, off I go with my soapy water and brass cleaning gear, up to the wheelhouse to get it spotless for home, on arrival Joe says what's that for? Come to clean wheelhouse skipper, not on this boat I do my own dirty work; you are here to work the deck. (wow great) but seeing as you got the gear you can do the brass,(not so great) ok skipper when I have finished you will be able to see your face in them. "With my mush

I better not".

So now on to a not so funny part of fishing.
We were into about the seventh day of fishing, and Joe shouts out of wheelhouse "stow the gear lads we are going in" very strange but no one asked why, you never question the skipper, but by the tone of his voice we all knew it was not good. Everything stowed and we are under way for home, Joe tells the third hand, no scrubbing just a quick swill down.
I was told when we were under way that the chief engineer's son had been killed, aboard another trawler
While I was making tea for the watch, (men In wheelhouse) the chief says to me make us one son I want to talk to you, any way I came back to the galley and sat opposite him, strange I felt a bit afraid of him why? Any way he told me that he had begged his son not to go to sea, but he would not listen, so I am begging you son get out of this job as soon as we get in, it's a waste of a life, and you can do a lot better.
He then went on to tell me his wife had begged his son not to follow his dad, what happened to him I said
His reply shocked me, don't know for sure but Joe tells me he fell into the trawl winch, while they were hauling and there is not much left for us to bury, anyway son he has gone, you got to think of your life get out of trawling now. My first thought was my mother, but when you're young you think no it cannot happen to me. We arrive at LT and the chief gets ashore, another man jumped aboard and we sailed,
Not in port for even one hour, but like Joe said there is eight other families to keep, sad but true, I never saw the chief again, I did here he stopped ashore for his wife. Four days fishing and trip over.
(Hey Trev can you lighten up this yarn a bit, I will try but never forget the danger side of the job.)
After about nine trips on Wilton, and still trainee? I ask the skipper if I was ready for a deckhand's job as all the lads I was at college with were now fully paid deck hands; Joe says you tell me are you? I says I think I am, he looked at me with them scary cod eyes, and said lad when you are good enough to sail deckhand with me you can go third hand on any other boat out of LT, ok skipper but I am on the breadline with trainee's wages.
Ok lad the next job is yours, and as it happened it was the next trip.

One of the deckhands left and Trev is now a fully trained grown up fisherman, (or is he?)The only difference from trainee to deck hand was you got less sleep, as I now had to take a watch every third tow, but it was a great feeling, guess what we never had a trainee that trip, so Trev had to take charge of needle basket, o well at least my wages had trebled and just doing the same job.

Well trip over and landing day, I go to the office to get my pay. WHAT? With my money I also got the sack, strange never done anything amiss, I ask why, they told me the skipper says you're not ready, too young for responsibility. I never saw Joe in the next three or four years, but I do remember thinking skipper I have learnt more today than the whole of last year. (Never think you are irreplaceable) thank you Joe Colson.

Not a lot left about 1964, I left the queen boats and joined a different firm, spent the rest of the year on a boat called the Mincarlo, she was also boat about three year old, and amazingly she is now a museum in Lowestoft.

To end this year off, I did two trips in Mincarlo and the cook a man named Ray, who I was to become lifelong friends with, was telling me about the anchor boats in GY (Grimsby) he was on about all this money the crews made, more than a LT skipper, piss off Ray if it's that good why are you on this boat.

To be honest Trev I am keeping out of somebody's way for a while, a very angry husband, (bad lad Ray.)

Any way off he goes and returned to the mess deck with his last three settling sheets, (wage packets)

I was astounded; wow can you get me on one of them?

On landing day he phones Grimsby, I spoke to a man called Peter Moss, ships husband (man in charge of crewing) and he told me I can start any time I wanted. I decided to spend Christmas with my family and go to GY in the New Year. I will try anything being young and daft.

    We'll all see you next year, and as I promised it gets better (well dafter.)…

1965

Hi hope you all had a nice xmas, (easier to type) well Trev is on the train to GY, a bit nervous and a bit extrasited, never been this far from home in my life, had me orders off mum, and advice off dad, but forgot what they were, never mind they will be remembered in times to come.

I gets off the train at GY and my first impression was hey it's all pubs, and I was right, well there was loads of them, kit bag over my shoulder, I stopped a lad and ask him the way to the fish dock, easy mate jump in a taxi and tell him to take you to fish dock. (why did I not think of that) so thanks mate, I will try that, any way he then ask me can I lend him the price of a pint, so I gave him half crown, (twenty five pence) in 1965 that was two pints. But he was a helpful chap.

Well I jumps into a cab, says to the driver fish dock road please, Tom Sleights office, me having a broad Suffolk accent he thinks got one here, off we go and I sit back and take in the sights of GY.

About two minutes into the journey he stops the car, and said there you go mate two shillings please, thank you mate, I gave him six pence tip and out I gets. (It has just cost Trev five shillings to do a journey of two streets) must slow down on this spending lark.

Remember dad's advice now, "be careful with your money son and watch out for the bums" been in GY half an hour now and stood there thinking thanks dad, sound advice will never forget it again (but I did).

As I went into the office there was an argument going on between a fisherman and the ships husband, (Peter Moss.) by the way I was to find out nobody called him Peter, it was Mr. moss, he was well respected in GY fishing , because he was a very fare man, any way the argument was, the fisherman wanted a job and Mr. moss says no, you have failed to turn up for sailing three times in the last five years, so look to a smaller firm, we don't need you're sort, and the fisherman left slamming the door EXTRA hard behind him.

So what can I do for you young man? Hi I am Trevor Potter from LT we spoke on the phone, about a job on one of your boats, there not mine but I run them. I noticed that, how did you know that man had missed three boats in five years? Laughing he opened a filing cabinet and says you all go in here, good or bad. (

Interpol did not have a record file anywhere as good as Peters,) oops sorry Mr. Mosses.

So I have been on the phone to LT and they think highly of you, keep it that way. We have a boat sailing tomorrow and I have spoken to the skipper, told him you have only sailed on trawlers and he is willing to take you. Great, do you need any money? (an advance on my first trips wages), no thanks I have got enough for I night, Mr. moss kindly booked me into the fisherman's mission for one night but no breakfast, (no breakfast tight sods), he tells me be aboard at three am, three? Lad GY is a dock not a harbor, we sail when the tide allows us to open the gates. Ok Mr. Moss I will be there, well if you're not

You will need train fare back to LT, that's me told.

Well lad the Maxwell is taking ice about now so put your gear aboard and meet the skipper, he directs me to the ice berth, and off I trots. There were four or five boats taking on ice at the same time, the noise was deafening, in LT only one boat could take ice at a given time, in GY up to eight boats took on ice at one time, (amazing). Well I found the Maxwell, as I looked at it my first impression was GET ME HOME...

She was a wooden boat, (I am used to steel) halve the size of a trawler, and the fishing gear was nothing like I had ever seen before. Well Trev you come this far give it a try; (told you I was daft).

I jumped aboard and met an aged man in the wheelhouse, try garden shed, hi I am Trevor new crewman are you the skipper? He smiles at me years ago son I am the watchman, if you want the skipper try the Albion

Or the Humber, both pubs near the dock, ok thanks I can leave my kit bag aboard? Yep in the cabin thank you, so I started to walk aft, (the back end) then he says you never been on an anchor boat before have you? What makes you think that? Another smile because there is about 150 snibbies (anchor boats) in GY

And I have never seen one with the cabin aft. Ok of I go foreword to the sharp end and find the cabin, HELP, what have I done talk about small/ claustrophobic/ and dark/ well I won't bother. Next job is find the skipper sounds a better job anyway.

Leaving the docks I set about looking for the Albion, do not ask a fisherman, or get a taxi, so I ask a nice old lady, and she points me in the right direction, same street about five buildings up, (thanks for advice dad). I had been in dockside pubs in LT, so I was not worried about this one.

On entering I asked a semi sober chap, is the skipper of the Maxwell in? Canadian jack that's him, and he points him out; hi are you skipper of the Maxwell? Yes lad why? Hi my names Trevor and I have just signed on your boat, great what do you want to drink? Well how nice, lager please, he shouts to the barmaid get my new cook a lager (COOK?), sorry skipper I am the trainee not the cook, it's the same thing he says and never call me skipper, my name is Jack, taking a very large gulp of my lager I then tell him I have never sailed on an anchor boat, so to my mind I would rather do a trip just to work the job out as it is so different from trawling.

Lucky for you lad, we are four handed so I will ask Nev (Neville Best) to show you the ropes, never mind the ropes, the cooking is my worry. By the way Canadian Jack? He spoke broader Scottish than Billy Conally, I will ask about that later. Three or four drinks later someone in my head says, you are sailing at three in the morning, and have you had anything to eat? (no mum) just remembered the orders, so I gets a taxi to the fisherman's mission, the next street, sorry dad but I am a wee bit drunk, hey I just met the man and I am talking Scottish! Time to add a pic of an anchor basher/snibby. The Maxwell you can see the difference from her to the Carlton, if not your as daft as me, no offence meant you did pay for this book?

MAXWELL MY FIRST ANCHOR BOAT

Wake up lad its two o-clock, there is a cup of tea in my office, and the taxi will be here shortly, taxi? I never ordered one; no he says the firm did. They pay for it just to make sure you are on time, nice firm wish LT had been as thoughtful, I had to travel ten miles then, again the docks are in the next street.

Well I am not paying so bring it on, taxi arrives, massive hangover and in I get in, hello lads nice to meet you, the skipper says this is Trevor ,a daft pud (fisherman from LT) called us that because LT trawlers fed you on suet puddings every day. Apparently it gives you energy, wish I had one now.

We arrived at the Maxwell and the deckie cook says to me right Trev first job check all the stores are aboard, (food). He hands me the list he gave the office, says make sure as you stow them that nothing is missing, and if there is I says, Its three in the morning what can we do about it? No probs the grocer will be in the shop, he is there every tide time, all was there and stowed away.

The engine starts what a fright I got, I was used to an eight cylinder, this Danish engine had only two, well we let go and past the lock gates at four am. Nev says to me take Jack a cupper then get some sleep.

With my hangover I did not take any persuading.

Come on Trev you're on watch with me, ok Nev how will we both fit into the wheelhouse? Laughing he says you will, I will make breakfast. (Strange lad he was always laughing), I arrived in the garden shed and the mate, (Melly Cox) said to me hi never been anchor bashing before then? No but I am ok to leave alone, took watch on trawlers, ok how do you stop her if you have to? Ring stop on telegraph, he cracked up laughing, no telegraph, and if there was no one in engine room to answer it.

He then shows me the wheelhouse controls, amazing why did the trawlers not think of that, no engineers to pay, (in time to come they did). Melvin was a nice bloke any worries at all Trev blow the fog horn, and someone will be strait up, great no worries there then, I looks at all the equipment in the wheel house thinking to myself no radar? No echo sounder? (A thing what tells depth of water) and no radio, NO RADIO? What about if something goes wrong? Doo there was one in the cabin not room for it in the shed.

Well all went well and we arrive at fishing ground, as I said it's a totally different way of catching fish,

But this is not a book on fishing methods; it is a tale of my life at sea, mostly the funny side but also some sad ones, well that's life. One thing I could not get used to was calling the skipper Jack, he hated being called skipper, I ask Melly why and reply was that all snibbys are the same, we are a family Trev not a crew.

Very nice, and it turned out we were a very happy one, Nev says you're a lucky man Trev, why? There is well over a hundred and fifty snibbys in GY and Maxwell is always in the top ten earners. Great ££££,

I hope, and we did fish very well that trip, we filled her up with big cod in eight days, (get in there Trev) we landed three hundred kit, (UNITS OF TEN STONE) and made a massive £2400. Wow I never made that in the Wilton ever, sorry Joe, but there you go size isn't everything.

Up to the office on landing day the cashier tells me they must think a lot of you lad, why? The crew has given you a full cooks share, 8% after running costs; you would think I should remember how much I got

But to be honest I cannot, but I do know I had never seen that sort of wage before, slow down Trev it was a record trip for the Maxwell, do not expect this amount every trip.

While we were in dock, (a full week) I lived aboard the boat as I had not found lodgings yet, I went out with Nev most nights, and met a few of his buddies and girlfriends, I remember they were a nice crowd, but used a pub well away from the dockside, THE WHITE HEART, he told me the dock pubs were ok on a dinner time but not nights, too much trouble Trev, and never bring more than a tenner out with you, £10.00. I told him I was stopping aboard the boat until I find lodgings; make it snappy you will see enough of her at sea. Actually I know a good house if she has room, and she has a very good name with the fishermen, her son is on the snibbys bit of a lad but ok if you get to know him.

Amazing, next day I was told the mate ,Melly had gotten a skippers berth (job), and the new man was no other than Barry Jensen, his mother was the lady Nev was telling me about, after meeting him (in the pub)

Off we go to meet her. The house was spotless, and she seems a nice lady, its five pounds a week in or out no girls in the house, otherwise treat it as you're home. Three weeks at sea, and one ashore that hardly seems fair , but all washing done, and two meals a day, cannot really complain also there will be times that I was ashore for longer than a week.

Her name was Maria Jenson, but known to the fisherman as Polish Maria, don't ask I never did, also the reason for only two meals was she loved her dinner time in the pub. In those days all pubs closed at three. Also she says if I cooked a dinner, would you be home for it at mid day?, (true) and another thing call me Ma, very nice felt at home already, except my mother never went into a bar unless it was a special occasion. Do not get me wrong mum loved a whiskey now and then.

Any way I was to spend the next eighteen month aboard the Maxwell, and earn very good money. Here we go again, off to sea, a couple of stories to make you smile, at the end of every day the fish stowed and everything on deck made secure, (in case of a storm) we sat down to dinner, meat and veg one night, fish the next alternating.

Anchor boats did not fish in the dark, so after dinner the crew turn in, (go to bed) bet you know what I meant? I had to stay up to wash and clean the dishes, also make sure nothing was moving about in lockers

With the engine stopped all was quiet, if the lads heard any noises other than the ones they were used to, like a tin or bottle rolling about, I was soon told. One night I had finished all my jobs, filled the kettle (it held about two gallons of water) and put it on the coal stove, so it would be simmering in the morning,

Then off into my bunk, great a short read then off to sleepy byes, wrong again? Yes.

Every time the boat rolled to port we could hear a bottle clink, shit so out I gets and check every locker, moving things about, the banging noise stopped, great back to bed, half way through the first page of my comic bang clonk bang, nooooo, Jack shouts for fu** sake Trevor get it sorted, yes sir. I am a bit fed up by now, after checking every nook and cranny moving things that did not need to be moved, I sat on the seat locker beside Nevs bunk, and says to him I will give it five minutes to make sure I have stopped it.

Yep he says it's annoying when you cannot put your finger on it, or your foot, strange thing to say, then plonk/ ping/ bang/. You bustard / (spelt wrong on purpose) Nev.

On his foot he had a large pickle jar, and when she rolled to port he banged it on the side of his bunk, never did forgive him for that one, well I must have because in the years to come many a cook I sailed with spent ages hunting for the elusive bang, back in my bunk I could hear a chuckle from both the other bunks, I found it hard to get to sleep that night, (plotting my revenge) but it will come.

A few days later I thought it had brilliant Trev, they will never find this one, that night after dinner everything wedged up, I goes on deck to dump the dish water and stow the bucket, then put my big (well thought of) plan into operation, getting a hard plastic headline can, (a float for the net) I hung it over the side, just in line with Nevs bunk, when the boat rolled it would leave the water and bang on the side,

Bonk/bonk/ bonk, Jack shouts Trevor sort it now, sorry Jack it's on the deck and that's Nevs department, leaning out of my bunk smiling, I said your turn Nev, his reply? You hung it over there you cut it free, (shit!!!) out I get and boots back on, off I goes and stowed it away. How did you know what it was? Because it's one of the oldest ones in the book, you will have to try a lot harder than that mate, do not bother Trev, just admit defeat, with a mischievous mind like Nevs you will never win. I never did. The next day while we were hauling in the ropes I was stacking the forward one, and Nev the aft one, Barrys job was to stand in between the two and keep the gear level in the water, that job takes a lot of experience and a long time to grasp it, he went by the angle of the ropes by sight, also he would press down on them alternately, if one was harder to press than the other he would hold that arm out, if it was my rope I had to pull a lever on the coiler, (machine that coils the rope) bet you all worked that one out, sorry anyway that stopped the winch on my side, and Nevs rope would then catch up and the net would be level on the sea bed. All clever stuff, I thought once it was level it would stay like it, but no two winch drums heaved at the same speed, as the ropes closed together we hauled faster and faster until the net came to the surface.

Hope I have not been boring you all, but had to explain briefly about the gear for future tales, as we were heaving faster and the ropes had closed together, Barry puts out one finger on my side (that means stop for just very short time, (about a foot of rope) he kept repeating this signal, and I kept slacking my rope,

This went on about ten times in five minutes, Barry turns round and shouts at me, for fu** sake man concentrate. But I am Baz no need to get nasty about it, (Bas was very proud of his hauling skills) and again, slack/ slack/slack what is going on? This has never happened before well not this bad, PING it hit me like big Ben, (the bell) as I was slacking my rope Nev was doing the same to his. Is this man sane or what?

He did not harm the fishing, just the mate's pride, and me getting a rollicking but I was used to that; wish we had a ships cat.

Well another trip over, and nice to have a home to go to, and clean sheets great, as we tied up to the landing jetty, Barry says o no please, what Baz? Ma is down to meet us in, what's wrong with that? She has brought the bloody cat, there she stood with a cat on a lead, it does look funny I says, FUNNY its fuc****

Embarrassing, hi boys I met you in because I know our Barry will be off to the pub, and Trevor will feel strange coming home to a strange house alone.

Nice of her, but I was going for a pint with Bas first, well make it look good off I trots with ma and the cat home to her house for a bath and some dinner, (its nine pm) and I hated cats, well did not get on with them anyway, hate is a bit strong. Never got a pint that night, next morning bright as a button off we go down for our money, when I say bright, Baz and Nev were ill, serves them right drunkards.

Two or three trips later, down to sail about eight am, I had to tell Jack that Barry will not be down for sailing, as the night before he was arrested, (drunk and disorderly) in that case I will go to the office tell them to get a new man for tomorrow morning, you go to the grocers for a case of lager, so we can have a drink before the pub opens.

But Jack it's not his fault, yes it is, did we get arrested? No so there you go, also Jack said I like Barry and he is very good at his job, if I do not sack him for missing sailing time others will think I am a soft touch and will all start doing it, true as I was to find out into my skippers career . Next day we sailed with a new mate, I will call him Bob (change of name for reasons to come), he was about Jacks age and a bit of a misery, also a very lazy man, for some reason Nev and I did not take to him, but there you go you cannot love everybody.

On landing day after a very quiet trip I went down to the office to find out Nev had left the boat, (strange)so after getting my wages I went round the bars looking for Nev, I found him in the white knight, strange, we did not use that bar often, hi Nev what's wrong I have been told you left the boat, nothing bad I hope, yes I am not sailing with a child molester, how do you know he is?, it's all over the dock he has just come out of prison for interfering with his own daughter. Well Nev, tells Jack, no way I will just find another boat.

What does Trev do? Down to the office and tells Mr. Moss find me another boat, I am leaving the Maxwell, not you as well reason? Just fancy a change, nothing to do with the mate then? (Peter is not daft), just sign me off, and I will be down tomorrow to see what boats need a cook, Peter looks at me with his I know what it is about look, and says why do you two not just tell Jack and he will sort it out. No way we will not undermine the skipper, he gave him the job, who are we to tell him he is wrong, maybe he did not know about it.

Next day Nev, Baz and I were in a bar called the Kent, in walks BOB, walks over to our table and says you two bustards (spelt wrong) just got me the sack, Nev, no we did not we just left, so get out of my face before I do give you something, he looked at the three of us and decided to leave. (Sensible move) next day we all went down to the office, any jobs Mr. Moss, smiling well the Maxwell needs a crew and a mate if you're interested Barry. Get in there the goon show are back.

Jacks not daft, he knows how to run a happy ship, and it was for the remainder of that year, Get In.

Come November most of the snibbys tied up till end of January, short daylight, and bad weather, seemed the best time for a paint up, and jobs done, this year Jack decides to fish the Moray Firth for the winter months. Nev and Barry both says no thank you Jack already tried that, being daft I gave it a go, well what else can I do, (try going to see my family for a start).
But being Trev I went to Scotland, Nev says your mad Trev, its night fishing and bloody freezing up north, hey i am a hardened fisherman now, I can do it no bother (WRONG AGAIN), Barry went on a deep sea trawler, Nev had two month holiday, (and I said he was mad???), what would you pick? Two month ashore or two month fishing off the Scottish coast, yes you are right (ashore).
Well we sailed for Scotland the new mate was an old guy, Andy Gun, he was from a small harbor in the north of Scotland called Wick, that's a coincidence the skippers wife is from the same town, it took two days to steam up to the firth, on arrival guess where we docked for ice and fuel? YOU GOT IT WICK.
After loading up Andy and Jack are off to visit relations, when you finished the dishes meet us in the bar,
And hide the cabin key.
All done, hide the key and off to the pub, not many in wick so they were not hard to find, any way the bar we met up in had a sign saying, (I meant reading) if you can drink a whisky from every bottle on the optics.
There will be no charge; there was only ten bottles in a line, so that's easy, anybody can drink ten drams,
Andy noticing I had a whisky in front of me says to Jack, does the lad normally drink whisky? No rum why? Well he is on it now, shit Trev you have not have you? Not what? Taken the whisky challenge? Why not it is only ten singles, (dooo a single in Scotland is a double at home).
Let him try it, he has to learn says Andy, and I did try, after three or four that's the end of the story, and of course ME. Next morning I woke up on the wheel house deck, and a very damp cocoanut mat, staggering on to the deck, and being violently sick over the rail, (polluting Wick harbor!) I go forward to the cabin
And find it locked, strange where is the crew? I decided not to go looking for them just went into my bunk to die in peace.
Well I awoke a long time later that day, the skipper and mate were

sat at the cabin table having a fry up, god the smell of it made me ill all over, (never drink again trev), where did you two get to last night? Jack glares at me, then said slept at Andy's mothers because our stupid cook would not tell us where he had hidden the key, so why did you not take me? In your state she would have killed us, she was dead against the dreaded drink, and (I don't blame her). Daft yarn over off we go to do some fishing, and Nev was spot on night fishing off Scotland was a killer.

We landed every four days in Wick, we were at sea on Christmas day, and new year's eve (Hogmanay) in Scotland, and we stayed at sea, I began to suspect my best skipper had flipped, but as he said the fishing was too good to leave, also being the only boat fishing over the holidays the price on the market will be extra high, and it was. Brilliant i am now a tea total god fearing fisherman, well for now.

Hey i am in the wrong year see you all on next page.

1966

Hi again did you have a good new year, as you know I did (NOT), we fished until the end of January, then back home to sunny GY. Steaming home we had to put into Aberdeen for minor repairs, Jack decided to land the fish we had, because the forecast was storm force winds for the next two days.

After landing fish and taking on fuel he tells me to go to the office, to see what the prices were like, on the way back I passed a fish house with about ten lassies, (I can talk Scottish now) filleting the fish, one of them shouts me over and ask me why I had girls hair, (it was past my shoulders) I told her it is the sixties look. She then says to me can I have a lock off it, being daft as you already know I let her cut a small lock off the end, she was a nice lass and she did ask, so no probs? Wrong again trev. Next thing they all wanted a lock, can you picture me? Running along the quay side, and a hundred (well ten) fish wives chasing me with eight to ten inch blades in their hand. I shit myself, running to the boat I jumps aboard crying to my skipper, HELP! I looked up and the lassies were laughing fit to bust.

We sailed from Aberdeen the next day, and I promised myself I would never go back, but as it was I would return twice again in my life, 1975 as a skipper, and 2010 on my honeymoon, (yes you read it right), that was to be my best visit to the granite city.

Well here we are steaming home in a force ten storm, Jack tells me to keep about one mile off the land as the wind was from that direction and the swell was a lot smaller, (waves). Ok skipper rely on me, so off he goes to bed. BIG QUESTION, how does Trev stay one mile off with no radar. Of course common sense everything ok for the first hour or so, but then I noticed something strange.

The wind had changed direction, or the compass was acting up, not being a total idiot I looked at the chart (map), sorry there might be the odd one that does not know, and saw that we were coming across the firth of fourth.

Trevor thinks, (TRY DID NOT THINK) why go all that way in just to come back out again, if I just keep on this compass heading we will pick the land up again in a few miles or so, very good thinking in nice weather.

Not advisable in a raging storm, well I lost the land but found some ginorm0us waves. Along the deck came Andy, clambers into the wheelhouse "what the fu** is going on?" i am bypassing the firth Andy saves a lot of time, true sonny very true if we make it, he looked a bit concerned . That made me VERY concerned. O I just remembered the navigation poem from fishing college. How did it go again?

IF IN SAFTEY BUT IN DOUBT CALL THE FUC***G SKIPPER OUT.

We arrive home safely to GY, no thanks to me! And off I goes to Marias house, hope ma has still got a spare bed, she had. She also had ten weeks lodge money, £50.00 and gave it to me. You have not been staying here but I thought you would be broke after all that time up north. No ma we done very well also spent the holidays fishing. Jack spent New Year at sea? Yes ma, "what is that man turning into not the Jack I knew" well ma he said the fishing was too good to leave and he was right.

I gave ma £20.00 back for a drink and sent the remainder to Mum and dad for a Christmas drink, or whatever she wanted to spend it on, well another five month on Maxwell, then Jack tells me she was to be tied up for a new engine, and wheelhouse, (about time too). The office offered him a brand new boat, the ASHVILLE, but jack turned it down, he loved the Maxwell and did not want to leave her, I thought he was mad to turn down a new boat, but he says to me "Trev better the devil you know, plus the old girl has been good to me, fishing and weather wise" I can now see his point.

It took me a few years to realise that but never think new is best, tried and tested is.

Well with Maxwell tied up I decided to go home to LT for a spell, had not seen my family for eighteen month or so, o I had sent mother post cards on a regular basis, one every six month with out fail, plus we never had a telephone at home, (no working family did), so I decided to have a couple of days with Nev and the gang and then home.

As we sat in the White heart that evening a lad walked in with a sky blue suit on, I says to Nev you do not see that in GY very often, typical trawler man, got to show off, (Nev and his pals were into the mod style) to be honest so was Trev, I then tells him in LT nearly all the fishermen wore brightly coloured suits, with pleats in the jacket, and half moon pockets, some had silk lining in and I have even seen a couple of tartan ones. (There was a telly program about it). The lads in LT said on the program, twelve days working and sleeping in the same gear it was great to be seen clean and bright.

Well I would not be seen dead in one, says Nev, or me mate, dare not tell him I had three in wardrobe at home. One light blue with dark blue collar and cuffs / one black with red silk lining / and a bottle green one with orange lining.

Thankfully I had left them in LT where they were not out of place. Next day bags packed and train ticket in top pocket, off I goes back to LT. well that was plan A, decided to have a couple of pints with Nev before the train left, now do not let me miss it lads, it leaves at three, no problem you wont miss it, glad to see the back of you, (nice friends). Well I awoke in this coach on the train, feeling very ill, and there was only one other guy in it. You awake then lad? "Well half awake anyway."

By the way trains in them days had six seats in each coach, and a corridor all along one side, (if you cannot imagine it watch murder on the orient express), I ask this chap if he knew what time the train was due at York, as I had to change their for the LT, giving me a very strange look, are you sure you want York?,

I check my ticket and say yes definitely, got to change there. Well your mates who helped you onto the train asked me to wake you just before the train gets in to Edinburgh.

EDINBURGH!!! I will fu***ng kill him. (Ex pal Nev the busterd), well I gets off at the next stop, over the rail bridge with three bags, (they did not have little wheels on in those days) and gets the next train to York. As we pulled into GY I looks at my watch six pm, great I have been travelling for three hours and this is where I started, know what it is? Never did get Nev back, but he was such a great guy why bother.

Well back home to LT, well I says LT but I lived in a small town called Beccles, about ten mile from the docks (sorry harbour), and thought sod it taxi. It was well worth the money after the day I just spent travelling.

Hi mum, hi dad, hope you are all well, I am now mother said eighteen month away and only two postcards, no mum three, o that's ok then, why did I worry about my teenage son? Well Alan and Ivan are away a lot longer than me; do you get on to them when they come home? That's different they are in the R A F. also a lot older than sixteen, (seventeen mum), dad said "will you let him grow up mother he is not a child anymore" wow thanks dad.

Well mum saw all the good gear I had bought and the new tape recorder, also my bank book, well son its great to see you have been saving well, and not wasting your money on other people, and drink, no mum I only had the odd pint with the crew on landing days, (fingers crossed), Looking across at dad he had that old, tell that to the queen look on his face. How long are you planning on staying he said, well the boat is having a big refit, so I am not sure, but for a while I will go back on the trawlers from LT.

Mother says great fresh fish again.

Yes mum and your first gift off me will be a fridge. Got one says dad, (show off) Janice will be pleased a lot less deliveries to make.

No she was not, I only found out today that she got more money off the neighbours than I was earning as a trainee in 1963, did not tell me until today, on the phone (February 2011), wow how time fly's.

After a week or two ashore, catching up with my old school pals, I decided to go back to sea, I did not go to the queen boats, I found a berth on one of the Suffolk boats, very smart boats they were, on my first trip back, the Suffolk ??? (cannot remember) for some reason the skipper never took to me at all, maybe he did not like anchor men, or maybe he was just a big headed twat, (posh name for a c**t).

Any way does it matter? I was not really in love with him, so on landing day I got the sack, been sacked off better men than him, like Joe in Wilton queen, it ended up quite funny, if you get the sack off a LT trawler the office had to give you a weeks wages.

Any way they told me that skipper had a bad name for being above himself, and gave me a berth on SUFFOLK ENDEVOR, very new very posh, you will never guess the next bit, on sailing day I jumps aboard the Endeavour, and there was a prick hanging out of the wheelhouse window, yes the skipper who had sacked me off the last boat. You are joking, "I am NOT sailing with him" a bit of a dilemma, do I refuse to sail and get fined, or do another trip with him.

Best choice was refuse to sail with him, the ships husband told me that the skipper had been given the boat as her regular skipper had taken very ill, but the office did see my point, and I exchanged jobs with a deck hand off another boat, also sailing that day. So every body happy and off I go to sea, on the Suffolk punch, she was an older boat but the skipper was great. Flash Fletcher they called him, and turned out to be a great laugh to sail with, sadly not a lot of money, but you cannot have every thing.

It amazed me in years to come the single fisherman preferred to sail on a happy boat, with mediocre money, than a miserable boat with more money, I spent two or three trips with Flash on the punch but could not get used to only two clear days in harbour, so I left.

It became the normal thing with single men, two trips in a boat then leave and have a full week ashore, great.

Plus the more different skippers you sailed with, the more you learnt different ways of doing the job.

SUFFOLK PUNCH

There she is a very happy boat why cannot all skippers be as easy going as him, but I think power goes to some men's heads, while others respect the crew and get respect in return. Another thing I would remember as I got to go skipper myself.

Well as I said I never done more than two or three trips on the same boat, after all I did have a life to enjoy, it is not all about big money, (can you tell I am not married yet).so I left the Suffolk boats and joined Clione fishing, their boats were named after a group of islands called, Bermuda /Bahama/ Trinidad/St Kitts /Anguilla/ and lots more, I have named the ones I sailed on.

Well one day on deck, the skipper shouts out of the wheelhouse, I am going to put the match on loudspeaker. Very strange most trawlers would not put the speaker on for safety reasons, it was a football match! And I had as much interest in football as I did in turning gay, apparently it was a big match England v Germany, still no interest why not put some pop music on.

Well England won and the crew went mad, why all the fuss over a game? We have just won the world cup o great, (I did not know there was one); I know you all do not believe that last yarn, but on my parents grave I swear it is true. A couple of years ago my son Barry said to me, it must have been great dad,

What? To be around when we won the world cup. Sorry Baz I can not remember it, he looked at me in utter amazement. I did not have the faintest interest in football until I was about 45 years old,

Now I love it. I support Millwall because that was my fathers team (dad was an east ender), and very proud of it.

Well that's about it for this year, just one last trip springs to mind. On a boat called St Rose, the firm had just bought her from France, she was also the largest trawler I had sailed on, any way towing the net coming in dark we had to turn on the fishing lights, as the door of the switch board was opened we saw that every switch was labelled in French.

Easy flick a switch and see which light came on, very clever us fishermen? Any way steaming home the skipper shows us his list of jobs that needed doing by the shore gang.

On his list he had written PLEASE REMOVE ALL FRENCH LETTERS FROM THIS BOAT.

Are we all mad? It helps if you want to go fishing. One other thing springs to mind, my elder brother Ivan, (5 year older) was also in the RAF, the same as Alan, well Ivan was serving with the air sea rescue, he was the radio/ radar man, he asked me if I could get any fresh fish, as the crew had to live and do there own cooking on the base, so I did and when Ivan came home to mums I asked him if the lads enjoyed the fish.

He told me that they said thanks, and if ever my boat sinks in the early hours of the morning they would only dip me into the sea one time, instead of two for getting them out of bed.

What a grateful crew he had, but in times to come I would put my life in there capable hands, more than once, actually three times.

I sometimes think if the RAF can run air sea helicopters, why can't the royal navy run the lifeboats. O well government again, but I salute you all and thank you all, because without you I would not be typing this.

1967

Hello again, try not to bore you this year, I did another five month with the same firm and mostly boring.

A couple of short yarns, then on to bigger things, I sailed on a boat called St Georges,(that's the one they blew up in one of the James Bond films, (think it was live and let die) but it does not really matter.

Well, came in from sea and mum had made me a thick knit jumper, great, bright orange, not so great bless her. That will keep you warm at sea son, it did for just one trip, then one sunny day (no oilskins needed) I went on deck at hauling time with just welly boots and water proof apron on, (hey clothes as well) was not ready for the rubber look just yet.

Shooting the gear away, I clipped the wire to the trawl door,(they kept the net open while we were towing).

Next thing trev is over the side, very wet and very frightened , then there was one of the lads in the water with me, great back on the dry side of the boats rail, I was a bit shocked but mostly RELIEVED that I was still a fisherman, and not a sea gull. (fishermen come back as gulls in afterlife,) or so I have been told.

All safe and dry I asked what had happened, your jumper snagged up on the wire so I cut it free.

Believe this or not I cannot remember the mans name who saved my life, mum will not be happy all that time knitting, and now a big hole in the front, well she was great with the needles so she can soon mend it.

When I told her what happened she dumped it.

The other yarn is on one boat, I was sat in the mess deck and the lads were talking about this great book they had all read , it was a western called MONTY WALSH, (brilliant try it), it was not a bullshit story It was a very true to life yarn, well I did read it and lost a lot of sleep in doing so, but it was well worth it.

The book was about an aged cowboy and his past life.

Any way at the end on his gravestone it said ,   Here lies MONTY WALSH a good man with a horse, bit sad really but as I said great story.

At the end of every trip the boat got a good scrub down in and out, after washing all the paintwork the very last job was the deck. (wooden) the evening before arrival at LT, the decks were scrubbed and then covered with a powder called chloride of lime, (illegal now) and left to burn in, when it was washed down the next morning the deck was like new.

But as Trev was leaving the deck that night the bright spark decided to get a brush and write in the lime, you got it, here lies Monty Walsh good with a horse, thinking it will give the lads a smile in the morning,

Trev has done it again (thinking without help). Amazing next morning about one hour before arrival in LT the skippers voice comes over the intercom in the mess deck, very good lads now get it off before we get ashore.

Get what off? One of the lads asks "the lime stupid "replies the third hand so breakfast over oilskins on,

Off we go to wash the deck down, every one of the lads laughed when they saw the deck, very good, wish we could leave it like this, but no the lime had to be scrubbed off, and the decks came up brand spanking new. Well except foe the parts I had brushed the lime off the night before. The owners were not amused when we tied up, but there you go cannot keep everybody happy all the time, I wonder if that's why they let James Bond blow her up?.

.St Georges`

Well come about May I decided to make a change to my life, I had sailed with a few men who had been in the merchant navy, and the stories they told of different parts of the world made me think, why not?
So I gave it a go. I travelled down to London, and dad came with me, mainly to see his relations than look after me, (I hope).
On arrival we stayed at mums sister's house in Hackney, went to the pool, (merchant navy office) and after a strict medical, (held my balls told me to cough) and passed me fit. They then offered me two or three different firms to sail with, and I picked Shell UK, a tanker, trevs done it again, bulk carriers spend two or three days in every port, tankers about one. I was to fly out to Singapore in two weeks time, dad stayed for a week and I was left under aunt Floes wing for another week.
I got a very big surprise the week dad was there, as all my young life I had never seen dad touch a drink, (one bottle of brown with Christmas dinner), hardly made him an alcoholic, aunt flo worked in a bar called the pembuary tavern, so dad and I went down for a few pints each night, we played shove halfpenny, and darts, and that was when dad told me he supported Millwall FC. Also some of the other tales, he told me about his life in the army. (Dad was a regimental sergeant major).
He served in India in the First World War, and was stationed in England for the second war, in a prison of war camp just outside Beccles, that's how he met mum (thank god). At closing time each night we stayed back to wait for aunt flo to finish her jobs, then walk her home.
The second night, (trev half pissed) hey dad for a man who does not drink, you are still stone cold sober,
Smiling he said "son I told you I did not drink, but I never said I couldn't". Wow ime seventeen and only just got to know my father, and what a man!
Well dad goes home and I stayed in London for another week, I had to go to the pool again to get tickets and flight time, as I was there I met a guy from Glasgow, he had joined the same ship as me so after all the paperwork was sorted we went for a drink or two, seemed a decent sort, but to find out later a right nutter.
The ship I had signed on was called SS HYGROMIA twenty thousand ton, and shell had charted the flight for a full crew change.

Forty nine of us, and we flew out the next day, (trev has never been on an aeroplane before) but all was ok.

We took off from London and after half an hour the skipper came on the intercom, sorry captain came on the intercom, good morning we have a very small technical fault and will be landing in Amsterdam shortly, please fasten your seat belts. Now I have seen movies with small technical faults, hope this is not one of them. The steward came round with drinks; (shell u k) was paying so large rum and coke please.

We landed into Denmark and all seemed well, this flying lark is easy, no worries.

We were then told the plane had a faulty something or other, and we will be staying in Amsterdam for the night, we got booked into a posh hotel, had a nice dinner and then out to see the sights, I say sights where we went there was some right ones. O well next morning up with the larks, (or seagulls) and sat down to breakfast, before the flight to Bangkok in Thailand, wrong again we landed in Tashkent in Russia, more technical faults? No, thank you, just to refuel, (phew).

It was a strange encounter, when we gets off the plane instead of nice airport personnel with big phoney smiles, we were met by armed soldiers, with not so phoney grim faces, they led us to a wooden building and gave us tea and biscuits, (no vodka then) after a while we take to the sky again, bound for Thailand, this time no technical faults and we had ample petrol, (or whatever this thing used) to get there.

Great on the ground again and just a short flight to Singapore, we took off after about a two hour stop, as the bus took us to the plane I thought hold on this is not our slim line jet? No Trev, it is your x war time four engine propeller driven second hand Singapore air line pride of the fleet. I was expecting to see Buddy Holly air line painted on the side, (ask your dad). Any way it got us there ok.

On arrival they told us the ship was not going to dock in Singapore for at least ten days, and we would be staying at a hotel. Wow a holiday on full pay, what more can a man ask, I then received two weeks pay in cash, and was told to stay with at least one other crew member at night time,?? Now I have grown up I can see why.

A Singapore dollar was then worth about twenty five pence, (in your money), so two weeks money filled about five pockets in my jacket, one dollar would buy one bottle of tiger beer, with a little change, wow.

There was no choice of drink over there, it was tiger or spirits, my brother Alan was stationed at RAF base in Singapore at the time, so I decided to give him a surprise (shock) visit.

Alan is the eldest of the mob, about six year older than me, he did not know I had left fishing, so here we go, jumps into a cab and ask the driver to take me to RAF Changi or what ever it was called, his eyes lit up.

No please not another GY taxi ride, but it was the opposite, any way he drops me off outside the RAF base and said ten dollars please, it was a long drive so I had no complaint, off I trots, (god it is hot) so off I dawdles, to the main gate and says to the guy, do you know a sergeant Alan Potter please? Well if he did not he should not be on guard, but nice to be polite. "Yes do you want to see him", (no I just wondered if you knew him), yes please I am his younger brother, but I would like to surprise him, will you tell him he is wanted at the gate.

Better than that lad, you go and sit in the café and I will tell him someone wants to see him after his shift, he finishes in an hour, "do not tell him who" ok lad no problem good as done, when Alan walked in I could see the amazed look on his face, wow hi Trev what are you doing here? I told him the fish prices were crap in LT so the office told us to land here, Alan's not that daft, "come on Trev for once in your life try and be serious", (he is asking a lot).

Well I tells him I had given fishing a rest and joined a shell tanker, he is now convinced I was daft, any way I stopped at Alan's house for two nights and always remember taking my two nephews to the shop,

I bought them a Batman &Robin outfit, they loved them. Mark and Ian if you're reading this can you remember that far back? Sister in law Noreen did not believe my fish story, another one not daft enough.

Alan asked me how I found the RAF base, easy got a taxi, how much? Ten dollars, WHAT?
Trev here you do not ask the fare, you just give them one dollar at most, what if he wants more? Tell him to piss off and walk away, strange setup but bruv knows best, he then tells me the taxi's over there were more like a bus at home, wave a cab down then tell him your destination, if he says no wait for another one. (Very strange set up).
Well I gets into a cab back to the town, Singapore was a lot smaller in the sixties, on the way we picked up another two passengers going into town, on arrival out I get and handed the driver one dollar, and he thanked me, with a large smile he said "hurry up and get sun tan" walking to the hotel I was thinking what a strange thing to say!, on arrival I asks one of the crew why he had said that, laughing "trev mate you are pearly white, and all the locals know you are new to this part of the world, and so an easy touch, green as grass.
Hold on in one afternoon I was told I was white and green and advised to turn brown, I am beginning to feel like one of them lizard things that change colour to blend in.
Also if I ever meet that taxi driver again HE IS DEAD ten hard worked for dollars.
Yes dad I remember your advice, but it must be the heat.

Well holiday over the SS Hygromia had docked and we joined her the next day, wow look at the size of it,

I am glad I do not have to paint it, doe Trevs wrong again! The lads all laughing tell me that is exactly what we do have to do. (Shit), yes the first job was washing all the paintwork, then we had to chip all the rusty bits, then dab with red lead, and after that paint it.

Might as well get a job on the fourth bridge. Well our first run was to the Persian gulf, not bad but tankers mostly tied up away from any built up areas, well the only thing I can tell you about that run was I got to build a sandcastle in the desert, the Hygromia was very posh compared to a trawler, I had my own cabin, and there was a swimming pool on the aft deck, I say swimming pool, it was about eighteen foot by eight foot, and five foot deep.

Big enough for me as I could not swim, (did I not mention that small detail), well if you spend your life one or two hundred mile off shore, what is the point in learning, better to get it over with, do not get me wrong I can doggy paddle, just to keep me up if I fell overboard, but more than that I did not see the point.

Some body once ask me how far can you swim. My answer was whatever the depth of water is.

Next stop Bangkok in Thailand, still great and we got to spend two nights there, one night off we goes (five of us), to a bar called the mosquito club, there they sold tai whisky for one dollar a bottle, wow

I will try that, shit I forgot about the hangover in Scotland!

Any way it got very foggy after that, the next morning I was summoned to the wheelhouse WHOOPS! Bridge, I forgot I am on a ship now not a boat, well as I walked in the third mate said to me "remember getting aboard last night? Well err no sir; did I do any thing out of order? "No lad you were very good straight on board and strait to bed" (phew) then he said "but you do owe the boson a dollar for the taxi you left standing on the quayside.

He then tells me I was to start taking the dog watch with him and an A B,

Sorry have to explain sea jargon again, AB able bodied seaman /EDH efficient deck hand / DHU deck hand uncertified/ (that's my rank by the way) SOS senior ordinary seaman / last of all JOS/ junior ordinary seaman/ . Hey there are two men under me and that's not counting the cat.

Well back to the dog watch instead of working the deck all day, I was to take the watch on the bridge from four am to eight am, also the same times in the evening, (no more painting get in there trev). Being on a watch was great, my main job was flag man, putting them up at daylight and down at dusk, no other ship can see them in the dark so why bother? Well it kept me occupied.

Two of our assistant stewards were gay, and they always sailed together, well whatever takes your fancy, but it was illegal then, (in England anyway) I forget what year they made it legal, but I was not going to hang about in England in case they made it compulsory . To be fair they were a great couple and did not flaunt it, so live and let live I say.

Every time the ship arrived in Singapore the beer girls came aboard, they used to sell bottles of tiger and any thing else you wanted, their shout was "hey Johnny you buy a bottle of tiger and I sleep with you for free", what? Never seen this on the trawlers, so if you were an alcoholic you turned in to a sex maniac, and if you were a sex maniac, well visa versa. I woke up one day with this young lady??, and tried to give her a few dollars, "no please no money" well if you insist why argue, then she said can I have that shirt, pointing to a white dress shirt hanging on the door.

Well yes you can but why? " it say England on it" well it did on the label, so I gave it to her, I saw her on the deck later that day and she was showing it off to the other girls, and they were all over her for a look.

By the way my sister Jean had got me the shirt for Christmas present, the year before from the John England catalogue, my sister jean is eleven month older than me and we have always had a love / disslove relationship. When I got home and told her it was the best present I ever had, (told her the story) she gave me that you are not right look. Any way thank you again sis.

Before I go any further in the story of 1967, I would like to say that I have NEVER been able to tell this to anybody. It is NOT pleasant or funny, I can say it was to be the worst experience of my life, and have always kept it inside, and it still affects me today. (March 2011) last year I got married to a wonderful lady
And I found I could sit and talk to her, and tell her things I could not talk to anybody about.
Not my x wives, or my six children, NOT EVEN MUM AND DAD. But for some very strange reason pat had this aura about her, and I feel so safe with her, also I can open up with her. So without her this part of my life would never have been mentioned. Thank you PATRICIA ANN PEACH POTTER.

Well we are all called to the ships mess deck, and told from today you are all on double wages, reason being we are going to carry aviation fuel to Vietnam, with it being a war zone you stay on board until we sail. Next day about thirty locals came aboard to clean out the tanks, there was twelve tanks and they had to be spotless clean, as the fuel we were to carry went straight into the American jets, and helicopters.
Also on sailing there was a strict no smoking ban on all decks, cabin only, on our first trip we went into Cambodia to offload and that was not too bad, we did have armed guards, (American troops) on board with a watchful eye on the banks of the river, on our third run we went to Danang, which was in south Vietnam, then I noticed a big change in the control of things.
First on watch, before we arrived I was given a new flag to hoist aft, that is where you flew you're red duster, (England's merchant navy flag), but not today, I was given the stars and stripes (U.S.A.), I was stupid enough to ask why, and told do not ask. So I did, (put it up).
Can I stop for a moment, to tell you the other day 2011 I was watching a program on telly about the sixties and on it they tell us that America had ask the British prime minister to send troops into Vietnam, his answer was no way, America said even an army band, just so the world will know you are behind us in this conflict, the prime minister at the time (HAROLD WILSON) stuck to his word, and NO WAY is Britain getting involved, what a brilliant chap.???
Well I am living proof that our Harold was either as thick as shit, and did not know Shell UK were running aviation fuel into Vietnam, or he was a typical politician.

Well back to 1967 and my life, on arrival into S. Vietnam, suddenly there was about ten fully armed GI,s on the deck, and when we tied up, to start pumping the gas ashore, there was also a small launch running up and down dropping grenades in the water, I ask one soldier why? He looked at me as if I had just arrived on a LT trawler. "If there are any divers under us with explosives, the grenades will shatter them, o great that's ok then sleep tight tonight trev?

With not having shore side pumps to empty us ,it took three days to get the cargo ashore,(ships pumps were a lot slower), I say three, but it took five days in all as the shore side pipeline was blown up twice.

Being on the dog watch it was my job to measure the speed of the offload, dropping a tape measure down the tanks every hour, and then marking each level on a blackboard in the office, and the pump man could then see what tank to empty next, (his job was to keep the ship on an even keel.) the soldier who was with me at all times, made Rambo look like a puff, that's how big he was, he told me he was a full blooded American Indian, if he told me he was from the planet mars I would have agreed with him.

By the way I forgot to mention a very small point, on the way in to the harbour on each side of the channel there was wreckage of another Shell tanker, which had been blown into small pieces by the North.

Well you do tend to forget the minor details of any part of your life, do you not?

As I said we were NOT allowed to smoke any where on the open deck,(who would want to), yep you guessed it stood amidships near the office door, right above half empty tanks (you could see the fumes never mind smell them), the nice Indian giant decides to light a cigar ! I pushed him into the office grabbed it out of his mouth put it in water, and then said to him are you are you fu**ing insane or what?

Think I must have been but, in them circumstances did it matter.

Any way he did not tie me to a totem pole, or any thing like that, he smiled at me and said "I am so sorry pal) PHEW! We both started laughing fit to bust, more with relief than anything. "Who needs to worry about the enemy with you on board"?

Steaming home to Singapore we were told we had one more run back to Vietnam, then back to carrying crude oil, great, one more run then shore leave, (we were not allowed off the boat on the present job), the down side was back to normal pay, to be honest it did not bother me I joined up to see the world not a small cabin.

On leaving Nam we filled all tanks to overflowing with sea water, (to clear the gas fumes), then after pumping them dry all of the deck crew were given buckets, and copper hand shovels, (no sparks off copper). We were then sent into the tanks and told to shovel up any sludge, from the bottom.

We were not given any masks, or any other form of protection.

Years later I was told off a guy, from North Shields, that he had done the same job on another Shell tanker but they were only allowed to stay in the tank for fifteen minutes max.

We were down for over an hour at a time, the very last thing I remember I was singing one of the Bee Gees hit songs (IT WAS CALLED WORLD), the next thing I remember was waking up in the sick bay wearing an oxygen mask. The next morning I was to go on watch as normal, got up at three am (still very shaky) made a pot of tea and then made my way to the bridge, half way along the deck I could smell the fumes and started to feel VERY frightened all over again, I dropped the mug and ran right back to the mess deck.

I had never in my short life felt so strange, (NEVER HAD A PANIC ATTACK BEFORE); I knew then that there was no way I could go back onto that deck. I went down to one of the A Bs cabin and banged on his door, the second he saw me he said what the fuck are you doing out of bed.

He told me I was as white as a sheet, and shaking all over, "I am on watch but I cannot do it" his answer was after yesterday you should not even be out of your cabin.

He told me that he would stand my watch, "go back to your cabin drink this (a bottle of rum) and stay there until I come back, it will help you sleep, (it did not), a couple of hours or so he returned with the chief steward, gave me more oxygen, and I drifted off into a very hazy sleep.

Later that day I was sat on my bed and a couple of the deck crew came in for a chat, to be honest I got lots of visits from all classes of the crew, but the two this time told me how lucky I was to be alive, why? I was then told that I was at the bottom of the tank then all of a sudden I was running up the ladder, with out holding on to it, can not remember the depth of a tank, but about sixty feet, any way to their amazement I was running up the ladder and one of the other lads grabbed hold of me, and walked me up to the top.
I can remember none of this.
The captain came to my cabin and said as soon as we dock in Singapore I was to be taken to hospital for a check up, which I was, and the next thing I was told was that I would be flying home the next day, that made me wonder, if there is nothing physically wrong why are they flying me home, or was I mentally ill.
The very next day I was on a passenger jet and back to London, NOBODY FROM SHELL MET ME.
I had to make my own way from the airport back to aunt Floes.
Going to her house I first got the tube train, or tried to as I stood on the platform and the train pulled in, as all the passengers were getting off, they did not look like a crowd of people but instead it was a wall of mud coming towards me, screaming I left my luggage and ran up the escalator, I could smell the gas again and I thought I was back in the tank. I came round in the station office, and some kind person had given them my luggage. They wanted to call an ambulance, but I told them it was a panic attack, (the third in as many days), so after a lot of cold water, they got me into a taxi, and off I goes to my aunties.
It was great to see a family face, I stayed at hers for two days then got a train home to Beccles, she knew something was amiss as the two nights I was there I did not go to the pub, and to be honest I found it very hard to even go outside.

On arrival home it felt so good to be with family, and friends (I felt safe), it was a bit strange as they had been told I was coming home after an accident, my little sister Janice told me years later that she was expecting her big brother to arrive in a wheel chair, but the problem was not in my body, it was my nervous system.

My dad took me to see a couple of different experts, (doctors and shrinks) and I was told do not worry, the worst thing that can happened to you whilst having an attack, is you will pass out for a while, (handy if you are at the top of a trawlers mast, changing a light bulb) well that's about it for the worst year of my life.

In 2010 I sent away to the archives, and asked for the ships log, and was told it could not be released. WHY?

I did get my discharge papers and they said I left shell because I wanted to work ashore, another said I wanted to go back fishing. Well what a nice firm, I had signed a six month contract and after three month they paid for a flight home. (Very strange). Here is the proof.

C.R.S. 56 (Revised 1954)

SURNAME: POTTER

Other names in full: TREVOR JAMES

Dis. A No.	Date of Birth	Rank or Rating
R863489	18.9.45	DHU

Home Address: 23 Rigbourne Hill, Beccles, Suffolk.

Information I have received has satisfied me that the above-named has ceased to be a merchant seaman.

His reason for leaving is :— Shore Employment

_____ Superintendent

Disposal of British Seaman's Card | M.M.O. Date Stamp

- (a) Attached.
- (b) Lost. C.R.S. 155 attached.
- (c) Arrangements to effect recovery in hand.

* Delete as necessary

Notice reason for leaving shore employment. How nice of shell uk.

And also another strange thing a second reason for leaving, I want to go back

C.R.S. 56 (Revised 1954)

SURNAME POTTER

Other names in full. TREVOR JAMES

Dis A No.	Date of Birth	Rank or Rating
R863489	18/9/49	DHU

Home Address 23 Rigbourne Hill. Beccles
Suffolk.

Information I have received has satisfied me that the above-named has ceased to be a merchant seaman.

His reason for leaving is:— Joining Fishing Fleet

Superintendent

Disposal of British Seaman's Card

* (a) Attached.

* (b) Lost. C.R.S. 155 attached.

* (c) Arrangements to effect recovery in hand.

* Delete as necessary.

M.M.O. Date Stamp

-6 NOV 1968 CUSTOM HOUSE LOWESTOFT

✱ BSC returned to Seaman 27/11/68

To rejoin the fishing fleet, and it is dated a year after? Well to me it is very strange.

The reason I have printed this, I never got to see the documents until last year 2010, and they will still not give me the Hygromia log book. Any way who am I to argue with the powers that be.

After a month ashore I went back on the trawlers, the second day at sea I was walking to the wheelhouse

Across the engine room, as soon as I had a smell of the diesel I took another attack.

Thinking I was back in the tank. I have fought against it all my working life, mostly beating it, but the odd occasion it was to win. What a way to spend the rest of my life, using valium and drink to get by.

Even my six children did not know why there father had such mood swings, and I apologise to you all for that. I was going to insert a picture of the SS Hygromia but decided against it. All I can say is thank fuck 1967 is at an end. Thank you PAT darling.

1968

Hi I am glad that last year is over, so here we go, as I said I went back trawling from LT, but could not face it.

I decided to get a shore side job, and guess what it was? A bus conductor. Bet you do not know what one of them is? Well before the days of a bus with doors at the front, and the driver taking the fare, we had open back ones and they needed a little man walking up and down shouting fares please, and you paid him, well that was me. To start with the Eastern Counties bus company supplied me with a uniform, (free of charge). Wish the trawling firms were as kind!

The first day at work I did not get to go on a bus, as I had to learn how to use the ticket machine, and to fill in the waybill, (a document to be filled in at every stop), how many passengers got on and how many got off. To me that was a bit daft, if it was a busy rout and I was on the upper deck taking fare's how the hell was I to know, well I am now skipper of my own bus, you would think the driver would be in charge, but he could not start without my say so, (jack off the Maxwell) would be so proud of me or would he?.

One ring on the bell is stop, two is go, very educated job, my first two or three days were a disaster, waybill filled in wrong, and ticket machine did not match up with money, but the kind cashier told me not to worry "it will come" I certainly hope so, and it did I stopped worrying and it all fell into place, well in my place any way. The driver told me at every tea break it was my job to pay for the tea and sticky buns.

I do not find that fair, we should take turns in paying, smiling he then said "ask the other conductors so I did and found out I had to loose the odd ticket, and that paid for the teas and so on, well I must admit at this point I got carried away with loosing the odd ticket, it was more a battle of wits between the inspector and trev, and I hate loosing. So here we go a couple of events that made it more a war than a battle of wits. It all started one day when my mum and little sister Janice got on the bus from Beccles to LT, no way would I charge my own mother for a bus ride, she said take the money trev you will get into trouble, sorry mother NO WAY.

What happened next, (sods law) on jumps the inspector, so I told him straight away my mother was on the bus and no ticket, "you cannot give free rides to just anybody", I ask him if he would charge his own mother and he said yes,(like piss off) either that or he had a bad childhood, any way I have a book witch allowed me an x amount of free bus rides every month,(not many tight sods) so I told him to mark the two fare's in my travel pass, he was not happy but I was new and daft so he let it go, with a promise from me that I would toe the line from then on.

Another amusing incident, one day I went up to a passenger and said fares please, (he was an elderly gent in his seventies or eighties), holding out his hand palm down, he says to me "I do not want a ticket son, that is for you not the bus company, on looking in my hand I saw one mint humbug sweet, aw how nice of him, I looked down at the dials on my ticket machine shillings? Yes, pennies? Yes, humbugs no, not on my machine anyway, so I just walked to the next fare and thought what a nice old guy, (try crafty old sod) I wonder how long he had been travelling free, also if he got a coach to London would he pay with a full bag of humbugs.

Back at the depot I told the lads, and they said one day the inspector got on asking for tickets and the gent gave him a humbug as well, did the inspector charge him? No he just let it go, must remember that for the future, as I told you I live ten miles from LT and had to be at work for five AM, and all I had was a push bike with three gears, not like those things you have got today.

First gear pedal on the flat/ second gear freewheel down hill/ third gear up hill, get off and push. Well I must have been fit in those days, as I peddled ten mile a day for three month, at the end of the shift I got the train home with my bike in the guards van.

Well as time went on instead of paying for just the tea and buns, I was to get the driver ten cigarettes a day, very kind chap that I am, his name was Bill Colderwood, and a great guy, the other clippies used to take the piss of him, called him the snail, because he was a slow (but steady) driver, like bill said we cannot leave until the time it states on the timetable, so why rush to get there, wish I was as laid back as him.

Reason I got him ten fags a day? If he saw an inspector at the bus stop ahead, he would hit the Brakes twice, so any dodgy tickets I had given out I had time to change them. Do not get me wrong never once did I fiddle a member of the public, quite the opposite.

Time to explain dodgy tickets, well if the fare was one shilling, I would charge one shilling, (five pence to you) I will be glad when decimal starts save me telling you the difference, then give them a one penny ticket, it had a one on and nobody ever complained, at the end of shift the machine had recorded the amount of money we had taken, so every body happy, and tea and fag breaks paid for.

One day as we were leaving Yarmouth bus station heading for LT, I was going up to the top deck and my ticket machine decided to go back down, and jump off the bus, (it came unclipped and fell) so I gave the driver the emergency stop signal, (about a hundred rings or so) on stopping I jumps off to rescue the poor thing. Well it had a broken dial and could not be used; as the passengers had seen this, I told them I would give them hand written tickets if they wanted; only about five of them did.

Entry on the waybill, five passengers, very few for a sunny day between two holiday resorts? Yes I thought so as well. On arrival at LT I took my little machine and waybill up to the cashiers office to get it replaced.

The cashier looked at it, then gave me a replacement to finish the shift with, looking at the waybill he said "piss off Trevor five people on that run" yes five and handed him the cash, as I was leaving the office I turned round and said, "what no receipt, hope you are going to be honest with the firm", I mean it would not do to fiddle Eastern Counties now would it?. I could still hear his bad language as we pulled out of the depot, twenty fags today bill.

As the weeks passed I dumped the pushbike and bought a motorbike, BSA Bantam, 125 cc, wow fifty miles an hour, (down hill) but it was better than peddling, and I could lie in bed longer.

One morning I was going to LT and it was snowing VERY heavily, and half way there I had to get off the bike and walk alongside of it, not pushing but letting the engine do the work, but the snow was drifting too deep to ride, never had motorways in the sixties, well not many, I arrived at work about ten minuets' late, I told them about the snow and that I did not think the bus to Beccles would get through it, as it was I had the first run there, and no passengers, as we start the run in Beccles, a bit daft really as Bill could have picked me up at home.

Well they would not listen to Trevor with my experienced fisherman's eye on weather, so off we go, as I told you no doors, and it was freezing, half way there guess what ? Yep the bus was up to its knees in snow, along with other traffic, and going nowhere, four hours we sat in the drivers cab to keep warm, and Bill said o well another two and we are on overtime, oh brilliant Bill, so what if we are sat here for two days?, in that case we will not be worried about money, cheerful chap my driver.

Anyway rescue came and away we go, (snow plough), on arrival at Beccles he phoned the depot and asked them what next? Will you do a run to Norwich? Yes but that takes over an hour, and then the same back. They then told him we were on overtime for the run so we did it. Hey bill we are on overtime rate anyway, but so far no money for tea and ciggies, well lets hit the road and make some.

There were not many passengers aboard going to Norwich, and I do not blame them in that weather, but we arrived there without any major hiccups, but going back to LT with only four passengers was a different story. Going along a small country road, the bus skidded and the back end went into a shallow ditch, well that was us stuck again, I will be glad to see the end of this day, try as much as he could the more Bill done the deeper we sank into the ditch. The bus was now listing to port, (sorry leaning to the left) forgot I was ashore.

I decided to go to a nearby farmyard to get some help (no mobile phones then), the farmer was brilliant, he got his tractor and back to the snowbound bus we goes, he also got one of his men to help, think it was his granddad, looking at him, putting chains under the front, he then advised me to get everybody off, in case she fell completely over, wise man. With the tractor towing and Bill driving it was still a struggle, then the farm hand shouts to me, "come on sonny help me" he had his back to the bus and was trying to push it, silly old sod it's a double Decker bus not a push chair, plus if it had toppled he could have ended up getting badly injured, so I pulled him away.

Success and back on an even keel, (level) thanking the farmer off we go on our merry way, with no more bother, I offered the four passengers their money back but they all declined my kind offer, so as they got off I ask them for their tickets, to show the cashier how many we had on the bus, and they gave them to me

And also praised the driver. Any way day over I took my waybill into the cashiers office and handed over the days takings, about £1.20, and the four tickets. Why are you giving me these? Well the passengers who got stuck in the snow demanded a refund, so I gave them one, shaking his head he told me to get out of his office, which I gladly did and after handing over twenty fags to Bill, off I go home for my long awaited dinner.

I presume you all guessed its nearly Christmas, what with the snow and all, and to be honest I was longing to go back to sea, but decided to stay on the bus until after the holidays, also the inspector was getting closer and closer to getting us to buy our own fags, tea, and sticky buns, and to be honest, (that's a laugh) I had petrol to pay for now. Just my luck, I got to work the Christmas Eve shift, it did not bother me too much as I am more a New Year man.

Well Christmas eve we had five runs around the broads, that's LT railway station, round in a circular run through Oulton Broad and back to rail station, it was one run every hour, it took us fifty minutes to do the run, and a ten minute break on each run, instead of a tea break I decided to have a swift pint, that turned out to be a pint every run (great job this), after the five runs we had twenty minutes break before the last run which was up to one of the housing estates.

Well that was the last bus, so it was full or nearly, Trev having had a few was in a very merry Christmas mood and decided to trim the bus up (with three rolls of unused tickets), as we pulled away I sat on the back seat with a fag and had put my ticket machine in its little case, it was to be the last time I was ever going to use it.

One passenger asked me are you not going to start collecting, nope its chrissy and we have decided to give you all a treat, free rides all round, but you must all join in with a song, well I do not know what the locals thought as we arrived at the estate, because about fifty people were singing Christmas carols, what a great night, as most of them got off they gave me a tip for being such a nice little bus conductor.

That is with the exception of one lad who informed me he was the inspectors son.

I will not tell you what I told him his daddy was, but I did scribble out my resignation on the waybill.

        O WELL BACK TO SEA HAVE A GOOD NEW YEAR ALL.

1969

Well off I go to the bus station to get my cards, wages, and hand in the uniform, saying a fond farewell to Billy, he told me he was going to miss me, how nice, "I will never get another conductor who buys fags as well as tea and sticky buns", hope that wasn't his way of calling me daft, I then popped into the inspectors office to say good bye to him, "well Trevor I must admit you were good, but I would have got you in the end", we will never know .

Well back to sea for Trevor, I went on a few trawlers in 1969, out of LT cannot name them all but I kept with Clione fishing company, and Trev is now boson, (third hand) so that's the cat told. The first boat I sailed on that year was called ST Lucia, and you will never guess who the mate was, Joe Colson, ex Wilton queen skipper, I was shocked to see him back on the deck.

Joe was in his sixties, when I asked him why? He told me they wanted young blood in the wheelhouse and the Wilton was to go flat fishing, come on Joe why do you not just retire? I know you can afford to, "well trev its not about money, I just love the sea, (strange man) but honestly it made me think, when I watched him struggle in the fish room, and on the deck, it made me so sad, that a man of his experience was put on the dockside by the firm he had sailed for all those years.

One haul the net came up with a rip in the wing, and part of it missing, so Joe and I started to sort it out, I was mending a part of the net called the quarter, it is the most intricate part of a trawl, and mostly the mate done that job, well mending away Joe stood rolling a fag and watching me put the quarter mesh in. job finished and we were towing again, we sat in the mess deck, Joe said to me Trev who taught you to mend a quarter mesh? You did Joe why? Because I never taught you that way of doing it, no but I find it easier that way.

Well lad I am sixty two years old, been fishing all my life and have just seen a better and quicker way of putting in the quarter. So Trevor remember that you are never too old to learn, and I never forgot those words, thank you Joe Colson. Joe left that trip and I never saw him again.

The man who took his place as mate was named Tony Scrivens, (Scribbo) from now on, and believe it or not he was as mad as Nev Best from the Maxwell days, maybe even more so, but if he took to you he was the bestest pal a bloke could ask for, needless to say with me being a bit strange myself we got on like a house on fire.

Nothing ever bothered scribbo, he had just passed his skippers ticket and said to me "when I get a boat will you sail with me" he has got to be joking put my life in his hands no way, but being me, I would.

When we landed that trip, we were lucky to get tickets to see the Rolling Stones, live at the big hotel on Lowestoft sea front, if I remember it was called the royal, (must ask little sis) any way I think the tickets were about£5.00 each.

Were they good? I do not know as we never got to see them, as the four of us, Scribbo, s wife and a lass I was going out with, Scribbo and me, (think that's four) were in the bar having a swift drink, before the gig is that what you young one's call it, well any way in walks three American oil rig workers, no bother they never done me any wrong, but scribbo was dead against anything to do with oil rigs, or Americans.

He said they were taking over our north sea fishing grounds, and in a way he was correct, but these guys did not own the rigs they just worked on them, well the two girls and me were sat at a table and Tony was at the bar getting another round in. next thing I know is we are sat on the wall outside of the hotel.

What the fu** happened Scribbo? Well this yank said he was hot so I cooled him down with the soda siphon, great and no refund on tickets.

On passing my motorcycle driving test, I decided to get a bigger bike, was a bit fed up with old dears passing my BSA Bantam on their push bikes. To be honest it was the mods, on their scooters that annoyed me most, I mean fancy a mob of rockers on Yarmouth sea front, behind them the mods on their scooters, and Trev bringing up the rear on his 125 cc, very embarrassing, especially when a little cat passed me, and he was running.

So I had enough and started to look for a bigger bike, a mate of mine was selling his as he was going abroad to work, it was called a Royal Enfield, and had a 500 cc engine, so I took it on a test run, at the time we were sat in this café where all the local rockers hung out, and I asked if anybody fancied a run to LT and back, a young lass called Mary said "I would love to" first off I warned her, I would be trying to see if the bike could do the ton (100 MPH).

It was not law to wear a crash helmet in those days, but I advised her to as the bike was strange to me,

So off we go, I only got up to about 80mph going to LT, but on the way back I did manage the ton, but only just. Leaving the new road, it was a new bypass and had just been built, I eased the bike back to about 60 mph. ahead of me on the country road now, I saw a car driving out of a driveway but I had the right of way.

According to the navigation poem anyway, (green to port keeps clear of you) remember it? Any way maybe he had not revised it, as he pulled out in front of me, SH**, I had to swerve to miss him and it was a very close thing. Well I am well ahead of him and fuming mad, so I slowed down to let him pass me, when he had I rode up along side of the drivers door, he had the window down and was speeding along at about 25 mph, I then called him every illegitimate swear word I knew, (his wife or whoever was sitting beside him). Then he turned to me and apologised, I could then see his dog collar. O dear sorry vicker, I did not buy that bike, instead I got another BSA, this time 650cc Gold Star, what a monster.

Well back to work Trev, I went into the office and asked what berths were going, and got a choice of three while I was pondering in walks Scribbo, hi Trev I have just been given my own boat, great got any jobs? Yes but not the deck, I only need a cook, never sailed cook on a trawler, but I managed on the snibbys so ok mate I will sign on, great the cook got all night in bed, and a nice warm galley to work in.

As we were on our way to the pub, I said to him "just one small point what boat is it"? SILVERFISH o no the fish boats were under powered, old, and well to be honest wreck's.

But to be fair to the proud new skipper, to him it was the pride of the fleet. They always gave new skippers the older boats, according to the office if you can make money with an old underpowered boat you had what it takes, I just hope scribbo can, he was a very good fisherman on the deck, but that counts for nothing in the wheelhouse, I have sailed with some big money earners in the past, and one or two of them were crap on deck.

Well off we go on the silverfish, and we done ok, did not break any port records but to my mind scribbo had what it took, it was a happy boat scribbo saw to that, but one thing sticks in my mind, the mate was a skipper as well but he did not make a go of it, and so he held that against scribbo, you can say he worked against us rather than with us, he was always picking faults with Tony's way of running the boat.

He also hated the fact that I was a mate of Scribbo, s why? Strange man.

As I said the cook got all night in his bunk, or was supposed to, every time the net was hauled the skipper came and woke me up to tell me how good, or bad the catch was.

So I give up and every haul I got up and took two pots of tea up to the wheelhouse, it saved him running up and down, any way one haul watching the lads on the deck Scribbo says to me 'Trev I am not being funny but when the crew can hear us will you call me skipper. Well of coarse I will sorry. Its just they think there is no respect, to be honest I agree with him, so from then on it was SKIPPER.

One night sat in the wheelhouse seat, behind the wheel, I was going to refill my tobacco tin, it was solid silver, and given to me by my aunt, her hubby was a fisherman, and he had it a long time, before filling it up with fresh tobacco I passed it to Tony and said dump that mate, and he did over the side went the tin.

What the fu**? You said dump it, the dust you prick, he said well why not tell me to empty it.

I surrender.

Mind you I went over the top with the skipper bit, whenever we were in a bar, or the office, or at home I always called him skipper, he hated it, but there you go he did tell me to, by the way one sunny day towing along, Tony and I were sat on the boat deck with a pot of tea, and I asked him how it felt being a skipper, with the worry and responsibility of having to make a wage for the crew, he did admit it was a bit scary, but then he looked up at the smoke coming out of the funnel and said, just think Trev all this power under my command.

Well I just cracked up laughing, I was to say those same words in my skipper's life, and the crew wondered why I always laughed, but scribbo was to become a very successful skipper, and take some very good boats to sea.

On landing day we all met up in the office to get our money, scribbo was with his wife, and said to all the lads off Silverfish, come on lets go to the Suffolk for a drink, first two rounds on me, well the Suffolk Hotel was not a bar you would take your mum in, one of the lads said hey scribbo you're not going to take the wife in the Suffolk are you? His answer "why what's wrong with that is she not good enough" told you he was nuts, any way let's get pissed.

There was another day we were having a drink together and talking about all the lads who were down on their luck, could not get a decent boat, or maybe some other reason, but fishermen knew the genuine ones and always gave them a westerly, (money for a drink), and scribbo said maybe they are better off than us, why? Well they do not work, and still get a drink every day.

We decided to put it to the test, standing outside a bar as fishermen were going in, scribbo told one or two of them that he was sacked, and Trev had been spraged, (given the cold shoulder of all firms) for missing a boat. Two lads gave us £5.00 for a drink, thanks lads it will not be forgotten, any way word got round and for the next two or three days we were given more money than you can earn in a trip at sea.

Actually it got so embarrassing we had to start refusing money and drinks off the lads.

On landing day we all had on brightly coloured suits, most LT fishermen had them tailor made shit I forgot to tell you about them. (GIVE ME TEN MINS) ok I am back you know about the colours now as I just went back to 1965 chapter and slotted the story in, hey typing this is like having a time machine, forget any thing you can just nip back and put it right. Well any way I have seen lads sail, and work in a new suit, dump it at the end of the trip and pick up the new one they had ordered the trip before, mad or what.

      Well come September of this year my big, (sorry Jean) elder sister decided to get married, so I took a trip off to be there, would not miss it for the world, get rid of bossy boots, any way on her wedding day (she married a guy called Malcolm Springhall) hope I have spelt it right but I can always come back and correct it. I am very happy she did she could have done a lot worse, he is a great chap (for a farmer) I wonder if he ever saved a bus with his tractor? And they were building their own house on a plot of land belonging to his family, (and are still in it today 2011).

After the wedding, the do was held at the town hall in Beccles, they both stood at the door as the guests were arriving, (think he was charging door money) any way everyone was congratulating them, and I walked in, I can never understand this bit, but when I gave my sister jean a kiss I broke down in tears, like big time, I do not know why but I think it was all the fights brother and sister have growing up.

Come tea time a lot of guests left to change, get kids settled and whatever you do in-between wedding days, and evening piss ups.

I went to the café and had an hour with the lads, my then girlfriend was in the café and told me how smart I looked, what she did not know was she was now my x girlfriend, any way just before leaving to go back to the town hall, for the night time do, I asked the lass who had tested the motorbike with me, fancy coming to my sister's wedding party, she said yes and that was how I got to know my future children's mother.

Well just one more yarn to finish off 1969, and here we go, one night a mate of mine from the same street, went to school with him, anyway Bernard Bowen was in the army, he arrived at the house in uniform, no way, take it off and put one of my fisherman suits on, why he said, why? Because all drunken prats want to fight a soldier. And not a fisherman, he said, no Bernie they know how nice we are, so off he goes and changes from a soldier into a colorful piss artist.

Before I carry on must tell you my dad loved gardening, and had spent years making a rockery in the front for mum. It was more of a model village than a garden; its center piece was a stone castle, that's what dad called a rockery, and in the sixty's it was featured in a gardening magazine.

The nice thing about it was nobody EVER done any damage to it, and we lived on a rough council estate.

Well it was called rough after I moved in, well night on the piss and got home about 1AM Bernie wanted to come in to get his uniform, but I told him to leave it until daytime, not him I think he thought I wanted to keep it, anyway first heated words, then we started fighting, (in the garden) mum comes out bang's our heads together, sent him home and sent me to bed, (with no tea).

When I got up next day, about mid-day mum went mad, get out the front and put the garden back how it was, as I was cleaning up Bernie arrives for his uniform, mum said no bother son, you can have it when you have finished helping Trevor.

My father in his garden.

1970

Hi again all if you have not dumped it yet, the book, welcome to 1970, lots went on this year so I will try to cut it short (do not want to bore you), well back to sea on a boat called the Barbados, yes I can sail on them wish I could afford to go to them, the islands I mean, any way one day as I was working the winch at hauling time the mate arrives, and we got talking about safety at sea,

He then said to me "can you see anything wrong with this boat" yes it's a wreck; no seriously can you not spot anything wrong with her? No what? He then said it was the only trawler he had sailed on with no guard rail round the winch, amazed I had not noticed it, but he was right, well I told you that because it comes up later. Nice to keep you all up to date, wish I was, think I have that thing where you can remember your past but not yesterday, it is called altzimers, anyway cannot spell it, so I must have it.

Well in dock at the end of the trip, a pal of mine asked me to go for a drink one night, not wanting to offend him I said ok just a few, we sat in this bar in LT minding our own, when two young ladies came up to the table "hi can we join you "well not wanting to be ignorant we said if you must, they were in LT on holiday and they wanted to know how us locals spent the night.

Drinking mostly girls, but we can take you on a tour of the town, like museums / art gallery's/ light houses, or what ever turns you on, I think they had decided by now that we were nuts, so we spent the evening chatting and drinking, they then invited us to a party at the caravan they were staying in, great ring a taxi.

Not tonight, tomorrow tea time, why not tonight? Because you will think we are a couple of easy ladies, we had come to that assumption already, but ok that's a date tomorrow at five pm, and shall we bring some jelly and cake, piss off just a couple of bottles.

What has Trev forgot? Yes he is sailing at 11AM tomorrow, SHIT! O well easy come easy go, I went down the next morning to go to sea and whilst I was in the ships stores, buying my bits and bobs for the trip, I told one of the deck hands about the invitation to the caravan, but standing behind me was the ships husband, of course he heard all and said no silly tricks Trevor, as if?

I threw my kitbag onto the deck thinking what a nice day for a party, but work comes first, (and my good name in LT) but on the other hand I am only twenty year old, all work and no play makes

Trev a dull boy, (or a silly twat) any way stood on the deck, sick as a chip, also no fish to go with it, I said to the mate "I do not fancy sailing today" he replied good on you Trev, I want an extra day in but if I refuse to go I get my ticket suspended.

All ready, the skipper shouts out let go, and I replied fu** off, what did you say? And I repeated go away in short jerky movements, well obviously all hell breaks loose, the skipper said what is the reason Trev? I could not think of one so I blurted out that the deck crew were not experienced enough, and that was a danger to others.

The ships husband said "nothing to do with the party then?" no way the job comes first, any way sat in the bar with the deck crew, they said to me hope you were not serious about us not being up to scratch, no way lads your great guys but it came to mind as an extras use.

In LT if you ever refused to sail It was a police matter, as you had broken the articles of agreement, so it was not long before two uniforms came in and ask for me, hi guys want a pint? Not on duty, that's why I ask, well do we need the cuffs? No I surrender, so off I go up to the kangaroo court, it was not a legal court, it was run by the boat owners from every firm in LT, and they were all sat at the table.

Reason for refusing to sail, unfit deck crew, but you have done one trip with the same crew why did you not leave on landing day? Err well err, BOING it hit me, GET IN TREV well your honours, I thought the winch guard would have been fitted while we were in dock, what winch guard? The one that is not there sir, ships husband runs out, returns five min, s later and said drop charge.

If there is a guard there tomorrow will you sail? Yes no bother, what about the deck hands? Good lads but I had their safety in mind.

Well I suppose you are wondering how the party went? It did not, the lads were so happy with me for getting them an extra day in they got me loads of drink, well I went home to bed and missed it.
Stop laughing! Any way off we go to sea, I went into the wheelhouse to take the first watch, I said to the skipper "I hope you are not going to give me a hard time because of yesterday" no way Trev but you do know you are sacked when we get in, I had thought that, well there are other firms, not for you.
What do you mean? I already knew.
Yes Trevor got the walk about, not one firm would give me a birth, fu** them, back to GY, but I would love to think that one day that boat took a huge wave and washed somebody into the shiny new guard rail and not the winch. That was the last LT boat I ever sailed on in my life.
Well I said my goodbye's to the family, and promised I would ring often, yes posh family now we got a telephone, and off I go must try not to fall asleep on the train, as I do not want to end up in Scotland again, (I have not forgot Nev) well in to the office I walked, Mr Moss was very pleased to see me, hello young man long time, but I knew you would be back.
How's that? Because you loved the anchor, and I have just the job for you, the Catherine Jean is looking for a cook, o great one of the oldest and smallest in the fleet, is that the only one? Well with you having the walk about in LT you can't be to choosey, how the fu** did you know that? He just smiled and said don't try it on here Trev; keep your good name in GY.
Going aboard the boat I met the skipper Jerry Lee, and the mate Tony Chester, Tony was to become very involved with my future, but for now I will stick to this year, well the boat had just finished trawling for sprats, and we were busy putting the ropes and anchor gear back aboard, just as we were finishing off Jerry asked me to go to the office, for the working by money before they closed for dinner. We got £5.00 a man for working on the boat in dock, that is new to me never got paid on Maxwell, but there you go times change.

      Well Tony and I decided to go for a pint in the afternoon and get to know each other, mind you Trev I do not want to stay long as I am off out tonight, well drink cider then you can drink a lot more of that and still be sober for tonight, so we did and as the day went on Tony said hey Trev your right this cider is very refreshing, I don't feel like I have had a drink, (we were three sheets to the wind) that's half pissed to you.

Tony did not manage to go out that night, and for the next forty years when ever anybody mentioned cider he said "oh that non pissy up making stuff". We sailed and Jerry was fishing for flatfish, ok but a lot slower than cod fishing, the trip was pretty boring, Jerry never had his nose out of a cowboy book, even while he was eating his dinner the book was propped up behind his plate, maybe he just did not want to talk to this particular crew, or did I mean peculiar?

One day the weather was so bad that we could not fish, we just lay at the anchor with a long storm chain out, that was to help keep strain off the anchor wire, after breakfast Tony said to me that he was off to rig a new net with floats and ground rope, in this weather? But I helped, it was better than looking at the cover of a cowboy book all day, I often wonder what Jerry reads now, he must have been through every one ever written.

For some reason I always remember what we made that trip £1400.00, not brilliant but a wage, I was a bit surprised we did not get paid in US Dollars like the cowboys. Anyway I left her and joined the Ling Bank with a chap called Barry Emerson, he was a cod fisherman and he was dead opposite to Jerry, every part of the job was done at top speed.

Also where we had four hauls a day flat fishing, we had six a day with Barry, and I noticed we wore out the gear and the crew twice as fast, the funny part was we also made £1400.00, but I bet by the end of a year the expense of running Jerry's boat was half of Barry's.

Every one to their own, but being a tight sort I said to myself, when I get a skippers job I was going to be a flatfish man, it seems a more laid back way of earning money.

That trip in I rang home to mum and dad, to let them know all was ok with life, it may have been my end but not in Beccles, they informed me that I was going to be a father, shock is not the word but after speaking to Mary, I told her I would find a flat and go down and pick her up.

No way was I going back to LT to work, anyway this I did and the flat was two rooms on Cleethorpes sea front, sounds posh but it was the opposite the rent was £4.00 per week, not bad for the time being, until I can find something better, well got the flat, and a mate of mine ran me home in his car, picked her up and straight back to GY, as I was to sail in two days on a boat called the East Bank.

We got back to GY and I gave her a quick tour of the town, the office would only allow us ten pounds a week sent home so I arranged with the landlord to pay rent monthly, plus my pals wife said she would keep her right, so at least I could sail knowing all was ok.

We sailed the next day the skipper was called Mick Jenson, but all the lads called him captain cannonball, I was to find out why when we got to sea, yes he was one of those all mouth and no common sense guys, but after a few days he found out that he could not give Trev any bullshit, I am not saying I was a tough guy or any thing, but I will not be shit on by anybody.

One day shooting the ropes out I had to do a splice, (join the rope together) as one of the forward ropes was stranded, as the rope was being shot away, I think to myself he will have to slow down a bit whilst I finish, did he? Did he fu**, and the rope was pulled out of my hand, I could see him, so no excuse, he could see me, anyway the spike you use was an expensive item, plus we always carried a spare or two, but that was not the point, he was talking on the radio to another boat when he should have been watching the deck. So I dumped the spike over the side, solid brass I think it sunk but I did not check as brass doesn't normally float.

He screams out of the wheelhouse what the fu** did you do that for, and my reply well captain (taking the piss) if we have not got time to splice we do not need it. Was that the window I heard slamming?

      I have always felt bad about this next episode, one haul we were pulling the net in and the cook (Peter) said something that annoyed me, now I do not believe in arguing at sea, as you look after each other, and to fight is not the way to settle things, you can do that when you get ashore, anyway Pete was on one ground rope ,me on the other, and captain Mick on the two headlines, it sounds like giving the skipper two ropes to pull in was a bit unfair, but his had floats on and ours were full of heavy chain, anyway whatever Pete said was not nice, so I dropped the net, then I dropped the cook. Mick looked at me a bit shocked and said there was no need to knock him out Trevor, true I should have let him pull the net in first.

Well we kissed and made up, finished the trip, and not a bad one, but Pete decided to get a different boat, I was expecting the long setting (the sack) remember, if not keep up with me please, well I did not, I wonder if it was because I was the only one dopey enough to put up with Captain Cannonball.

Or maybe he thought I was not too bad at my mate's job, well it was my first one, and it did not go too badly except for losing the spike and the cook, and giving the skipper a rollicking, trev you must behave in future.

Well that trip in I got married to Mary, strange type of wedding as there was only four of us In attendance, well six if you count the registrar, and the baby, after the glitter and pomp, we went for a Chinese meal, and then for a couple of drinks in a bar across from the flat, I could only have two or three as I was sailing that evening, well being married I had responsibilities, so five o'clock, or five pm, or 1700 hours, off I go to sail into the sunset. Actually we were steaming east so the sun was setting behind me, never mind cannot get every thing right.

As you know we had a new cook, strange sort of chap he was built like a brick shit house, a Scottish lad cannot remember his name, but I did wonder if the captain gave him the job as his bodyguard, during the trip it turned out quite the opposite.

As we were steaming out of the Humber river I went up to take the first watch, and told Mick that I had got married that trip in, congrat,s Trev was it a good night? Don't know mate, it was ten this morning, he says to me, you should have said we would have had another day in.

Why I need the money, so get fishing, his look was a picture, should have had a camera for the wedding album, the new cook like I said was a giant, but we seemed to get on ok, he had never been on an anchor basher before, but he had done a lot of fly shooting out of PD (Peterhead), the only difference was the anchor gear, but he picked it up the first day.

On an anchor basher, at night all the crew turn in and the engine is stopped, its very quiet and the anchor light was rigged up to an alarm, so if the bulb blew it woke us, I mean who want's to be sound asleep in pitch dark with no lights. Also on all snibbys the alarm clock was rigged to another electronic bell, so we never slept in, trouble is captain cannonball did not trust the bell, so he had it wired up to a very loud claxon horn, it was under the cabin table, so you had to get out of your bunk to turn it off, I forgot to warn our new cook about this, also captain Mick had his own berth, behind the wheelhouse.

Well you can't expect him to live with us scurvy underdogs can you? The cook was claustrophobic, so instead of sleeping in a small closed in bunk he slept on the seat locker, beside the table/ beside the klaxon/ beside the EXTRA loud claxon.

Next morning all hell broke loose, when the alarm went off so did the cook, he ran strait up to the wheelhouse, and was busy strangling Mick when I arrived, well I begged him not to kill him, as we needed to catch fish and earn money, well he decided not too, (phew) the trip went without any more trouble, plus no more klaxon, the cook dumped it, just one last thing , one day we were hauling up the anchor gear, to move fishing ground and Mick said to me, that shackle looks loose (big bolt joining wire together) so I let it go round the winch a couple of times, to hold it solid stopped the winch, and passed the crock over to Jock, (sick of calling him the cook) now a crock is a spanner about four feet long, and fits any size nut.

Jock tried to tighten it but no way, plus it was rusty, no way would it have come loose, but me and my mouth again, "come on put some effort into it" well Jock goes mad at me and shouts come on then tough guy you turn it, well I walked round the winch and fitted the spanner to the shackle, knowing if he could not tighten it, I had no hope in hell.

Do not know if it was fear, or what but I just knew I had to move it, and I did half a turn, wow was I relieved when it moved, Jock treat me as his bestest ever pal after that, at the end of the trip we both left.

That trip in dock my son was born, Tony Trevor Potter, I have never felt so high in my life, me a real dad, wow wet the babies head time, wet it I drown the lad, I named him after my old friend from LT Scribbo.

    I was so proud when they came home, Mary was cleaning the flat so I took Tony for a walk along the sea front, it was July and very hot, so I decided to pop in for a swift pint, the gaffer allowed the pram in so all was ok, until my little lad run out of milk, well he comes first in life, so I put a drop of nut brown ale in his bottle, he enjoyed it and popped off to sleep. (what a good lad) well Mary decided to walk down to the beach and meet us, as she was walking past the bar, she looked in and saw Tony's red pram, also when she saw his bottle she exploded, strange things women, I mean he was sound asleep /in the shade/ and seemed happy with his new life, o well she is the skipper, so off she goes with the pram, and I decided to give her an hour or two to unwind.

The next boat I sailed on was called the Dorny, it was the first one I had sailed on where the skipper was also the owner, Paul Sorenson, he was Danish, but there was a lot of them in GY, also he turned out to be one of the best men I ever sailed with, always in a good mood whatever went wrong at sea, I stayed with him for the rest of the season.

Paul was also a flat fisherman and only four hauls a day, but he earns a great deal of money, she was a very small boat, and only had a one cylinder engine in her, so as we were steaming along, or out shooting the ropes the low revs of the engine used to shake the boat, like as I stood on deck my feet used to leave the deck on every stroke of the piston, very strange experience, and when I got ashore I seemed to hop instead of walk.

The next trip was to be the hardest I have ever done, after a few good days fishing on the Dogger Bank, it's about middle of the north sea, and very shallow, nasty place to be in a storm, if it's from the north you get off, like quick, that is if they forecast it, sometimes it hits you and no way would you try to get to deeper water.

We awoke one day, the weather was horrendous from the north, so we put the storm chain out, and just sat tight, normally in a storm it's not to bad, as anchor boats are designed to put away bad weather, but in shallow water, the sea gets confused, by that I mean the waves hit the edge of the bank and start to break out of normality.

Three mile from us was another snobby, she was called the Morina, and same as us had to ride it out, I will never forget that night as long as I live, Paul left the engine running and the pumps going all the time, he also set a watch, but even if he had not none of us would have gone to bed anyway.

Come the early hours of the morning the wind dropped, and the waves started to subside, as daylight broke we could see that the deck was covered with about two inches of sand, washed up from the seabed, I have been through lots of storms but had never seen this, Paul said it was the depth of water, picking the sand up with the huge waves.

Paul then told me the Morina had lost her lights during the night, must have lost power, or I hope she did, but he looked very grave, and was scanning her position through his glasses, he then said "I do not like this at all Trevor" no not one little bit, no way would he have tried to move, I said maybe he parted his anchor gear and has drifted away south, well I certainly hope so son, take the anchor, we will go and have a look.

      This we did but the mood on the deck was terrible, we would normally be laughing and joking after that sort of weather, (in relief) but deep down we were thinking the worst, as I stood behind the winch I could hear Paul calling her on the radio, but in his voice I could tell he was thinking the same. Anyway we arrived at her anchor position and saw nothing, we then started to run to the south, witch is the way she would have drifted.

Sadly the first thing we found was the cabin table, Paul had been in touch with the coast guard, now he could confirm the loss, within less than an hour the RAF Nimrod, and two air sea rescue helicopters arrived. And a few hours later there was about twenty fishing boats in sight, there was a lot of wreckage picked up, and one of the helicopters found the life raft. It was dead ahead of us but Paul told Jerry on the Catherine Jean to get it, as Jerrys brother in law was the skipper, sadly it was empty, we searched for another 48 hours and then it was called off.

We had another weeks fishing to do before the end of the trip, you can imagine the mood on the deck every time we came out of the cabin we had to pass the table, and the skippers bunk side, plus other bits of smaller wreckage, very sad. When the crew were named the next day I found out that Pete was one of the crew, (the lad I hit at sea), but the only solace I had was that he did not join Morina after leaving us he went on another boat in between. Any way lads REST IN PEACE.

I spent the rest of the season on the Dorny, and did very well, when she tied up for the winter break I joined a boat that was going trawling for sprats, she was called Trendsetter, and was brand spanking new, only one very small problem the skipper was no other than Captain Cannonball.

Well I have put up with him before, maybe he has mellowed (had he shit) but as long as he made money who am I to make waves, somebody must trust him as he was given a new boat, god he will be even worsera.

The other crew member was a lad one year older than me, and believe it or not nuttier than Nev Best, his name Fred Sayers, not sure if I have spelt that right but its only a name, any way from now on it will be Fred, at least when you are sprating there is no gutting or ice, you just open the net over the fish room hatch and let them flow, GREAT what an easy life, sorry forgot Cannonball is in charge.

To be fair to the Captain, we did very well in-between the disasters, to be grudgingly honest I picked up more money a trip than I ever had in my eight years at sea.

So I salute you Captain Mick, just think what I would have got if he knew the job of pelagic trawling.

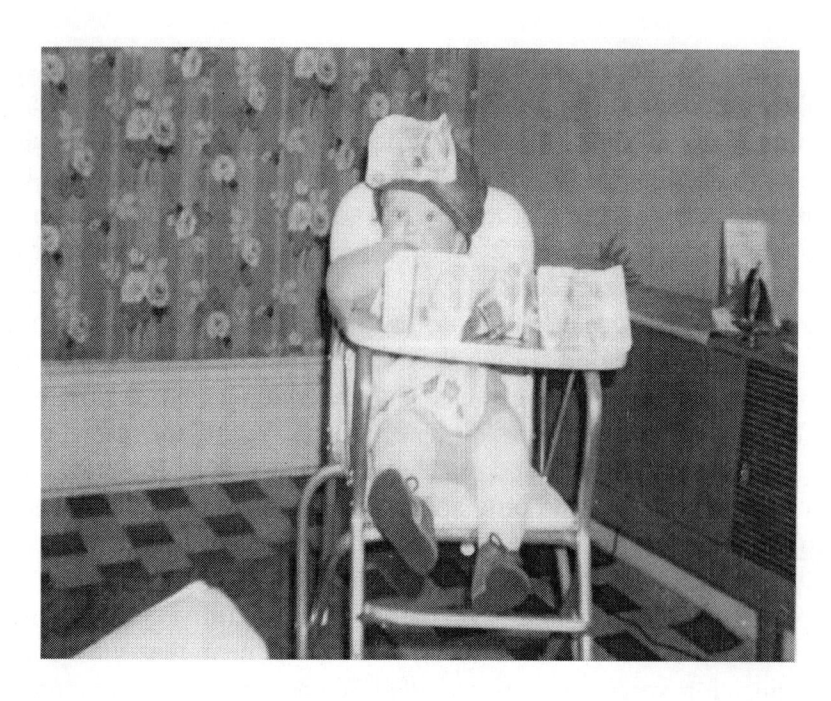

1971

Hi again, we had a great Christmas, Tony's first of many and with the money we were earning that made it even betterer. By the way I spent my 21st birthday on Dorny, so as they say I am a man now.

After New Year back to sea on Trendsetter, we were fishing off the Tyne, and still doing very well, mind you the sprats were so thick that year you could catch them with a bucket on a rope, one night we hauled and the net was full to overflowing, as we were hauling on the dog line (a rope from the cod end to the wing) used to haul up each lift of sprats, and in this haul I estimate about 70 ton, the boat only held 60, on the first lift the dog line parted, it was flat calm weather, and we had to put a wire round the net let it sink and hopefully lift the cod end up, but it took us about 12 hours to get the haul aboard, the other boats had been into North Shields landed and back out twice, while we were piss farting about. At night the sprats came to the surface to feed, they were that thick that you could see them being pushed up by the shoal underneath, (very strange sight).

While Mick was putting the wire round, for about the tenth time Fred said to him "look Mick they are coming up to laugh at us" that did not go down to well. Glad I never said it.

Sprat season over, Mick told Fred and I that he was going pair trawling this summer, Fred was all for it but I had grave doubts and decided to go back anchor fishing. It turned out to be a very smart move on my part, plus a full season with the Captain and it was defiantly the funny farm for me.

I joined a boat called Coral Bank, the skipper / owner was a man called Dennis Mc Kenny/ better known as Mac, don't know why, maybe you all can work it out? Mac started his working life as a school teacher, and a lot of the lads called him that, he was certainly going to teach me a lot about catching fish, Mac was also into the communist way of life.

All men are equal but I am more equal than you type of communist, as it turned out I was to stay with him for two years, and NEVER land without a decent wage, mind you the first trip was nearly my last as steaming home the cook called me out, and said breakfast is on the table, is it my watch? No, well shove it; I was that knackered that I would have a snack before going up to the wheelhouse at watch time.

    I must have been dead to the world because when I awoke, (nobody called me) I had been sleeping for ten hours, I made a cuppa ,and as I left the cabin I saw that we were towing another boat, how the hell did I sleep through that? And why didn't anybody tell me? And why did the cook not wake me for my watch? And why was Mac very cold towards me when I arrived in the wheelhouse? And why the fu** am I asking all these stupid questions?

Any way Mac said to me "why did you not get up for breakfast when the cook called you, did he not tell you we were going to pick a tow up", no he did not if he had I would have been straight up,

Must remember to kick his head in when we get ashore, well Mac turned in and I did an eight hour watch, so he could catch up on sleep, when you are towing another boat only the skipper and mate take the wheel the other two lads do the running about for us, like fetching tea and checking the engine room and fish room were pumped dry.

    You cannot leave the wheel while towing another boat, for obvious reasons, any way Mac got up and asked me if every thing was ok, I replied that it was, and also told him how sorry I was for the let down earlier, also that I did not want a share of the towing money, the insurance pays the boat towing a set amount per mile, and that is split the same way as our normal wage.

Anyway landed fish, and went down to the office for my money, and the sack, got a surprise, no sack and got towing money as well, off to the Albion bar, when I walked in Mac asked me what I wanted, lager please, and why did I not get the sack, he answered you turned out very good fish, and you can bring the gear home better than most.

But never get too big headed about that, no Mac I will defiantly not, by the way can I have a small rum chaser? He shook his head and ordered one, get in Trev.

Mac was a strange bloke, a lot different from any skipper I had ever sailed with, like if we were laid for bad weather he would start a quiz, or get the monopoly board out, now that may sound strange, with the boat rolling and tossing in a storm, but if you bought a house or hotel, we dipped it into the butter so it would stick to the board, had some great times playing that and lost a lot of sleep.

 Actually I could write a book about the two years on Coral Bank, and you would never stop laughing, but it's not her story, it is mine, as I said he was the owner of the boat, but you would not think so at times, like at the end of the trip on all boats we scrubbed down all the paintwork, as we did on this one, but I arrived on deck with a bucket of diesel to scrub the winch, and Mac says what are you up to Trev, like he did not know ,going to clean the oil and grease off the winch, no way leave it on, why its manky (very dirty) yes but oil and grease protects iron and steel, so if you leave it, it cannot go rusty.

I saw his point and less work for trev, what a sensible man, do not get me wrong Mac kept a very clean boat, but his priorities were more sensible than most. (I found that out in my last boat as skipper).

One day in the dock Mr Moss said to me, Trevor the boat is clean but why is the winch in such a state so I told him that Mac would not let me wash it down, well he says it lets the whole boat down, so my reply to Mr Moss was ok Peter, I bet you £10.00 that if we both put a shackle on the hood way ,hand tight clean yours in diesel first, and I will rub mine on the dirty winch, at the end of next trip the first to get it off is the winner.
He did not take the bet, and I do not blame him, I know I am not talking about shore side much but Coral Bank was that funny I tend to get carried away with it, Freddy from the Trendsetter days did a couple of trips with us, and while we were hauling in the ropes we invented this game with a plastic headline can, they bounced very well off the wooden deck, the idea was to throw the can over one rope and under the other, throwing it at different angles, it is a wonder one of us never went over the side.
Mac never said anything about all the cans we did loose, as long as the job came first, and it always did.

One day he even came out on the deck and took on the winner, what a happy boat,(a lesson for you (Captain Cannonball) it is very strange that sometimes it is not how much money you earn, it is if you are happy earning it, another thing I was to remember when I started skipper, one day I was down the engine room trying to hacksaw a large rusty length of chain, it kept slipping in the vice (the brand new, got it fitted that trip vice) and it was giving me a lot of grief, plus it is hot down an engine room, without the bother of using a hacksaw, so getting mad with myself, the chain, the vice, and the heat and the skipper for telling me to do it, I decided it was time for poor little sweating Trevor to take command
Of the job.
For the 500th time I put the chain in the very new vice, tightened it as much as I could then gave it an extra tap?? With a big hammer, well it worked the vice was now in three bits, well he will buy the cheap shit.
Taking it into the wheelhouse I said "are you one of these owners that moan at every mishap? Yes what have you fu**ed up now, just the vice, and he said, knew I should have got a better one. PHEW.

One day in a gale of wind, we were riding it out on the storm chain, Mac sat at the cabin table talking away, and I happened to flick a teaspoon into the sugar bowl, I hit the spoon with my finger, it spun over and just went in, bet you can't do that again, so I tried it and missed, then Mac tried it and it went into the bowl.

Wow we have just invented a new sport, and called it spoonies. For most of that day we were to keep at it, taking turns we hit the spoon, if it went in the bowl you got another go, hey stop laughing, we do anything to stop the boredom in a storm, well after about an hour we found that our fingers were getting sticky, with the sugar so we changed it to a bowl of salt, that was much better.

Any way it took off big time, every day at tea breaks we would play spoonies, hey we even wrote out a set of rules, like distance from spoon to bowl, and your high score had to be witnessed by another crewman; yes I can imagine what you are all thinking, grown men having strict ruled tournaments, with a teaspoon. And a bowl of salt, but have you ever been on an anchor boat in a storm? No? Well stop taking the piss.

Well as trips at sea went on we started to play spooney tennis, the rules? Four half pint mugs were in a line, in a rack that stopped them rolling over, and two players hit spoons at the same time, one point for the nearest, two for the next, and so on, the first to thirty was the winner, sorry to say the game did not go into the Olympics, but it kept us, and one or two other boats happy.

Well let's talk about shore side for a while, the flat we had was over a café, and they complained about Mary hanging the washing out during the day, as it did not look nice for the punters to sit and look at nappies while they were eating, why they were clean? Well the landlord asks us to come to a compromise and hang the washing out when the café was closed.

Trev was not happy about this and told him so, his reply, they pay a lot more rent than you, also I can easily get another tenant for the flat, true so I said I would try to get Tony, not to fill his nappy while the café was open, but my little lad was as stubborn as his dad (good boy).

A few days later Mary was filling the washing machine, (it was a twin tub) with a rubber hose from the tap, Tony decided he was fed up with just laying about all day with nothing to do, so he starts winging and crying, I think it was because daddy had gone for a pint and did not take him along.

Giving him a cuddle and filling him full of bullshit about if he went to sleep he would go with me tomorrow, or whatever mum's tell babies to keep them quiet, BANG/ BANG / BANG, somebody at the door, she used to catch on quick.

Yep you are spot on, washer was full and floor was full, and one of the tables in the cafe was full, all with water from the forgotten hose, well that was the straw that broke, Trev had to find somewhere to live, and in those days there was no such thing as tenant's rights.

Well do you remember Ray, the lad who got me started on anchor boats; he had a four bedroom house, he kindly let us stay until we could get a permanent home, very nice of him and his wife, but one very small detail, Mary was expecting again, so flat hunting again.

In these modern times if you had a child you get a house instantly, but not in 1971, any way we stayed with Pat and Ray about five month, very good of them, cannot thank them in this book as they have both passed away, but god bless you both.

Back to sea, I was talking to Mac about the difference in cod and flat fishing, (Mac was a flatfish man), in most ports you always seemed to get a better price for flats than round fish, and also flat fishing was kinder on the gear, he said to me always think of the chickens, chickens? What the fu** is he on about, well he says if you have about twenty chickens, and you want them in for the night, you spread out your arms and slowly guide them in, right! So now spread your arms and charge at them, what will they do? Well I am not daft as my father kept chickens so I said to him they will scatter all over with fright, there you go Trev fish are the same, I remembered that for the rest of my fishing life. But I did say to him why doesn't cod scatter, all he said was do I expect him to know all, no Mac sorry.

CORAL BANK

Well Mac said, as I did earlier, that flat fishing was cheaper on the gear and the fuel; he made me smile when he said flat fishing is so laid back, cod fishing was tow like a bastard heave like a cunt.
I also said there must be times when you do go for the cod, he replied yes in February, as the cod were spawning, and they congregated on a ground south of the Dogger Bank; it was about 100 square miles of sandy bottom, with hardly any wrecks or obstacles to get your gear fouled on.
 His actual words were, shoot anywhere I am daft, again I smiled to myself, it was his way of saying it was just luck if you done well, and that was very true, I have seen beginner skippers fill the boat up and very experienced ones go home with hardly any fish at all.
   We landed one trip of fish on the 22 of September, and as I was watching the fish being laid out on the market, my second child was busy arriving into the world (I did not know at the time) when I got home to rays house he told me. So after picking up my wages, off I go to see the new little Potter.

A girl, and was named Angela Louise Potter, Mary and I had this agreement that if the children were boys I would name them, and she the girls, so sorry Angie do not blame me, at the time the cook with us had told his mother about us expecting our second child, she had kindly knitted a cardigan for the baby.

After a couple of celebratory pints, off I go to see my little girl, Kevin (the cook) came with me as he lived in the next street to the building where they find babies, so I said to him "you take the pressy in" and tell Mary I am still wetting the babies head, and he did, while he was in the ward chatting to her I went to see Angie, there were four other proud fathers stood, as the nurse asked our name she brought the baby to a window, as there was some kind of bug going round and they had to be cautious.

To me that was very sensible, any way after the first two babies were put on show, I said to the other dads "I wonder if she is showing us all the same one just to keep us happy" and letting the others sleep, (I would have) and this coloured gent behind me said I fucking hope not, we all had to laugh at that.

After introducing myself to Angie, I went along to the ward and as I walked in there was about six other men visiting, when Kevin saw me he gave Mary a kiss and on his way out said to me that he would meet me in the bar, ok, nice offer, as I walked up to the bed I said in a voice louder than normal "hey I don't mind your boyfriend visiting you but not on the day I get home from sea".

I can still hear the sniggers now, and the look I got off the wife, well put it this way I wish we were sailing that night, after I left she told all the new mummy's that I was always joking, but I think only half of them believed her.

The next day, on visiting she had calmed down a little bit, but I was still In shit street, o well maybe when she got home, I popped in to see Angie and she was not talking to me as well, are all females like that, no sense of humour.

Well back at sea thank fu**, Mac asked me when I was thinking of sitting for my skippers ticket, to be honest I have never given it much thought, well don't leave it to late, put your name down for the winter it only takes ten weeks, and your job will always be open here, so I did, but that comes next year, we had two or three trips to finish this one.

Another daft episode, on Coral Bank, Kev and I decided to make a kite each, and see who could get there's the highest, after about three failed attempts, (kev had given it up as a bad job) I made one that was spot on, it was brilliant, and as it got higher I was letting the ball of mending twine slowly out, Mac came out of the hood way and stood beside me, looking up at the kite, "very impressive Trevor" yep thanks mate, I knew I would crack it, but then there it was GONE! Mac had a knife in his hand and had cut the line behind me. What the fu** was that for?

Kite's need wind fishermen don't, and there was me wondering why he had not joined the challenge, true Mac I can see your point, but I was going to take it home for little Tony, Mac laughing said he would buy him as many as he wanted, and he did.

I have just remembered one trip it was the day of the Grand National, I said to Mac I am sick, I forgot to tell the old woman (wife) to put a bet on, in those days being stupid I often used to waste money in the bookies, his reply "I will take it", it is 10-1 are you sure, no problem name the horse, so I did Red Rum, that won last year I replied and again this, no way said Mac.

Well he took on the bet and it was £10.00 to win, so if it did he then owed me £100.00. AND IT DID get in there, Mac laughed and said "I wish I had put it on myself" so whatever I picked up at the end of the trip I had £100.00 bonus on top, but I did promise to get him a drink on landing day, all heart me.

Some trips we would fish in an area that was on the main ferry route to Denmark, we saw two ferries every day, a bit nerve wracking at night, hope they kept a keen watch, anyway each haul we always got about half a basket of empty beer bottles, (the little short ones) well we got into the habit of throwing one high into the air and then another one to try and hit it, it was very hard I would say one in every twenty was a hit, but it kept us amused.

One haul Mac came on the deck picked up two bottles and said to me, "right Trev one go double or nothing with the money I owe you" great the odds were about 15 to 1 against him, (there I go again letting my daft hang out) anyway I took the bet, he threw the bottle about two foot up and smashed it with the other one,

Hey you that was cheating! No he said the height was not stipulated.

To be honest I had to admit he was right and also started to wonder if I was really ready to go for my skipper's ticket. We finished the season off and Mac gave me £200.00 bonus for the year, no other skipper had ever done that in the past.

By the way he got Tony a kite, and his dopy daddy lost it in somebody's television Arial, well who the fu** fly's a kite in the middle of the town, yep your right again Tony's daddy.

Well the Coral Bank, and the Ling Bank, decided to go pair trawling for the winter months, was I glad I was going to school instead, anyway getting ready, like buying the books I was to use, and getting my name tag sowed into my coat, I was to start on the first week in January.

So I will see you all at playtime. O and I must remember my dinner money; there were no free school meals, but I would have a liquid lunch.

1972

Hi again god its bloody cold this winter, got two sets of under pants on (with name tags), well I could not get a flat, but I got a caravan, about six miles outside GY, that is ok in mid summer, but a very dopy move in mid winter, but at least it was home, the rule on site was only one child, (we have two) so every week when the rent man came we had to hide Angie in a locker, she would not fit in the oven.

Well its off to school time for trev, I got the bus into GY every day, and was surprised to see that there was no conductor, the driver took the money, so trev had wasted money on a bag of humbugs, o well something to eat in class.

There were three of us sitting for the skipper's ticket that year, Derek Ireland and a chap called Mick???? (forgot) it will come to me, any way with it being such a small class, most lessons they put us with the lads sitting for third hand tickets, lads off the trawlers, but a lot of the classes it was just us three, such as navigation/ Morse code/ signals/ and first aid.

Well the first two weeks was very interesting, but the next eight was mostly repetitive, dinner times we used to pop to the local bar for a couple, (we did not get free school meals), I did wonder why I was being taught Morse code /the sextant / and all the flags from A to Z, as the anchor boats did not carry any of them.

I mean for a start the sextant went out of fashion years ago, one day we were in the mock up wheelhouse, I asked the instructor why we had to learn it, as all fishing boats used the Decca navigator, he looked at me with disgust, and replied that electronic aids can go wrong, he then said, if your Decca went off how would you find your position, I said I would ask another boat, he had a piss take grin on his face and said that is why I am teaching you to use the sextant.

But captain I replied I have been fishing for ten years and sailed on about thirty different boats, none of them had a sextant aboard. By the way a Decca navigator picked up radio signals from three different positions, you then pinpointed your position on a chart. He was not amused, and told me it is in the exam so we have to learn it, what a total waste of time and money.

Mick??? Asked him if he would be teaching us the Decca and he said no, I piped up with "Mick he does not trust them" Mick's answer, bet he can't read one, the captain said class over and stormed out of the wheelhouse.

Next day we were called to the headmasters office, (college principle) and told if we wanted to finish the Course we must behave and not upset the captain again, phew I had put a book down my trousers expecting the cane, so on with the class this day we were doing buoying systems, they taught us the different shapes and colours of buoys, and light ships, and which side to pass them on, very interesting but it baffled me a bit when it came to one type that you could pass on any side, so why have one?

I was then informed of such a thing as a wreck marking buoy, and also wreck marking vessels, they were always painted green, and at night they flashed a green light, so Mick Love (just rung taffy and he told me his last name) said to the instructor, what about fog? His answer was that it rang a bell, and I piped up is it a green bell? This instructor was an ex fishing skipper, so he had a sense of humour, he replied I wish just one year that nobody asked that.

As I said it was a very harsh winter, one evening I got back to the caravan and found Mary crying, "What's up?" the water tap is frozen, I cannot make the baby a bottle, one outside tap was used by six different vans, and they were all moaning about no water, for fu** is there no common sense left in this world.

After melting a large pan of snow, tipping it over the tap, all was up and running, (no pun intended) and we had a cup of tea, Angie had a long awaited bottle, I cannot understand why little Tony did not do it for them, but he had had his dinner and must have thought, sod them I'm ok.

Well to be honest I was annoyed at my self for the condition the family were living in, so I got Ray to run them down to her mothers, until I could get a decent flat in town, which he did and I stayed at his house.

Back at school Mick and I were finding it a struggle with our chart work, we were still on chart one.

And the other guy was on chart three, anyway Mick asked him for a bit of advice on the chart ,his reply "I have not got time" (what a prick) so much for fishermen sticking together, well all the way through the term we found that he was defiantly not one of the lads.

On Thursdays we were with the third hands, doing net mending, and splicing, with rope and wire, the mending side was simple for me, (thank you Joe), and when Mick had a struggle I done his for him, the other guy could go and fu** off, wow Trevs being a meeny, (well that's how the Beatles spelt it) and one of them got a knighthood.

Next wire splice, this had me struggling, but one of the third hands did it with no problems, the instructor looked at his and told him he could finish for the day, (lucky sod) in the corner of the room stood an upright piano, the instructor threw the finished splice behind it, yes not being daft us anchormen Mick retrieved it, wobbled it about a bit and took it to the teacher, not brilliant but it will hold so good effort, and Mick winked at me and said see you in the bar.

Well a couple more got put behind the piano, I decided that my effort at wire splicing was never going to pass, so retrieving one of the other ones, after dumping mine, I showed it to sir, good attempt Mr Potter you can go, thank you sir, he replied "I will look at your real attempt when you have left" and we thought we were the clever ones, he had seen it all before.

One day I asked him why there was a piano in the mending room, he said it's to throw the bad splices behind, no be serious, so then he said I have to learn to play it in case I am sinking, like they did on the Titanic, is nobody in my life ever serious? No thank god.

Every week at 7.30 pm on a Wednesday we were taught first aid, so instead of going to rays I went for a pint or three after school, about the forth week the doctor who was teaching us, said tonight is all about alcohol at sea, and how it affects our wisdom and timing, so he goes on, and said tonight we have an expert on the subject, and introduced him, yep me, would you all welcome Mr T J Potter.

Very funny? Maybe he had a point, or do I mean pint? Whatever keeps him happy, on the serious side I picked up a lot off that doctor, which helped me, and others in my skipper's career.

Chart wise after six or seven weeks, Mick and I were still struggling on chart one, Derek the swat (the prick) was on chart ten or whatever, could have been chart one thousand as far as we were concerned, but give the lad his due, he was good at chart work, (please remember this bit for the future) thanks jot it down if you must, but I will remind you.

Well I found a flat and it was very good for the money, Mac paid the deposit thanks again mate, it had three bedrooms, well it was more a house than a flat, the only room missing was the front one, that was a turf accounts, no they did not sell grass, it's a betting shop (please keep up) well I moved the family in and got on with my schooling, hey I never played truant once, well not often.

Sorry but now the sad bit, about a week before finishing the college a policeman came to the door, and told me my dad had a heart attack, we went straight down to Beccles to see him, I will always remember him laying in bed and saying to me look after your mother trev, and I said to him you know I will dad, then he says to me you are the only one to say don't be daft you will get over it, and he thanked me.

That made me feel very bad, I wish I had said the same as the others, but maybe not, he then asked how I was getting on at college, I sit the exams next week dad, "great I always knew you had it in you.
Well next time I come down I will show you my ticket, he said even if you don't pass this time keep at it, and I promised him I would.

Well a week went by, and exams took three days to sit, first chart work, (o shit) next day signals and Morse code, the last day oral exam, lights/buoys/ and general rules of navigation, well the first two days over, on the third morning as I was carrying Angie down the stairs, Mary stood at the bottom and she was crying, she had a telegram in her hand, and did not have to tell me what was in it.

Sorry Angie I nearly dropped you, I felt very cold and empty, but all I said was dads gone, anyway she told me to ring the board of trade office, and postpone my exam that day, no way! Dad wants to see it (strange thought) but it was a strange day…

At the end of the exam the three of us were told our results.

Mick passed all three, trev failed on orals, and Derek failed on chart work, yes you read it right Mr big head failed on CHARTWORK, you see the funny side, he spent ten weeks flowing through all them charts and the exam was set on chart one, Mick and trev could have plotted that course in our sleep, Derek had forgotten it.
I suppose the moral is take you're time and get it right, if you rush things there are mistakes to be made, well we were told we only had to sit the part that we had failed on, and we had to wait at least a month before applying, ok by me.

Well dads funeral, and all the family were there, I did not cry at the grave and I had not let my feelings out, very strange, well good bye father, will see you again one day.

When I got back to GY I was told by the office that Mac needed a cook, and that they were laid in SN, (North Shields) it was strange to go cook on a boat that was holding the mates job open for me, but I went anyway, I could swat up for my next exam, also I had never seen shields before, yes I had been in there to land sprats with cannonball but we never got a night in.

Well on arrival, walking out of the station looked at the taxi rank, remembered my first day in GY so I popped into the nearest bar, which was called the railway hotel, so you can work out that it was not far to walk, anyway I went into the bar and ordered a pint, standing there with my kitbag, (a fisherman's trade mark) this old guy said to me, hello son are you a fisherman? I thought to myself no I am a fuc**** bank manager, but being a very polite lad I said yes.

I then asked him how to get to the fish dock, and he replied if you have never been in shields get a taxi, now why did I not think of that, (sorry dad) well I found the guys in the bar to be very friendly, I even sat playing dominoes with them, like for three or four hours, I did eventually get to the Coral Bank.

When I got up the next morning thinking about the Maxwell, and all my stupid vows about the evils of drink, Mac and the other two crew were sat at the cabin table, I can imagine what they thought about their new cook, but the way I felt fu** them, Mac said hi cookie what's for breakfast, and my reply was go and look in the fisherman's mission.

He laughed and said already been, after pulling round a bit Mac informed me that the net was on the quay and kneaded mending, ok then lets crack on, I knew my skipper could not mend, sounds strange but anchor men never often split a net, if they did they just changed it, anyway I said to the mate is it a big job? Don't know he said I cannot mend nets, WHAT? Well I knew Kevin could not either so that leaves Trev, what would you have done if I had not joined you? Mac replied pay a local to do it.

After filling a few mending needles with twine, (left over from my kite) I went onto the quay and got stuck in, as soon as I saw the net I realised I had a two day job on my hands, as I was mending away the crew off our partner boat Ling Bank came ashore, great they were all trawler men, and I expected to get finished by mid afternoon, with their help (wrong again) they said it was our net and not up to them.

I was fuming and ready to get the next train home, but I have a little bit of pride, (stupid pride) but there you go, what annoyed me most of all was when I went down the cabin to get a cuppa, and warm up a bit I said to the mate, "ok you cannot mend but at least you could fill a few needles for me", he replied that I was being a childish prick because he had my job, no way you are welcome to it, at least you would be if you could do it, that must have upset him a tiny bit as he then hit me.

After Kevin sat him up and wiped the tea and blood of his face, I told him I would be on the quay if he wanted to take it further, mending away about an hour later he did arrive on the quay with his kitbag and not saying a word walked away, I never saw him again, shit what will Mac say, as he is short handed again.

At about four it was getting dark so I stopped for the day, and went for a pint or two in a bar on the fish quay called the Dolphin, it was not open but one of the local lads told me to knock on the window and I would get in, (GET IN) you know what I mean.

I informed the two skippers that we were short handed; Mac said he was expecting it as he knew what my temper was like. Skipper of Ling Bank then told his crew that the net would be finished off by them the next day, gave me £20.00, and all was well.

Next day net finished and off we go to sea, we had got a local lad to sail, anyway pare trawling is boring so I will not go on about it, just one amusing thing springs to mind, while the Ling Bank was taking her net on the last tow of the day, we were waiting to see if the haul was good enough to stay, or move fishing grounds.

The weather was not very nice but ok to fish in, well trev was busy mending a rip in our net, Mac was watching our partner from the wheelhouse window, all of a sudden I am knee deep in water, then the wind was on the other side and it was ok, but it was very strange as one min I am in the shelter of the wheelhouse then the next knee deep again, this went on for a few times so I looked up at my skipper and said "what are you doing Mac I am getting drowned here".

When he told me I was amazed, well the trawling flag on the forestay is wrapped round itself and I can't see it, so I decided to turn the boat round the opposite way and let the wind unwind it, o that's ok then but did you know I am getting drowned in the progress? If you are that worried about a flag IN THE DARK, I would have climbed up and done it for you,

That was one of the few times I saw him embarrassed, well pare trawling over with, and back to the anchor (thank fu**).

That trip in I sat the last exam again and passed, nice I am now officially a skipper, no boat but that's a minor problem, anyway out to celebrate, I got as pissed as a fisherman, but on arriving home I sat on the couch and looked at the ticket and it hit me, I broke down and cried like a little baby, I had lost dad, and he never saw it, but I would like to think he will know.

So dad you always called me TOSH, (you're little bit of nonsense) I hope I have made you proud.

Well back on the anchor, we had a new cook, this lad I could write a book about, Dave Barret, my god what a man, do not get me wrong he was a hard worker, and never answered you back, but thick, well don't think about two short planks think of about six.

I will tell you just a few of his achievements as a fisherman, I think Mac kept him to amuse us on long trips , any way for a start he was as blind as a bat, wore bottle bottom glasses, and if you asked him to jump over the side to see what the weather was like he would do it, what made us twig on that he was a little bit, to be very kind, thick as shit, one night fishing over for the day, we sat down to dinner, that is about 10PM, after the meal and sweet pudding, he said did you enjoy it? Yes very good thanks, and the custard? Well yes very nice, then he said well I have never done orange custard before.

Mac looked at us, and Kev and I looked at Mac, and kev and I looked at each other, then all three of us looked at the pan holding the remainder of the custard, of coarse trev being the inquisitive one said, "Dave that was normal custard, not orange" and kev piped up yes it was defiantly vanilla, no says the cook it was orange. They do say the last person to upset on any boat is the cook as you do not know what he is putting in the meals, but we had to know, so Mac told him to show us the custard powder.

On reading the label Mac said this is normal vanilla, Dave then told him to read the flavour, which he did, and it read original flavour, gave the tin to Dave and ask him to show us, so Dave did and he read it as, ORANGE AN ALL, so Mac looked at us two and said "is he taking the piss" I replied I do not think so mate.

Another one was on a very foggy day we were towing back to the anchor gear, it was also choppy weather (medium to high waves), when we got close to the dhan about half a mile off, Mac could not see it on the radar, as the radar was picking up the waves at close range, well the four of us were peering into the fog searching, I said to the cook go up the mast and see if you can see it over the fog, which he did, after ten minutes past Kev said to him "can you see anything"? Dave replied no it's foggy up here as well, so why the fu** are you still up there, well Trevor is the mate and he never told me to come down, I just shook my head in utter despair.

We did find it and carried on fishing, the next haul before we let go of the anchor to shoot the gear, Mac told me to tie a bag of rags soaked in oil onto the dhan, so when we were towing back he would pick up the oil slick, and follow it to the anchor, what a clever simple trick, but the simple one's work most of the time and this one did, I would use that little trick a lot in the future,

But I would let them think it was my own idea, bad lad, anyway at the end of that trip we were steaming home, it was still thick fog, the cook called me out for my watch, and I asked him who was in the wheelhouse, nobody says he, well why the fu** are we still steaming flat out, if it is foggy you are supposed to stop her, while we change watch, why? Did he say why? Well Dave we might hit somebody who is at anchor, his reply believe it or not was, if I stop her some one might hit us.

Is this guy for real or is it me? I sent him back to the wheelhouse, while I made a cup of tea and pulled round, then I went up to take my watch, on entering the first thing I looked at was the radar, shit no radar, Dave how long has this been off? He said about two hours, well why have you not called the skipper out?

His reply was, why? Well son lets think about this for a bit, if the radar breaks down in thick fog, you call the skipper out, he has the responsibility of the boat, and the crews life to think about, also if it is just a fuse he can get it going again, no it is not the fuse Dave said, how do you know?.

(I hope you are ready for this bit because it is beyond belief) "Because the whining was doing my head in so I turned it off", at first I did not believe him, then I turned it on and it was perfect, just a small UN important thing, there was three ships within six mile of us, (how am I here to type this).

When Mac got up he called me a liar, no way would he believe it, all I said was think of the custard,

The next trip we fished very well, after only about 14 days we had about250 kit of flats aboard the boat (1 kit = 10 stone) and Barry on the Ling Bank, told Mac in code, that there was a lot of cod fishing with him, so we steamed all night, in the morning dropped our anchor two mile off him.

That day we caught another 100 kit of codling (small cod) one small problem, we did not have any ice left, that would have been ok in calm weather, but I am afraid it was very poor, spreading the fish on the tops of all the fish pounds was ok, but the last 40 kit had to go into pounds with no ice.

Well to stop them moving about and spoiling, after every four baskets I laid a sheet of net over them, I even cut the net we had been fishing with, anything to keep the fish semi solid, and the fish on the tops were packed that tight that they could not move far.

Anyway day over and off in to land, to be honest I was a bit worried about the catch, as I had a very good name for my fish, (the way I looked after them) and of course the better the fish the better the price you got, well after landing and all the fish laid out on the market, I was VERY relieved to see that all was well, the fish looked great, they did not look very happy, but they were fresh and clean.

We got a decent price, and Coral Bank brook her record, sorry Mac broke his record, and it was also the best trip I had ever settled on, so everyone was happy.

We made £5991.00, if I had not allowed the crew to have some fish for home, we could have cracked the £6000.00, but there you go what is £9.00 between friends, in the pub that day, Mac told me he was very surprised how good the fish looked, as he was expecting it to be a bit chafed, o thanks for your confidence mate.

The Ling Bank landed the next day, had about 70 kit more than us but made £1000.00 less, no the market had not dropped it was the fact that we had a trip of flats to back us up, and Mac said to me "always try to get a bottom of flats first trev, and top up with cod at the latter part of the trip, plus if you have a mixed trip you stand a better chance of at least getting a price for one or the other, that man should have been a teacher, o forgot he was.

A couple of days later I went to the office, Mr Moss told me I was wanted in the cashier's office,
So up I go and was asked to go through to the director's office, frightening! Anyway the head guy said to me do you feel ready to take on a skippers job, I had a long think for about half a second and said yes.

He then said because you know the Coral Bank so well, we are willing to give you her sister boat, Ling Bank, but what about Barry? He is off to Denmark to pick up a new boat that has just been built, the problem is his crew are staying with him, so you will have to find your own, I said I will leave that to peter, that is what I wanted to hear from you, well good fishing, "thank you hope I don't let you down"
His reply was don't let yourself down; on leaving he said do you call him peter to his face? No I call him Mr Moss, glad about that I am head of this firm and I would not call him peter, its respect Trevor.

That night Mac and his wife came round to the flat, he had with him a case of lager and three books, having a quiet drink, he told me that all his anchor positions, wrecks and obstructions, were in the books normally they are a skippers treasure, and certainly his life's work, and no way do you just give them away, but according to him I deserved them for all the shit I had put up with.

His polite way of helping me with a start in my skipper's career, I said to him that I was surprised to be given a start in such a good boat, beginners normally got the old wrecks, to this he laughed and ask me if I thought Coral Bank was a good boat, yes Mac she is great, and the Ling Bank is the same age.

One small difference he said, "my boat has had only one skipper where as Ling Bank has had quite a few", he then told me that they had a new engine, and wheelhouse in, ready for a big refit, I had not been told that, he then said for a start her engine was on borrowed time, and they were testing me to see if I could make her pay, before she blew altogether, nice blokes running the office, but they had given me a challenge, so, bring it on the worst I could do was fu** up an old clapped out engine.

Well Mr Moss eventually got me a crew, it is hard nobody wants to sail with a beginner skipper, and I do not blame them, I knew the cook it was Freddy Sayers brother, had done a couple of trips with him on Coral Bank, the other two I had never met, maybe a good thing, freds brother was Keith Sayers,

Anyway on the morning of my first trip, (very scary) I had started the engine and was stood on the deck, watching the pumps working on the fish room water, (melting ice) and this lad about 30 came on the deck, kitbag in hand and said to me, hi my name is Tony and we shook hands, then he said is the skipper aboard, I replied yes I am the skipper nice to meet you.

He picked up his kit bag, and I have never seen him to this day, that was scary, he had not met me and did not want to sail with me, (cannot say I blame him) so another day in to get a mate, nice start Trev, I went round Fred's house and asked him to join me, his reply, "we are good mates Trev lets keep it that way" so it is left up to Mr Moss.

He got a bloke to sail mate the next day, I would hate to see his record in Peters file, but there you go so Trev try again, I thought beginner skippers had to worry about catching fish, not getting a crew to help you, well I went aboard that day started the engine and had a full crew, we were laid alongside a boat called the Well Bank, and the skipper said to me "that engine of yours does not sound right" he had the same type in his boat, when I said I know but I have to sail with it, he looked at me as if I was daft, I wonder if he thought o well another know it all skipper.

To be honest I was that nervous I had to sail or I think I would have given it up as a bad job, so off we go two miles out of the gates and it came in thick fog, sods law the radar decided it had finished with life, so we have a first trip skipper in the fog, in one of the busiest rivers in England, and no radar.

I decided to carry on as ahead of me was the open sea behind me was very small lock gates, and very shallow water, more luck than judgement I got clear of the river Humber, (never heard any green bells) so all was semi ok, we steamed about 60 mile and still thick of fog so I decided to drop the anchor, hoping that all the other boats and ships had working radars, at least laid at anchor I would not ram any thing, so if there was a collision it would be their fault, see Trevor is not as daft as you thought.

The next morning, still thick fog I decided to try a haul, the mate asked me how I would find the anchor without radar, well I said tie a bag of oily rags to the dhan buoy, and I would follow the oil slick, never heard of that one before, no I just thought of it (sorry Mac) but I am only trying to put a bit of confidence their way.

First haul three kit, wow very good, second haul the same, this fishing lark is a piece of piss, third haul towing back to the anchor we parted the rope, so hauled in the loose end about five coil, then steamed back to the anchor to pick up the rest of the gear from the other end, (easy) was it shit, back at the anchor I found that the other rope was slack in the water, so heaving in that end I got seven coil of rope back.

Well when I started that haul I had three mile of rope and one net, now I had, about two mile of rope and no net. Still think this fishing is a piece of piss Trev?? Well if you loose gear on the sea bed you then tow a grapple hook over the position you dropped it in, and just catch it back, so no big problem, while towing the creeper the fog cleared, great and all around me there was about two million beam trawlers.

To be honest there was only three, I spoke to one of the skippers and he said that none of the trawlers had picked up my gear; he had no reason to lie, as he said they could have towed it miles, without knowing.

Every three hours we would talk to other boats on the big set, (long range radio) tell a load of lies about how much we were catching, or not catching, but the main reason for keeping the three hour schedule was to let everybody know you were still floating.

Anyway I told Mac about the loss of gear, and that I would have to go back to GY for more rope, Tony Chester then came on, and told me he had six coil of rope that he could give me, Mac had four spare, and another skipper Jeff Todd had four, so great all I had to do was steam to each boat and restock.

Tony Chester now had his own boat called the Immanuel, which he had bought after a year long trip in the Merchant Navy, so Ling Bank now fully rigged, (for how long) and on with some serious fishing.

The last boat I got gear off was Mac, he was fishing ok, 300 miles north of GY, but distance was nothing to him, we fished along side of him and were plodding along ok, in-between minor hiccups, like fuel injectors, and broken cogs on the winch, after three days of fishing, we got up one morning to find about five foot of water in the fish room.

That's it, says the mate get me home, why what's up are you feeling ill or something, feeling ill, no I am pig sick of all the trouble, and cannot see us getting a wage out of the trip with all these things going wrong, I then asked the other two what they thought, one stuck by the mate, and the cook said, I will stick it out.

So I had to make a stand, (or try to) come on lads give me another couple of days, the answer was no way, we are not working any longer. MUTINY on my first trip, so do I take the boat home, or am I allowed to hang them from the yard arm, small problem anchor boats do not have such a thing , so homeward bound, with the grand total of about 30 kit of fish, not even enough to pay for the rope, and net I had lost.

On the way home the mate called me out to take my watch, well I told him to fu** off, if you want the boat home you take her, he did not know that when Keith, the cook was on watch I was up checking on the position and every thing, Mr mate then informed me that he was going to report me to the board of trade.

What he did not know was that I was getting sound advice from Mac on how to handle things, so I knew I was safe as far as my ticket was concerned, and the office, we arrived at GY after two days steaming, and the mate said to me it is not you Trev it is all the jobs that want doing on the boat, if it is all sorted I will be happy to sail with you next trip, I will not type my answer! Well we landed the fish, if memory is correct, I think we made about £2.50p, maybe a little more but why bother.

After talking to the owner he said you can have another go, if you think you're up to it, I said I do not think! I now know I am. Well there I was sat in a bar called the Kent Arms, with no crew and a drooping confidence, when Fred Sayers sat down beside me and said, "Trev I know we will loose our friendship but I have decided to sail with you" who said I wanted you to? Laughing he replied you do not get a say in it.

Well that reminded me of Scribbo, so Freddy just two more and we can sail, no Trev one more I can get us a forth man, who? He then called this lad over to the table and said this is Taffy, and he has only done two trips at sea in his life, (great) and I asked Taffy what boat he had sailed on, in answer he said you will not know the name, as it was on the west coast, well Taff no promises if you want a job you start the same as I did, trainee, and you get paid according to how you work, Taff said ok by me thanks for the start, Fred then said well Taffy it is two lagers please, one for me getting you the job, I was to sail with Taff for over 15 years, and always rely on him to do his best. His real name is EIFION OWEN ELIAS, so now you know that for the rest of the book it will be Taff.

On sailing, it took me about ten minutes to twig that Taff had never been to sea in his life, so glad I only gave him trainee wages, to every ones shock the trip went ok, well except for about ten lost hauls, with all sorts of miner problems, but we done ok by plodding away on 2 or 3 baskets per haul, and not leaving it to look for bigger things we landed 160 kit of mixed fish, and made about £3600.00. It was a very big confidence boost, also the office were very happy with it.

The next trip went even better we landed 240 kits, and made £4600.00, wow do not get big headed Trevor you have not proved yourself yet. The next trip I went straight back to the same ground, on the first day we only caught three kit of fish, I said to Fred, "its unbelievable they have all gone", and he replied "yes Trev we took them to GY" (silly me) so off we go to another fishing ground,

It is called the Nameless Bank, (stupid name) I must remember, if I ever get to own a boat to call it that,

Well it is just north of a large oil and gas field, there were about five rigs together, at night it was so lit up it looked like a small town, we were catching two or three baskets of flats per haul, remembering the Moray Firth I tried a haul in the dark, and there was the same fishing as daylight, small problem, we do need a little bit of shut eye.

It was flat calm weather and we all agreed to work three men up and one in bed, so we all got six hours sleep, that was except for Trev, as Fred could not shoot the gear, if he could he would have his own boat but strangely when I asked him, he said he was happy on the deck, let you dopy guys do the worrying, he had a point there.

One haul Taff and I were sat on the platform, (after deck raised up for hauling the net) flat calm and sunny, chatting away I was telling him about the day on Silverfish with Scribbo, and I now know how he felt, proud but scary, any way I remembered his words, so I looked up at the funnel and said "just think Taff all this power under my command" Taff choked on his tea, "POWER all I can see is begging letters coming out, I choked to, and even now 39 years later we both still talk about it, and still laugh.

Well it had to happen the weather turned bad, (end of night fishing) and we had just let the net out, most of the second rope when the poor girl just gave up on us, one big bang and a lot of white smoke and the engine had finally popped her clogs.

Do you remember Jeff Todd, he gave me rope on my first trip, anyway he was on his last day fishing, also well north of us, so he said he would tow us home, great but I had three mile of rope and a net on the sea bed, plus I was not at the anchor, come night time we had a full storm on our hands, and were laid broadside on to it, (not advisable) after about two hours, we had been blown along and the fishing gear came tight.

On tying the rope to the forward post we then swung head to wind, brilliant a lot safer, now I just hoped the rope was strong enough, but being at anchor with three mile of it out it had plenty of stretch, actually it seemed better than normal storm gear.

Next day Jeff arrived, he had a brand spanking new boat maiden voyage called Halton, she was a beauty, any way the storm had faded into a gale, so I passed him the rope and he had to pick up all my fishing gear, also the anchor gear, it was the first time I had ever been under tow, it was ok as you did not have to steer the boat, so after the last two days I had put in it was sleepy valley for Trev.

On arrival at GY I said sorry to the owner, he replied that he was more than happy with what the boat had done, and coming up to the end of the season she would have her refit, and not loose fishing time, I then asked him about the crew, they had landed in debt, after making two very decant trips for you, he told the office to settle us up on an average, great that was £3500.00, and we only made £1800.00.

The office then asked me if I wanted to take the Ashville away for the rest of that year and I did not refuse, they also told me that the owner had decided to give me the Ling Bank back after her refit, and well can you remember the Ashville? It was the new boat that Jack off the Maxwell had turned down, so I was to sail in her after all, she is now seven year old, but that is still new for a wooden boat, a couple of anchor boats in GY were fifty odd years old, small snap of Ling Bank

That is her after the refit, if you look at the picture of Coral Bank, last chapter that was how she looked before, god I am boring myself now, let's go back to the amusing side of life, we sailed in Ashville and Taff was now cook, we were only three handed, but it was short daylight.

The mate was a guy I had never met before, Bob Mc Queen, well from now on he is big Bob ok, for some reason he took a dislike to Taff on the first day, and to be honest he was not in love with me either, but there you go cannot get on with everybody, in a few years he would be known through out GY as Billy no mates, but that was his doing.

I soon realised that he hated all skippers, as he was colour blind, and not allowed to sit for a ticket, he thought he had problems, what about poor dopy Dave, first trip semi ok except for Bob winging on about Taff all the time, until one day I exploded and told him to lay off the man, as he was a very good worker and when I told Bob to mend a small hole in the net, he made a fu** of it, I told him to get his own job right, before picking on others, (reminds me must teach Taff to mend) Bob went mad and said he had sailed with better skippers than me, my answer "well fu** off back with them" if you can.

Things calmed down and he stopped picking faults with Taffy's work, so we plodded away for the rest of the trip, one night Taff came into the wheelhouse and told me that it was fish and chips for dinner, and it was not a takeaway meal, (they refused to deliver for some reason) any way Taff said take your fish from the port side of the platter, I did not ask why but remember never upset the cook.

We sat down for dinner and it was very nice, but I did notice Bob kept picking bits of food, or whatever out of his mouth, I thought it was fish bones, but found out later that Taff had not put the bad weather catch on the oven door, so we, (or Bob did) had French fish. It's called FISH ON DE FLOOR.

Mine was ok but as I have said many times, Never upset the cook, I can not remember what we landed or made that trip, but it must have been ok as we went for another, and I said to Bob thought you did not like sailing with Taff, he is ok when you get to know him, phoney bustard (that's a bird) what he meant was he could not get another boat this late in the year

This was our last trip of the year, the fishing was very bad, O by the way I forgot to tell you that the Ashville was the worst sea boat I had ever sailed on, known in the trade as a dirty cow, and to be honest Jack certainly made the right move by not moving, if you know what I mean, well we had about a week to pull a trip out of the bag, when we were hit by one of the worst storms I had ever been in.

Mind you fishermen say that about all storms, but to be honest this was a very naughty one, as it happened the Coral Bank was laid three miles south of us, and we kept in constant touch over the vhf, short distance radio, well as you do, I was thinking of the last time we had been beside another boat in a storm, (on the Dorny) I stood in the wheelhouse and said to Taffy "I wish I was aboard her and not this one" I was nearly two years with Mac, never at any time did she worry me in weather.

But strange things happen at sea, Mac came over the vhf and told me they had took a bad sea, and parted her anchor gear, also it had smashed a lot of his deck boards, lost the net and platform with it.

Now I was really concerned, he dropped another anchor, cleared the ropes off his deck, he put them all down his fish room, he also told me that her engine room had more water in it than he had ever seen before, I remember his words "I hope it is the wave that filled it, if not we are in deep shit.

Luck was on his side, I know that sounds stupid but you can pump water out if it was a wave, but any damage under her was bad news, well he gets her dry and we laid the storm out for another two days, when it finally dropped away Mac told me he was heading home, and being a common sense sort of guy I decided to escort him in, we had 250 miles to go, but everything was ok and we docked.

Never had a lot of fish, but time of year and the bad weather the prices were sky high, we picked a small wage up, to be honest we were just glad to get in and have Christmas with the kids.

Hey it has been a very eventful year, what with one thing and another but trev got through it, am now 23 years old, I feel more like 53 is it worth it? Yes I would never change this job to sit at a desk.

1973

Well getting old now, you think that at 23 but when I look back I was still a child, as the boats were laid up for the season I had two month ashore, what can I do with myself? Well Freddy had a job in a cold store, twelve hour shifts, so go for it Trev, better than wasting time in the pubs, or is it? To be honest (that's a laugh after the bus episode) any way to be honest I would rather be working than sat on my backside doing nothing.

The job we had was mincing up the fish heads and bones, freezing them, and that was it, how challenging, any way it was a wage and a good laugh, I even got a bike and had a packed lunch, so I am now an official shore worker, the job did have its perks, and Trev is pretty good at finding them.

Like on the fork lift, after the fish came out of the freezers I had to take it into the main cold store, it was a ginoramus place, and all the different stuff waiting to be shipped out (like large salmon) were just laid there waiting to be saved from the cold.

A couple of doors down from my flat was a butchers shop, one day I asked the gaffer if he was interested in a large salmon, for Christmas, he asked me how much, so deep thinking and telling him how hard they were to get I decided to give him a trade, right you get one large fish, and I get a turkey and a leg of lamb ok, he was happy with the deal, so the next night I saved a salmon from it's freezing environment, and got the Christmas dinner as a reward, (am I not a kind chap?)

Freddy and a couple of the other lads did the same, so whoever bought the pallet of boxed salmon would not have been amused, but I look at it this way if you can afford a pack of 100 salmon, then you must be able to afford loosing a half dozen or so, plus we were not relying on this job for life, to us it was a pastime, another thing, (all firms should stop this bullshit) if the mincing machine broke down we had to get an engineer in to fix it, and with us being on the night shift we sat in the tea room and waited about three hours for him to arrive, when he did it took about five minutes to put right.

It was just the safety pin in the big cog, I said to him that we could have changed that, WHAT no way, and health and safety will not allow it, so eight men sat on their bums for three hours, (on pay) just to keep 1 man in a job, and we wonder why this country is in the shit.

Of course Fred and Trev decided if we wanted a nap just drop a metal bolt in with the fish, and lay down for three hours on pay; hey I could make a life long job of this lark, but to be honest give me the sea any day. About 6.30 am I was peddling along on my way home, (no traffic) went down a one way street, next thing I knew I was stopped by a nice police cuntstable (not an error), he said to me where have you been this time of the morning? I was going to say sunbathing on the beach, but with having the salmon I decided to tell the truth.

Anyway he had stopped me because I had no lights on the bike, and was also going down a one way street the wrong way, but being a kind sort of chap (after I gave him a fag) he just gave me a warning, don't worry if it came to a push I would have given him the salmon, and then reported him for taking a bribe.

Next day I went into the office and was told that the owner of the Ling Bank had decided to send her pair trawling, so all the promises of make her pay and you can keep her were bullshit, Trevor was not amused at this but there you go he did own the boat, and I am now an unemployed fisherman.

I then asked about the Ashville, sorry we have given her to another skipper, they don't hang about these guys do they? Not that I was that sad about not getting the Ashville back, rather go back on the deck and that was my next question, but the office did promise me the next skippers job that became vacant.

That is how I felt that day VACANT, but there you go I could always go into the salmon business, but I do not think it would last, and it did not, Fred got caught the next day, phew glad I had left.

On New Years Eve Mac had a party at his house, and I mean a party, there was cases of beer stacked up to the ceiling, (drunken sods) at the party I met the man who was to take the Ashville away, and he said to me "hope you do not hold it against me", laughing I said mate you are welcome to her, dirty cow, and I was not being childish, he was very welcome, his name Nat Herd, and we were to become close friends for life.

I even (nearly) asked him for a job, but if I go back on deck it would be in a better sea ship than her.

Well it was kept from me, but Mac and Jeff had bought a boat from Denmark, so we had three boats and three skippers, small problem the Halton, (ONLY THREE MONTH OLD) belonged to somebody else and he had a say in who was skipper,

Mac wanted Trev to take Coral Bank/ him the new one, Homeward, and Jeff too stay in the Halton, but Jeff said that was stupid as why put his money in a boat and take another one to sea, (I can see his point) well without even asking me, (the underdog) it was decided that I would take the Halton, Nooooo, too new and too much worry.

On the other hand it is only a boat and they all do the same job, after the owner was informed that I was reliable, He agreed to give me a try, so what have we got here, a brand new boat/ a brand new skipper, and a lot to live up to, (please can I have the Maxwell) at the time Jeff Todd was spratting with the Halton, so I had to go up to SN to take her away, Jeff stayed with me for a week until I got to know her, right she is the sister to Trendsetter, and if cannonball can catch sprats what have I to worry about?

Well for a start the sprats had decided to leave the NE coast, or they had all been caught, anyway the fishing was very sparse, I think our best landing was 30 ton, and the boat held 50, so all was not ok, mind you it did not reflect on my catching skill as none of the boats were doing great, by the way Taffy was with me and I cannot remember the other lads name, no worries, anyway we had about ten ton aboard and all the boats were going into Shields while the strong tides were running, (full moon).

Taff was on the wheel, the other guy and I were having a meal, during dinner he told me a joke that cracked me up, (forgot it sorry) and on my way along the deck I was still laughing, but I did notice the lights of a coaster behind us, also heading for the Tyne, no worries he is the overtaking vessel, and also I had the fishing lights on, in case we marked sprats on the sounder, half way through telling Taff the joke we saw a big black monster going across our bow, SHIT, no time to think all you can do is go full astern, that's reverse to you lot, and prey and hope and beg and wish, but none of them things worked, so it was the inevitable collision.

As if that was not bad enough the prick never stopped to see if we were ok, he just carried on into the Tyne, but he did have to stop and pick a pilot up, and that was to help our argument in time to come, the pilot boat had commented on how well our boat was lit up, (well she was new and no bulbs had blown up yet) checking the damage it was bad, we had lost the stem and opened the foredeck about a foot.

On the plus side we were not taking in water to fast, so the pumps could handle it also we were only two miles off the harbour, arriving in Shields we had to offload the sprats, to lift her head and stop the water coming in.

While the lads were unloading the pilot cutter came along side, the skipper told me that the boat that hit us denied all knowledge of a collision, he then took me and another skipper, Mick Overend across the Tyne to confront the captain, on arrival at his ship (a small tanker) the first officer said to me that we had rammed him, his first mistake as he had told the pilot there had been no collision, I then asked him where the captain was, he said ashore, on leaving the ship I met another crew member and asked him the same, he said "in his cabin, very fishy! We found his cabin and went in; he was as drunk as a skunk.

I woke him up and asked him why he did not stop to see if my boat and crew were ok, he asked me what the fu** I was on about, well Trev lost it and flew at him, I was that mad I just did not think of what I was doing, lucky for me Mick and the pilot skipper dragged me off him, the pilot said to me "come on son I am a witness to all", so you do not have a worry in the world, and hitting him will not help you're case in court.

It did not go to court, the owners of the tanker took full responsibility, and paid for all repairs and loss of fishing time, I bet that man never got another ship to command; well I would like to think so anyway.

With Halton needing a couple of months in intensive care, I had to find another job, but as luck would have it the skipper of the Reef Bank had just lost his dad, and went to Denmark to be with his family, hey that came out wrong, sorry Peter Oust (he was the skipper owner).

I had her for two trips and done very well with her, he was pleased anyway even if I did loose a net one trip; we more than paid for a new one, she was a nice boat, one of the smaller types of snibby, but like I said before size is not every thing, the funny thing that springs to mind about the two trips, was the mate he was also Danish, he picked up the English language as he was reading comics, he loved the old war picture ones.

With those being aimed at the schoolboy market there was no bad language in them, so there was no bad language from the mate, it was quite amusing when we had a flap on, or parted a rope I would say what a bastard, the cook would say fu**ing hell, and the little Danish mate would shout blooming heck, for a long time after that I would say the same in a disaster.

After her I took a boat called the Bekima for one trip, and what a total disaster that was, on sailing day I jumps aboard and guess who was the mate, DOPY DAVE, why me? And how the fu** did he get a mates job, just wait for the next bit, his brother was the cook, to be fair I was condemning him without a chance, any way he could in no way be as daft as his brother, PLEASE!

Well this was the first time I had ever sailed on a boat with the new fangled rope drums, (instead of a coiler, and no stacking ropes) I have seen them but never used them, any way these drums were made in Scotland, the skipper/owner had made some sort of deal with the firm that made them,

They had been successful on the Scottish fly draggers, and they wanted to break into the anchor boat market, so the drums had to be smaller, well off we go, after three days fishing, blooming heck, the drums conked out.

The nearest port to us was Shields, so off we go, landed twenty boxes of fish on the market, and five for the lads, it is called stocker, a little bit on the side, like cash so we did not have to get into debt with the owner, (told you how thoughtful I was) any way the cook decided he did not like me and went home to GY, one down one to go, rope drums sorted, a Shields lad I knew a bit joined us, Paul Richie better known in Shields as Bandela, yep you're right always had a band around his head.

Well we sail again and I steamed 100 miles north to where Mac was fishing well, another two or three days good fishing and bang they conked out again, (good advert) I rang the owner and he told me to go into Aberdeen, he would meet me in there, great we landed about forty boxes, got a good price, but I was thinking about the trip we were loosing.

After landing the fish Paul went and picked up the crew money, (stocker) and the owner arrived the next day, I let him sort it with the engineers, they told him the pump was under powered, brilliant how did they not test it when they made the fu**ing things, another day in, well Jimmy Howard the owner informed me that he would be taking the boat and I could go home.

He told the lads the same, but Paul told him to fu** off "I signed on with Trev so I will only sail with Trev" thanks mate but after the last two attempts I would have gladly got the train, it ended up that I took her again, we got three days fishing and the same trouble, I said to Paul sod this it is GY time.

When I rang the owner he told me to return to Aberdeen, but one problem, we were one mile from GY at the time, on arrival I told the owner that Paul needed train fare home to Shields, and some money for helping us out, he was not pleased about this but I did manage to talk him round, as I was passing Paul's kitbag up to him the ships bell rang, (from the bag) anyway I can be a little deaf at times so I never heard it.

That was my career in the Bekima over, but did I give a jot, (sorry just came home from Scotland) no I did not, also the Halton was ready for sea, anchor bashing so Trev is now return skipper of the queen of the fleet, (frightening) on stepping aboard the Holton the manager of the firm said to me "the VHF is hard to use as the knobs are sticking" my reply was WD40, he asked me if I was taking the piss, and I replied "yes man the boat has been laid up for three months", he took my point.

From that day on I knew I was on borrowed time.

Well let's get back to sea, Taffy rejoined me and a mate of his, an Irish lad called paddy, yes I know but in them days you did not ask awkward questions, and the mates name Billy Macuton, from now on Billy.

On the first trip it was a slow plod a bit boring really, but fishing can be like that sometimes, paddy was all strength and not one bit of fishing brain anywhere, do not get me wrong he was in no way thick it was as he said to me himself, Trevor I do not do technical, but I work my self to death for the right sort of gaffer, so I knew if it was technical do not call for paddy.

We only made £2100.00 that trip, not good enough for any boat never mind a new one, but I did get a brilliant homecoming present, while we were at sea my third child was born, a tiny little girl, she was under weight so had to stay in an incubator for the first two weeks of her life.

Well welcome to the clan Caroline Mary Potter, Pat and Ray had the other two while they were in hospital, I think Tony and Angie were over the moon, as they were spoilt rotten and no nagging mother to contend with, it was a bit strange coming home as the two kids did not take to me straight away, it always took them a day or two to come round, like the first day home no cuddles, the second (after new toys) the semi friendship was there, by the time they got used to me it was time to go back to sea.

The second trip in Halton, same thing slow fishing, but it was top class fish, like lemon sole and large plaice, so I decided to stick it out, quality always pays, (at least Mac said it did) we got up one morning and one of the anchor bladders was missing, (I explained about them earlier) but if you got a memory as bad as mine it is a large plastic ball to keep the anchor gear afloat, think of a football about four foot high and you got one.

Well anyway the spare had to be blown up with a foot pump, not a job I would wish on anybody, but we could not nip to a garage for air, so we had to make our own, then my little brain came to life, it came to me the fog horn was run by an electric motor, pumping just the stuff we wanted, yes AIR.

The pipe for the horn was too short to reach the deck so the bladder was blown up in minutes, err one small problem, yes it was in the wheelhouse and we wanted it out, yep we had to let some air out to make it fit the doorway, it was only yesterday (April 2011) that taffy was talking about it he has NEVER let me forget that balls up. (Did you get that? Balls Up)

After a weeks fishing I was wanted on the radio, and was told to get in touch with the office in GY on doing so I spoke to Mr Moss, he informed me that he had a mad father in the office asking when we were landing, so I told him "in two weeks" peter, then told me to get the boat home like NOW, very strange! He then said has the mate (Billy) not told you his wedding is in two days? No hold on, I called Billy into the wheelhouse and asked him what was going on, his reply "don't want to get married".

O my god Billy why did you not tell me before we sailed? I then ask Peter over the radio if the mad father had a shotgun with him, in answer Mr Moss said "Trevor just get that boat home now".

So I did much to the annoyance of the crew, all I could say was at least we can get to a garage now for air, that did not make the lads break a smile, o well, guess what we made? Yes £2100.00, I know it was only one week fishing but the owner does not look at it that way.

To top it off we never got an invite to the wedding, after landing the fish we got a case of lager and sat down the cabin to drown our sorrows, well any excuse! A young lad called Dave Larsen joined us, and it led to a bit of a party, what young Dave did not tell us was that he was sailing that morning on a boat called Saxon King, and by the time the lager had run out the lock gates had closed, so Dave missed his boat, and got sacked, well we needed a mate so no problem let him join us.

On taking him to the office to sign on the ships husband from his old firm, Arcona Fishing Co, passed us in his car, when he stopped he was shouting the odds about me stopping one of his boats from sailing, so Trev is getting the blame for another mans letdown, no way! And I told him so, I think my reply was something like "get in your car and fu** off or I will put you in it through the windscreen" well something like that but anyway he went away in short jerky movements, Dave then said to me "my father will go mad now" why? Well the Arcona firm only had seven boats and his dad was skipper of one of them, it's like this mate your dad did not threaten him I did. The ships husbands name was Captain Corsak, he was Polish, remember him a lot to come about the pole, especially for ME.

Sailing day again, I was very surprised to see Taffy so drunk, he had never before came down for sailing in that state, well put him to bed and let go, as we left the dock gates I turned on the navigation system, it must have been out with Taff, as I could not get it to work, it was dead, so back we go and the gates had closed, but there is a place called the basin, outside the royal dock so we tied up there, or tried to, as we were approaching the quay side I told Taff to get the shore rope ready, now I did say get it ready, but Taffy being a tiny bit drunk, must have thought I had said take it ashore, so he did.

Splash, Taff walked off the stem into open air, then into very cold water, if it had not been so dangerous it would have been funny, well I was going full astern, praying that he would not foul up the propeller, and the other two were busy throwing him some more rope, phew we got him out, I think he was a bit soberer (a lot less drunk) hey that's better than black coffee, Mr Moss was on the quay with an expert navigation aid menderer, (think that was his title) well taffy on way to hospital to pump the dock water (and rum) out of him, the expert came into the wheelhouse and mended my sick navigator.

Really all he done was turned the main switch on, what a show up, I never thought of that, how the hell did I get a skippers ticket? But be fair I never turned it off normally, so somebody else is to blame.

We got to sea the next day all sober, Mac and Jeff were on the Nameless Bank, still a stupid name for a fishing ground, Mac gave me the down in code, (where he was) and I joined them, the fish were laid along the edge of the bank in a certain depth of water, something to do with the pressure, I know how they feel under pressure, I certainly am.

We fished very well with no problems and ended up with a big trip of fish, and it was top quality, but get this, Mac landed on a Monday230 kits and made £7600.00, Jeff the next day 240 kits and made £6800.00? The market had dropped a bit, more fish and less money, we landed the next day with a brilliant 260 kits, can you guess? Yep £2100.00, the markets had collapsed, and so had Trevor.

Our fish was in perfect condition but there you go. A very small consolation to me one of the top boats in GY, the Well Bank only made £1800.00, he had more fish than us, anyway it just shows that fishermen do not only rely on catching, they have to hope the market is ok at the end of it.

On going into the office Mr Moss said Trev they want to see you upstairs, I could guess why, and I was spot on, sorry Trevor the owner wants a new skipper, my reply was tell him to give her to Big Eric, (skipper of Well Bank) any way they told me I can take one of the smaller boats, as they still had confidence in me, but feeling that it was not worth the worry and stress, I politely told them to shove it up there *****, well the director was not amused at that, but as I said, if I can catch more than one of the top men in GY and get the sack why bother to keep trying, he said that the owner does not look at it that way, so what you are saying is that he does not trust you to find the right skipper for his boat, any way back on deck for me. On leaving the office Mr Moss said, "to be honest Trev I advised them not to give you her" and asking him why, he said Trev you had only done six trips skipper and they gave you too much responsibility for a young man starting out, I agreed with him all the way, and wished that Peter was the head man as he had a lot more common sense. He then advised me to take a day or two and think very carefully about my next move, he said do not throw away all that you have done over one disappointing trip, bit late Peter I all ready have, he smiled and said do not worry they will want you back.

Well I had a week or two to get to know my new little girl Caroline, but she was not very talkative well not in the daylight hours anyway, (why do they become so awake in the dark) and I also bought Tony a plastic fire engine, a big one but he decided that he did not want it, might have been the wrong colour? So anyway in the flat we had an open coal fireplace, he had been told not to go near the fire as it was hot, and was a bad thing, so like I said he either did not like it or he might have thought the fire engine would put it out. (As it was bad) yep on went the engine and the real fire brigade had to come and help him, what a mess and embarrassment, especially when I told them what had caused the fire.

Yes we did have a guard but it had taken a day off, that's my excuse for being a bad baby sitter anyway, back to fishing or the lack of it, I was sat in the Albion having a dinnertime pint, not that I wanted one but there was more jobs to get in the dockside pub than on the dock itself, in other words catch a skipper while he is half pissed, they are not so fussy about your past record.

Not that there was anything wrong with mine, well shall we say shady, NO I had a good name for the deck so I will be honest, I wanted a pint and a bit of a rest from kids and fires. Well in walks Dave Larsen and he told me that the Saxon King was now without a skipper, so why don't you go for it, just one small point Dave, the last time I saw the gaffer of Arcona Fishing I was threatening to put his head through a window, Dave said he might have forgotten, and I choked on my lager.

About an hour later Dave came back to the table and told me that Corsak, (the ships husband) wanted to see me, in my own time, nice so I gave it about three minutes, did not want to let them think I was too keen, and then away down dock, arriving at his office the first thing I said was sorry about that episode with Dave, he held his hand up and told me to forget it, he should not have blamed me, and I agreed with him.

Anyway about the Saxon King, he told me that he was running the two boats for Banisters Trawlers, they had about seven or eight large trawlers, and two snibbys, Saxon King and Saxon two, as they were anchor boats they were run with the Arcona firm, anyway he took me down to the owners office and introduced me to Mr Banister, funny sort of guy he wore an eye patch, and straight away I thought yep got a right pirate here.

But he turned out to be a very fair man, I started to tell him about my skippers attempts, he stopped me, saying "Mr Potter I have all your past trips in front of me, I cannot understand them letting you go, wow I suddenly felt great, he went on to say, "if you catch fish on the King like your past record you have a job as long as you want one, so I am a skipper again, the King was another sister to the Coral Bank, they built a few of them in Scotland in late sixty's early seventy's, the King was four years old.

The crew? Dave / Taffy / and Paddy, will nobody else sail with me? O well better the devil you know and they are a good bunch, first trip went great, and I loved the boat, a very good sea ship, and no problems, (so far) we made about £3000.00 and the office were over the moon, it was no port record but a steady living, and that's what counts in this job.

The next trip at sea, after about three days fishing, flat calm weather, the compass fell out of its housing and smashed, very strange, well all compasses are filled with alcohol to stop them freezing, and the smell sent me dizzy, well even more dizzy than normal, and of course no spare, there were no boats nearby but having a ticket I knew that the sun rise was from the east, so shooting the gear was not so bad.

Sods law, the next day was cloudy but the wind had picked up and listening to the forecast I knew the wind was coming from north east, so if I was shooting the gear south west I just shot down the wind. And it did not turn out too bad, not spot on but hey we caught fish, (and they never had a compass either), we got through the trip and made £3600.00.

Ok by me we were earning a bit anyway, when I went into the office for the settling, the cashier told me I was wanted in the owners office, what now, (am I being accused of drinking the alcohol from the compass) or have I to pay for a new one, no to my shock the owner Fred Banister presented me with a bottle of whisky, thank you but why? He told me that the Saxon King had just made her best trip since she was built, well thanks Fred but it is not a port record by a long way, he laughed and said no but hopefully that would come, but for now it is her best trip, and with £3000.00 last trip just keep it there and we will get on great, what a nice man.

When I went up to Captain Corsak, s office he was throwing whisky down my crew as well, so everybody happy, and off to the pub to celebrate, I cannot even remember if I ordered a new compass or not, o well we did not need one last trip and we done better, I know it was luck, but you can get too technical cant you?.

End of year again, time flies when you are having a good time. The office gave me, bottles of whiskey and rum, a turkey, and a large box of chockies for the wife.

They also gave the crew a bottle of rum each; never saw that in the other firms,

1974

Another year, another dollar, well I hope so, to be honest not a lot to say about this year, the King behaved her self and so did Trev, we plodded along ok, and the office was happy, and that's the second most important thing, the first is the bills were paid.

O by the way we had a new addition to the tribe, some time between March and May, he was a spitting image of his dad, (or so my mother said,) and I named him after Barry Jenson, from the Maxwell days.

So welcome to the world, Barry John Potter.

By the way, if my mum was right, I must feel sorry for him, to be honest to me he was just like the other three, always hungry, and always crying, but the girls took to him, I do not think Tony was that amused,

Well he did not seem to take to him, not at first, and to share the bedroom was the last straw, but hopefully as he grows older, they will get on, they may even work together one day.

I can put that bit in because I now know that they do, and I think on the quiet, they are good pals, as well as brothers, mind you Tony is the quiet one, and Baz, well, the gabby one, I meant gobby, but spell check will not pass it, well anyway the most important thing is that they all grew up, and no Police, or any other bad things parents have to put up with.

I wonder who they take after. Certainly not Daddy, maybe there Granddad Hall, and Granddad Cole,

Barry said in later life that I had named him after a plonkey, (alcoholic) and that annoyed me a bit, I said to him, "Barry, he might be one now, but he was one of the best fishermen ever".

That is another thing; the folks ashore look at the drunkard's and say how disgusting they are, but do they know what them guys have been through, NO, some have lost family, or close friends, at sea, or ashore, (like coming in dock to find the wife had left) so please do not judge them, for the drink.

Remember the chief engineer on the Queen boat? Well there you go.

Do not get me wrong, we did get the odd bum, but you soon got to know who they were, the rest of the year went very smoothly, and we made a decent wage, and all the bills got paid on time, I remember one trip, Mac was fishing well on a ground called the

Finger Bank, stupid name again, but if you saw a chart of the north sea, it was a bank of shallow water, in the shape of a bent finger, (good job there was not two of them) any way I went to join him, he was doing well with large Cod.

I anchored about five mile east of him, and caught all flat fish, strange! But the water was about two fathoms deeper, (12 feet to you lot) and the strange thing was the amount of catfish, about ten stone of them every haul, small problem, they did not sell very well in those days, but they helped to fill us up.

Well we plodded away on mixed fishing, quite boring really, so I said to the lads, let's have a bet, who can make the best kite, (sod Mac and his superstition) well after a few failed attempts, the mate won, shit another£5.00 down.

I should have won that with my kite making expertise, but there you go, next day we got hit by a North Westerly storm, so no fishing, the wind was that strong, it bent my eyesight, true, I was seeing round corners, typical fisherman's tale, another one was, sonny I have been on one wave longer than you have been at sea, and another, I have emptied more water out of my sea boots than you have seen.

No way could a young man outwit the older guys, (except maybe Nev Best), o and another thing, sorry about this gale Mac, but we were making kites yesterday, see told you, I can never win, (but I never told him) so he was still my pal.

On landing we made a decent trip, but everybody was talking about all the catfish, (sixty kit of them) one older skipper said to me, "been in the shells then Trev, stupidly I said how do you know? Smiling he replied "that's what they eat" we got a bit of a shock, as they fetched a decent price, if you ever see one in a fish shop, try it, very tasty.

Well we had one more trip left to finish the season off, stupidly I told the crew that we were to sail at three, in the afternoon, bad choice, should have made it three AM, no pubs open then.

Sailing day arrived but Paddy did not, I was not amused, he arrived about half an hour after the gates had shut, so I had to give him the long setting, (the sack) remember LT trawlers, when we went up to the office and got a sub, (£10.00) for a drink Corsak said to Paddy "why did you miss the boat, now I have to find a new cook for just one trip", he then gave Paddy £10.00 and asked him if he wanted a job on the Saxon King.

Hey I have just sacked this guy, now you are offering him the same job, he said "true Trev but you want him back really as you four make a good crew", how right he was, I said ok but give him another £5.00 as he is getting the first two rounds, then the bad news Dave Larson's father took bad and he left, so we were still a man short, no problem got one the same day, Roddy Mc Donald.

Off again, we sailed the next day and being late in the season I was not expecting big fishing, and I was spot on, for the first week it was a very hard slog, averaging about one basket of fish a haul, (HELP) I am glad I shouted that as Tony Chester let me know that he was fishing big off the south west coast of Norway, he was catching haddock, they were not a big seller in those days but it was better than being empty at the end of the trip.

After two days steaming we arrived at the fishing ground, I dropped the anchor about two mile north east of Tony, in the morning he came on the vhf and told me that the best fishing was in his northerly hauls, that was fine as I was NE of him, I never had any chart for this spot, but he gave me the position of just two obstructions that I could reach with my gear.

The first two days we put about 80 kits of large haddock down, (very nice) there was no other type of fish to back it up but there you go, not even one single cod, on the third day Taffy woke me up and said Trev there is bad news, then there Is very bad news, go on Taffy I can take it, well we have a north west storm, ok and? And the net has been washed over the side. (THE HADDOCK NET) designed to catch high swimming fish like haddock, like the type we were fishing for haddock.

We only carry one haddock net and there it was gone, as if that was not bad enough, I told Taff I would come down the cabin for a cup of tea and decide on our next move, walking down the cabin ladder Taff was telling the mate about the lost net and I heard him say, good now we can go home, well Trevor exploded and started to throttle the prick, lucky for him paddy dragged me off, so I cup of tea and a calming down period, I told the lads if it was ok by them that we would shoot the gear with hooks on the ropes in an effort to get the lost net back, the reason I asked them is that the weather was that bad it was their choice, (well it was their lives in danger) and they agreed, the mate knew better than to refuse.

So that we did, hooks on the ropes and a heavy flat fish net, I shot the gear and hauled it in very slowly, not thinking about fish I was fishing for our net, and we got it, I say we got it we certainly picked something up on one of the hooks but as it left the seabed it dropped off.

When the hooks came up one had a small bit of the net on, but the main net had torn free in the massive swell, well when the flat net came to the surface I got the shock of my life, up floats a very large catch of fish, and it was all big cod, there was about 30 kits of them, the speed I had hauled the ropes in, it was against all the rules of cod fishing, or maybe they had decided on a mass suicide pact.

We did not fish any more that day but I told Tony what I had caught, well next day still blowing a gale but not as bad, we had three very big hauls and all cod, we left Tony still catching haddock, (strange) and headed for home. I let Mac know and he went and took over the anchor spot, he also fished very well.

When we landed we made just over £4000.00 I was a bit disappointed to be honest, but the haddock did not sell too well, but there you go a lot better than £2100.00 anyway, Fred the owner wanted to adopt me, well that's the anchor season over for another year.

We moved into the new house just before Christmas, the office wanted to help furnish it out, but I said no way not more debt, and I stuck to my guns, (stupid sod) they wanted to advance me £1000.00, but to me that was unwanted debt, also the stuff from the flat was mine and it did ok in there, so why get new.

Back to fishing, as I said the two Saxon boats were starting their first time on the sprat trawling lark, and the firm invested a fortune in four nets, and all the other gear needed for the job, the nets arrived at GY two each, and I got the lads down to rig the first one up, ready for the water, that took most of the day but after putting it on board I said to the lads "ready for a pint"? (Stupid question) I will let you guess the answer.

Well I was, but I did not like the idea of leaving a brand new sprat net on a pallet, on the quay, so sorry boys, we will at least spread it out and put a mark on it, so I would know the net if it went for a walk.

The Saxon Two did the same, well almost the skipper rigged his first net but never put it on board the boat, also he left his second one still packed up on a pallet, on the quay, I said to him "why don't you put a sign on it saying please take me", but he just laughed at me.

He would not listen to us baby skippers, next day there it was gone, oops the office were not amused but I kept out of it, the mate of the Saxon two was an old Danish fisherman, a great guy, nothing bothered him, all he said was o well one less to rig, so Tinus (that was his name) can go for a pint. The skippers name (also a Danish chap) Skull Kay, no I do not think it was his real name but that is what everybody knew him as.

So off we go on our first trip sprat fishing, it is a great job, no gutting, and no ice, you just let each haul go straight into the fish room, by the way I had sacked Roddy the prick, we only needed three of us for this job, so it was the Englishman / Welshman/ and Irishman/ what a squad, but a happy one, we steamed up to the mouth of the Tyne and joined the fleet, I saw a mark on the echo sounder, it looked very good, so we moved upwind of it and shot the net away, I had seen the depth of the fish so I knew the length of wire to let out, after only ten minutes towing we hauled, and got 40 ton of sprats, wow I feel like cannonball, sorry I did not mean to say that, I mean who would want to be like him.

This next bit I feel bad about telling you, but the Saxon Two had also towed through a good mark, on hauling as the doors came out of the water, Tinus was ready at the winch handle, when he gave it a tug to stop the winch, it snapped off, and with no winch handle you cannot stop the winch, Bang Port wire gone, BANG Starboard wire gone, so all the gear gone. I was told later that all Tinus said was "o well me go to bed now" the Skull never did get the net back; to be honest I don't think he wanted too.

We done another couple of landings and then it was home for Christmas, and a well earned holiday with the kids. One last thing to finish off the year.

. SAXON KING

1975

Hi I'm back; just had a week or two off, not for Christmas, from typing this book, but back now.

Back sprat trawling, this time I had been told there were sprats in the wash, (small bay off Norfolk) so it being closer to home, I decided to give it a try, and there was lot's of them, problem is they were very small, and the oil content would mean lower price, but we filled the King up in just two tows, being on the fish, I decided to fish for a deck cargo, the third haul was that big we filled the deck, also we let about ten ton go free, (god aren't I kind).

Steaming back to the Humber we bumped into a northerly gale, and with a deck full that is not very wise, I was pondering about letting it go when the weather decided for me, she dipped her nose into a giant wave, all I could see was the mast, (I shit myself) but the old girl was not ready to go, and slowly she recovered, when the water cleared it took all the sprats with it, (thank fu**) well we continued into the Humber, but I was told by the office that GY could not take any sprats, so I had to carry on up river to Hull.

On arrival there were about five boats waiting to land, so we had to stay the night, o well off for a pint or three with the Yorkies, (people from Hull) and a good night was had by all.

Next day after landing we steamed back to GY, but on the way the engine started to stop, (if you know what I mean), when we docked the engineers asked me if I had let any water into the engine room, well I told them that I did not let it in, it just made it's own mind up, and who am I to argue with a ginoramus wave.

Any way they let me off with that one, but she was In need of a new gearbox, the owner said that while she is tied up he would fit a power block on her, (hydraulic crane to pull the net in) great but why did they not invent all these things when I was on the deck? Well Trev had about four weeks to pass while the boat was ready for sea, you would think that I would be happy to spend more time with the kids, and I was, but in those days about 80% of fishermen's wives, used us as a threat to the little ones.

It was; your dad is home tomorrow and I will tell him that you burnt the house down, or the shed, or broke the camera, or whatever they had got caught doing wrong, SO instead of them looking forward to daddy they dreaded him, to be honest I hated that, I wanted them to shout Daddy's home! Not o shit here he is again.

Well the skipper owner of a boat called the Arcona Champion wanted a trip ashore, so who do they ring? Yep Trev the spare, but it was only for two weeks, and she was on the sprats, so all ok, or is it? When we sailed the next day I found that the crew, (father and son) were both from LT, so that is three of us, bet we get on great, WRONG AGAIN, we filled the fish room in one day, I then said to the lads "we will have one more tow for a deck cargo", and they said NO WAY, when I asked why, they said their skipper never did that.

I reminded them that I was their skipper, (after the King you would think I had some sense) but no way do I ever let the crew dictate to me, and I told them so, we shot the gear again, and it came up empty, the sprats had gone, or they were sticking with the crew, never mind great catch and back in to GY.

Next morning I went into the office and was told that the crew did not want to sail with me again, nice to know us LT men stick together, to be honest I was not bothered what they thought about me, I mean do I look bothered, (sorry Kath Tate).

So the next move with the King still in hospital, for major what ever I was asked to take the Saxon Two anchor bashing, great I am up for that, it was only for one trip, so what can go wrong, (there I go again)

Trevor you must stop this thinking lark.

The Two was only one year older than the King, but to me she looked and felt like TEN year older, what a mess and so sad to see a boat neglected like her, after four days fishing and more going wrong than the Ling Bank ever dared to, we awoke to find the engine room half full of water, (and it was flat calm)

After pumping her out I decided that these fill in jobs were not for me, so I took her back to GY, telling the office not to ring me until the Saxon King was ready for sea.

Captain Corsak was in agreement, about time somebody was, well another week with the kids. Nice.

They had not broken any thing or killed any thing, so were semi pleased to see their dad, awe how nice,

At last the King is ready for sea, and back on the anchor, the day we took ice and stores aboard, I gave our Tony a treat, I took him down to meet the boat, but I was very worried about his safety, and told him "do not go near the rail" as he could squash his fingers or even worserer, (that means worse than worse)
But did he listen? Either no, or I have a deaf child, I looked out of the wheelhouse and saw him leaning over the side, do they never listen? Any way I said what are you looking for Tony, he answered the boats name, so father let him see it, I picked him up and hung him up side down over the stem, he was not happy, but he never went near the rail again.

To this day Tony still tells me off about that bit, but it was for his own safety in the future years, well all stored up, ready for the first trip and down to sail, Mac (Coral Bank) had other plans for us, him and skippers from all over the UK had decided that we were fed up with cheap fish entering the country,

Mostly brought over on the car ferries from Denmark and France.
So it was no fishing for us, it was blockade the major ports, all around the British Isles, any way, this we did, at least the King had plenty of food aboard, but that was not a plus as a lot of the others had none, so we were now the suppliers for the Blockade boats.

Our port to block was Hull, so the King and thirty other boats set sail, the rest of the GY anchor boats closed down Immingham and Grimsby Royal Dock, well it lasted about two weeks, all we got was a lot of media coverage, and the threat of loosing our boats, it did not matter to me or the other skippers, but the owners were getting a bit edgy, and I don't blame them, well anyway it was called off and the fishing boats all went home.

On talking to the office on the VHF, I was told that Fred Banister, (owner of the King) had woke up dead that very morning, I think it was the stress of giving Trev his bestest boat, and the worry of the Blockade on top, any way I was advised not to enter GY, as all his fleet of trawlers, and the two anchor boats were to be laid up, until all the legal bullshit had been sorted out, so I tied her up in the basin of the Royal Dock.

On going up to Corsak's office he said that I had two choices, one take her to sea and land the catch abroad, two bring her in and see what happens, well for a start most of the ice had melted, and also not much food left, I was very tempted to give it a go, but Mac advised me on the legality of my taking her to sea, and also was she now insured.

That made my mind up for me, so when the gates opened the next day I took her into GY, as soon as the ropes were ashore, two guys jumped aboard and told us to get our personal gear ashore, they then slapped a writ on her mast, and that was to be the very last time I stepped aboard M.F.V. Saxon King, and I was very sad about that, as she was by far the best boat I had taken to sea.

I did not go to Fred's funeral as he would not go to mine, so that was the end of Banisters trawling co.

Sat at home I decided to see if Chessy, (Tony Chester) was still up for the offer of the Immanuel, he was at sea, so I would wait for him to land before I made any daft moves, not that I made many, (ha ha) but with all the ones I had made it helped me to stop and think.

This you will not believe, I was sat in the Albion bar the very next day and one of the lads said to me "did you hear about Chessy? "No what?" well the Immanuel sunk, and the crew were picked out of a life raft by the Frem.I was dumbfounded; not because I had just lost another chance of a skipper's job, but I did not think they made inflatable rafts big enough to carry Chessy, I mean he was a great big lad, and all the fishermen used to take the piss of his size, one of his crew once said "hey I saw this guy and he was huge, about one and a half Chessy's). Tony went mad at him and said "don't use me as a measure" well after that all through the fleet every body was using it, half a Chessy, or two Chessy's.

So after that he sold his car and got a peddle bike, give him his due he lost about half a Chessy in two month's, but then with such a fast weight loss the lads said that he had cancer, and Tony let them think it was true, when I asked him why he said "Trev mate, every bar I walk into someone who feels sorry for me buys me a drink, so why let them down" crafty sod, Tony might not have been a top skipper, but business wise he was one of the best. I asked him whether he was getting a replacement boat.

And he replied just thinking at the present; he also said "it's hard to find a decent skipper nowadays, that made me think, is he asking or testing, we will see.

I was sat in the house one day, and who should arrive, none other than Mr Moss, he came in had a cupper and asked me what my plans were, I said "Peter I do not make plans Anymore, they always go wrong", smiling he then said to me, "they want you to go on the Halton" not skipper but mate, I said to him and you are the one they send? "Yep I am the only one you will speak to, not wrong there Peter.

Well the job was to use my skippers ticket, as the man taking the boat never had one, who is he? It was no other than Bob, he was mate with me, in the Ashville, Peter then told me that the boat was in Shields and the regular skipper had had a fall, and broken his arm.

When I said ok I will, Peter looked at me in amazement, "but Mr Moss on my terms", he asked me the terms, I said, ok full skippers share, gas and electric bill paid, one month's mortgage paid, and none of this to come out of the settling at the end of the trip, Peter asked me if I thought the owner would agree to that, and I said "not if he can get another skipper".

I did not think they could, not at short notice, Peter told me that he would ring me with the answer, that afternoon, also as he was leaving the house, he turned to me and said " Trevor I am proud of you" why?

"Not for taking the boat but for screwing the bastards" well I was shocked, never herd Mr Moss say that word before, and they did agree, yes get in there Trev.

So on the train, going to Newcastle, Bob (sorry Skipper Bob) and I had a few cans of lager, only to pass a boring ride, when two young ladies asked if they could buy a can or two off us, being a kind chap I gave them one each, (lager) get your minds out of the gutter, any way they were very friendly girls, and asked where we were off to, they were getting off the stop before us.

Chatting away and Bob, after telling them we were fishermen, (and he was the skipper) they seamed very interested, until that is Bob got his new chart out and tried to teach them navigation, god what a boring sod, any way that was the end of the chat up, and the end of any hope of taking them out for the night.

O well my marriage was still safe, thanks to my new skipper, when we arrived in Shields, I met the other crewmen, (both Geordie lads) one was called Aden, and the other was the head, well Mick Mc,Ginty I had met the head before, but not the other lad, why did they call him the head? Well it was out of proportion to the rest of his body, but he was a great lad, also a brilliant cook, ex merchant navy chef.

Any way we sailed, and I said to Bob, you are the skipper, but any help you want just ask, or call me into the wheelhouse so the lads do not hear, and he did tell me that he was a bit worried about shooting the gear, well I said, if I was on my first trip, I would start at the Nameless Bank, as there was very few obstructions, and you can plod away on a couple of kit, until you feel that you are ready for tighter areas to fish in.

Then he tells me that he had no chart for that area, lucky I got mine with me then, so off we go to the Nameless Bank, (still a stupid name), and as it was there was a steady plod of two or three kit per haul,

Things were going ok, and Bob started to feel better, but the plod was too good to leave, his only trouble to my mind was that he treated the crew like they were dogs, and Trev was not up for this.

A beginner skipper does not want much sleep, and if he did the worries of the job did not let you, so Bob thought the lads were the same, (ok I remember the night fishing in Ling Bank), but the lads got a watch in there beds, but sadly not with Bob.

After about five days even Trevor was feeling knackered, like big time, we were only getting about three hours sleep a day, and that is dangerous, any way, that night after dinner, Bob sets the alarm, then goes off to his bunk, behind the wheelhouse, when he had left I looked at the clock, and it was set for three hours time, well I had to sort this out, and I turned it off, the two lads said Trev he will go nuts, fu** him boys if he wants to finish this trip, he does so with out killing us.

Well next morning, (try mid day) we were awoken by some screaming maniac on the deck, getting out of my bunk, told the cook to start breakfast, and I will go and talk to the skipper, the two lads looked at each other as if I was daft, but this time I was not, I was fuming mad, before I left the cabin I made two pots of tea, (not a peace offering) Bob was busy starting the engine.

So I put the mugs in the rack, and sat in the wheelhouse chair, in comes Bob, he did not look amused,
He said to me "what the fu** is going on we have missed two hauls" any way I told him to calm down a bit and listen to a bit of advice, I then told him that he treat the crew like robots, and I asked him why he did not wake up earlier, before he could answer, I said, "because you yourself are knackered Bob".

I then told him he had two choices, one slow down a little, and finish the trip, or carry on as you are, and we go home, I wanted to finish the trip, but I did not agree with his way of doing it, he then said, ok Trevor, but we must get the gear In the water, true Bob but after breakfast.

The rest of the trip was a lot happier, and when we landed we did ok, we landed 138kit and made£3500.00, great trip Bob thank you, three or four days later I was sat in the Albion, with a few of the lads, and in walked Bob, he was not amused, "what's up Bob" he threw the Fishing News on the table, and said, "third top for the weak, and they have put you down as the skipper".

All the boys in the bar laughed at him, and one guy said that you need to take the boat alone Bob, then maybe they will name you, to be fair Bob went on to be one of the top skippers in GY, when he could get a crew.

After that trip I took the family down to see Mum, and after Bob I needed to unwind, well I have not mentioned him yet, (sorry) but my little brother Paul was there, (five year younger), and a foot taller, he had been in the army since he left school, but now he was a policeman, well who else would take him? It was great to see him again, and we caught up with a few missed pints, anyway yapping away one day and he told me a story about a fisherman in LT, he told me that him and another policeman were on the beat one night, and they were walking past the fisherman's mission, well the mission had a strict rule, in by eleven, or you are locked out, they did not want men coming in, after the night clubs causing bother, and I do not blame them.

Any way Paul told me, that this guy shouted to the whole town, let me in, I want to sleep, Paul and his oppo then told the lad, there is no chance of you getting in there mate, so quieten it, the young lad said to our Paul, arrest me then, and Paul's answer, "sorry mate you have done nothing wrong, plus the station is not a hotel, we cannot arrest you for nothing, (think Paul takes after me) two or three yards on, and Crash, in goes the mission window, so the lad got a bed, but it would have been cheaper to get a posh hotel.

Another funny tale, Paul asked me, do I wear tights? (strange question) so I said only on a night out, he then said be serious Trev, stupid thing to ask of his brother, any way I ask him why, and he said that on a winter night, walking the beat, on LT sea front it was so cold that they wore ladies tights, to keep them warm, he was asking if fishermen did the same, and I answered, no bruv, a dangerous thing to do on a trawler.

Any way, even to this day I have to stop myself from asking the policeman, "Have you got your tights on"

Not the best way to stay out of the cells.

May June and July, I sailed on the deck, and to be honest, it was like a holiday, let somebody other than me do the worrying, mid July Chessy, (Tony Chester), came round the house, and told me he was thinking of buying a boat, it was called, ISLAND, a very well known boat, as she had smashed a few port records, with the skipper owner Jens Bojen, that was pair trawling, and now she was back on the anchor.

Jens had two brand new boats built, that's how well he had done, and good on him.

Well the deal Tony gave me was very attractive, the Island was up for £6000.00, and I was to take her skipper, as, and if, I made the same amount profit, he would then sign over a half share to me, who would be dopey enough to turn that down, this time you got it wrong, I took the deal, (see I'm not as daft as I thought), but I did say to Tony, lets slow down a bit, she is twenty six year old.

So we agreed that I would take her away for one trip, and then decide to buy her, and this I did, well she had a few faults, but nothing major, we landed 160 kit and made £3600.00, but the fish did not turn out very good, to be honest it was crap, and we had ten kit condemned, unfit for sale, to be honest the boat had a name for poor fish, so this needed looking into, I felt sorry for Taff as it was his first trip as mate, and not a good start to his mates career.

On speaking to Chessy, I told him that the boat was ok, but she needed a little spending on her, but to my mind she is worth the money,(well his money), glad you like her, because I have already bought it, so much for waiting for my approval, he then told me that we made £800.00 profit on the first trip, or so HE thought, I tells him that the fish room was rotten, it wanted drying out, a repaint, and 200 new fish pound boards.

He told me to slow down on the spending lark, and I replied, Tony get somebody different, if you do not trust me, but no way do I sail with a bad fish room, after calming down, and seeing sense, he said get it done, and I replied, "now who is wasting money?" so next day the lads and I, and Chessy set about repainting the fish room.

All done I went to the office and drew £80.00 for labour, gave Taff and Paddy £20.00 each, same for Trev, and gave Chessy his £20, Chessy then moaned at me for paying our self, so I told him to think of the tax man, he smiled, and said "you are learning mate".

We plodded away for the rest of the year, but at that time, the trawlers in GY, were having a domestic with Iceland, something to do with how far off their coastline we could catch fish, they called it the cod war, but to me it was bullshit, as our government backed down, why? Well they said it was the fish stocks, and the fishermen, said it was that the U.S.A. had an air base, in Iceland.

Same old story, we gave up, and thousands of men were now out of work, they do say that for every fisherman, at sea, there is four men working ashore, that was true, instead of us taking their offer, of X amount of fish, per year, like a lot of other countries did, if we had done the same, at least there would be about ten freezer trawlers fishing Icelandic waters to this day.

But no, we spit our dummy out and lost the lot, on top of that, Norway did the same, so that is the British trawler fleet fuc***, now we had 150 anchor boats, and 3000 fishermen looking for jobs, at least I could now be choosey, but back to the Island, the mate, Taffy, the deck hand was a lad from Blyth, and the cook was called, bambolini, well that's what taff called him, do not ask me why,

Anyway, about little Charlie, if you have ever seen the Muppet show, think of the mad drummer, well that's him, ginger hair and beard, small, and gabby, he was ok, stood four foot eight, but two vodka's and he thought he was visa versa, (eight foot four), the trouble I got him out of is beyond belief, and the trouble he got me into is, well, FRIGHTENING, hey why are the little ones always the worst.

Let's get to sea, before I get filled in again, Charlie was a very good worker, he also got on well with the crew, Taffy, and Paddy, and so the Island was now known through the fleet, as the Muppet Show.

I had just got a chart for a fishing area, it was called the North East Bank, and not many had it, it was like gold dust, you could lay on the same anchor spot all trip, and still catch fish, do not get me wrong, they were not the best quality fish, but when fishing was slack, in the north sea, it was a great area to pull us out of the shit, reason for the poor quality, they were feeding on sand eels, so they did not last long in the fish room.

But like I said, there were only about five skippers in GY that had the chart; it was such a small bank with stony ground all around it, if a skipper decided to try fishing it they always came up with a bag of stones, so not many bothered with it. Well here is the ISLAND.

See you in 1976

1976

Well still afloat, still fishing, and still trying to pay Chessy the £3000.00 I owe him, to be honest I only owe £1000.00, and then I will be a half owner of the boat, steaming out that trip, I decided to test paddy on his watch keeping ability, so I rigged up three daft tests, one was a piece of twine leading from the main switch of the depth finder, which lit up, and made a loud noise, to my bunk, (that was behind the wheelhouse) number two was an electric cable, from the fog horn, also to my bunk, so when I touched the wires together, the horn went off, and the third one, another length of twine, through the porthole, down to the engine room, when I pulled on this one the engine would slow down.

So, Paddy now on watch,(all alone) I gave it about an hour, for him to settle down, and let him think I was sound asleep, then the test, first the fog horn went off, Paddy looked out of the door, and in the radar, then ten minutes later the engine eased in a couple of times, (that is when you are to call the skipper out), all of a sudden, the echo sounder went on, I could hear him muttering to himself, but all he done was turn it off, fog horn again, engine again, and at last ,he said are you awake Trev? I said no.

Then I got out and asked him what was up, when he told me that every thing is working on its own, I said "have you been drinking" he told me to piss off, then he said that the boat had a mind of its own, I replied no Paddy it's the old skipper, his ghost looks after the man on watch, then he told me that the engine kept slowing down, "well Paddy that is just a fuel filter, next time that happens call the skipper out" he said ok, "but if it starts up again I am not staying up here alone", It was a struggle not to laugh, but Taffy was on watch in an hour, and I went back to bed, thinking, at least he will now call me, if anything out of the ordinary happens.

About an hour later Taffy came on watch, Paddy was busy telling him about all the strange events, Taff said to him "it will be that cu**, testing you" well Paddy stayed up the wheelhouse with Taff for a yarn, and they were doing my head in, chatting away, keeping Trev from his sleepy bye's, so time to get them to shut up.

This was a STUPID thing to do, but we all have our daft moments, whilst they were chatting away, I crept out of my bunk, and with a full tin of lighter fuel (petrol) I ran it over the bulkhead, (wall to you) and it run down onto Taffys hat and down the back of his shirt,

I heard Paddy say "can you smell petrol Taff"? Taffy answered, "it's the fumes from the engine room you idiot".

Even I got a fright, when I lit it Taffy burst into flames, he was that shocked, and he ran out of the wheelhouse door, if it had not been for Paddy grabbing him he would have jumped over the rail, into the sea, what a stupid joke. Sorry Taff but you did insist on me telling all, about blowing up the anchor bladder in the Haltons wheelhouse, and I have a lot more to come, in future years, by the way Taff and I have had a life long thing about getting one over on the other.

Well that trip we made £4600.00 the trip after,£4100.00 it was great, as I had now paid Chessy off and had a couple of grand in my boats account, so I am now the very proud half owner of an anchor boat.

Do not get me wrong, it was not time for big cars, or holidays, in the Bahamas, as you never now when something on the boat needed replacing, as with all machinery, they can be expensive to upkeep.

By now there was about 200 anchor boats in GY, nearly all of them had rope reels, but Island still had the old coiler, but the crew did not seem to worry about it, so why should I, especially as a set of reels cost around £6500.00, hey the whole boat never cost that much, even Chessy told me he was ready to invest in a set, but I told him to give it another year, that way we did not go into bank loans.

Tony said to me that I would struggle to get a crew with the old coiler, laughing I said "not a worry Tony I will just keep this bunch" they were daft enough, also I did not want to confuse Paddy, with all this technology, to be totally honest they were a brilliant crew, and had said to me, that as long as they were picking up a wage, they were happy dragging and stacking ropes, now it is confirmed, Trevors crew are dafter than him, great, another plus ,all the boats getting reels on board, were giving away loads of coiler spare parts, so I never even had to buy them, great I have enough for about twenty years.

As I said, always keep a bit of money aside, for mishaps, and the next trip we had a big one, we were steaming out, when all of a sudden she started to vibrate, and then jump about madly,

We were lucky that we were all awake, sat in the cabin telling lies to each other, I ran up to the wheelhouse, Paddy was just sat there, taking no notice of the boat doing the tango, I pulled her out of gear, well I thought that the prop had picked up some floating net, or rope, any way as soon as she was out of gear she stopped dancing, I then shouted to Paddy "why the fu** did you not stop her straight away", if it had not been so serious I would have keeled over laughing.

Paddy said to me, "Trevor it was technical, so I ignored it" can you believe that? Well it is true, on leaning over the rail, I could not see anything in the screw,(propeller) but there was a burning smell down the engine room, and a lot of smoke coming from the gearbox, it was also red hot, (o shit) towing job for somebody.

As it was a boat called Scanboy was on her way home, she would pick us up in as little as six hours time, when she arrived, the mate was no other than Ray, the lad who started me up in GY, on arrival the engineers confirmed my worst fear, yes the gearbox had died, and we needed a new one, shit more expense.

Well I got the insurance man down, told him we had seawater in the gearbox the trip previous, when he looked at the dipstick, (not me, the one in the box), he said that the oil was clean, and no sign of seawater, time to think (like fast Trev), so I said to him," the first thing I did was clean it out with flushing oil, then put fresh oil in".

Well anybody would have done the same, the outcome was, and the cogs were sent for analysis, (hey this spell check is great) I would never have got that one, and the result was, she had saltwater damage, so a free gearbox, I say free, bet the policy goes up, like lost my no claims bonus, o well the gearbox was £4000.00.

Well at least while they were fitting a new gearbox, I could take the kids to see nana and Marys parents, also it was quite nice getting to know them, or rather them getting to see daddy, without his overalls on,

So we got the train to LT, the reason I am telling you this bit (a rest from fishing), no, it was to me very funny, ok little Angie had a wollygog, (gollywog in English), but maybe you have not seen one, (they got banned), any way it was a black doll, and Angie loved it.

She had never seen a coloured person in her short life, sat on the train an African woman got on, and sat in the seat opposite, well Angie looked at the lady, then at her doll, then another look at the lady, I thought to myself please Ange do not ask, but to my relief the woman asked Angie the dolls name, her reply was Golly, but daddy calls it, stop there Angie do you want a drink?, phew she never told the lady, but I bet she guessed, by the way, in no way am I a racist, there is good and bad in all countries.

Well another break over, time for Trev to get back to sea, reading this, you would think that I was happier at sea than being at home, well to be totally honest, I was, things were not going too well in the marriage department, to be very blunt, Mary was seeing other chaps, while I was away, (that happened a lot in fishing), but their you go, five years married, and four of them spent at sea.

I stayed with her for another five years, but was a changed man, not for the better, I started to get so that I would rather be on the boat, than in the house, while I was fooling myself that it was for the kids, they suffered as well, but like I said, there were more divorce's in the fishing industry, than any other job I know.

Sod that lets get back to sea, the next trip we sailed, there was big fishing going on at Helgoland, that's a small Island off the Belgian, German, coast, it was only about two square miles, in size, and it was part of Germany, well the fishing was very good, but no secret, most of the fleet was there, (not Mac) he was doing the sensible thing, catching flats, while Trev and the other morons were catching very small cod.

It was easy to catch them, but hard to sell them, at a decent price, god will I ever learn, well I will but it takes time to sink in, it was easy fishing, and no moving anchor, as the tide was that strong over there the fish were on the move, after only two days, we had caught about 150 kit, Island held 300, so hopefully very short trip, (there I go again) mouth open and brain shut.

Nat, (remember him from the Ashvill), well he now had an anchor boat from Shields, the Nyborg, anyway his rudder fell off, I say off, but it was hanging on one bed, instead of two, towing job.

So I started to tow Nat back to Shields, (300 mile), with his rudder hanging over to port, the tow was very hard, normally when you tow another boat, a very long tow is used, not only does his boat, hold a Course, but the towing boat is easier to steer, the problem we had was that Nyborg wanted to go to port, and that automatically pulled us to starboard.

So thinking caps on, one thing we had going for us was the weather, it was flat calm, no wind at all, so we changed the tow from a very long one, to a short nylon rope, this would be unsafe in any choppy weather, but as I said the sea was like a mill pond, we nearly got there without a mishap, that is until Nat decided we were not going to get in before the pubs closed.

So he decided to speed the job up a little, ten mile of the Tyne, he engaged his clutch, two engines go faster than one, well that was his thought, but with his rudder being jammed, well his boat went hard over, with having a short tow, that was not a brilliant idea, (glad other skippers can be as daft as me).

Well! crack, the tow ripped off our aft rail, and a couple of the ribs, the damage was VERY bad, after sorting out another method of towing him, (the pubs were now open for the evening shift), we got him safely into Shields, the funny thing was his rudder fell off, in the river, I wish it had done that at the start of the tow.

In the morning ,Nat was landing his fish, I decided to land in GY, the insurance men came down to asses the damage, luckily it was all on the Nyborgs insurance, and as you do, I found more damage, and broken tow gear, and loss of earnings, the only thing I did not claim for was the extra fags I had smoked,(with the pressure, so we now had a boat with no aft rail, and it would take about three weeks to put right.

The insurance man told me, after patching up the holes in the deck, that I could take her back to GY, but to keep close to the land, if the weather got semi bad I was to pull into the nearest port, yes sir, defiantly sir, you are the boss sir, so we set off for GY, wrong, there is a spot of ground 60 mile East of GY, with only having 150 kit, and the weather still very kind, I decided to give it a look.

We fished for two days, got another 100 kit, then went home, as I was told by sir, well on landing we only made £3600.00, not bad but the market was flooded with small cod, mind you with the towing job and the extra damage, also new anchor gear, plus two new storm nylons, then the loss of earnings, we ended up with £9000.00, not bad , by the way Nat got the sack, wonder why, I think he was expecting it as he gave me a brand new net, worth another£2000.00.

By the way as I said before, about marriage breakdowns, it happened to Nat, that is why he is now living in shields, only one of many, but that is fishing, after the towing job and all repairs done, we managed five more trips to finish the year, nothing out of the ordinary happened, (new for me), we averaged £4000.00 a trip so everything rosy.

One of them trips we were fishing south of the Nameless Bank, (still a stupid name), I wish somebody would name it, anyway, we were four mile south of the Echofisk oil field, there was now about eight rigs sat there, sorry stood there, towing back to the anchor, a small inflatable raft came alongside and the lads ask us for some fish, great, in return they gave us cigarettes, steaks, and other goodies, no drink, (strictly banned on the rigs), we tied the raft alongside, while we sorted out a kit of mixed fish for them.

I was still towing the rope but thought to myself, (there I go again), anyway I thought to myself, if this rope breaks we would charge ahead, and put the raft in danger, so I did the opposite, I eased the engine in, and the stretch in the rope pulled us backward, (o shit) the inflatable got dragged along with us, then filled with water, I am glad they had gave us the fags and other goodies before it happened.

Well they were back afloat and semi dry, so we gave them two baskets of fish, I do not think they were expecting so much fish, as they only had a plastic bucket to hold it in, I shouted to the lads "just tip it into the raft, so we can get on with this haul" this they did, brilliant sight, four rig men, trying to stand up in a rubber raft, and 15 stone of slimy fish, sliding about under their feet.

Strange thing they never came back for more later in the trip, or maybe they were not fish lovers, but we enjoyed the T bone steak, also the American fags, I just hope Scribbo does not hear about me giving fish to the oil rigs.

The rest of the season passed ok, that is except for our last trip, Paddy had to leave, instead of replacing him we sailed three handed, Taffy, and little Charlie, we went to the Finger bank, (that's were we caught all the catfish, in the King. Anyway we were nearing the end of the trip, then the weather changed to very bad, (it was a hurricane force 12), and believe me, you do not want to be in one of them.

The wind was from due west, problem was, we were on the eastern side of the north sea, and the wind had 300 mile to make very nasty waves, well the first 24 hours were bad enough, we were dragging the anchor, (that is a good thing), if you were dragging, you had less chance of parting it, (breaking the wire).

One big problem was that we were drifting to the edge of the shallow water, when the sea hit the edge It just boiled up, as in the Dorny, I set a watch, one man awake at all times, also kept the engine running, and all pumps, the Island was a very good sea boat, but there is only so much any boat can take.

And by fu**, she had taken a lot in the last 24 hours, in the early hours of the next morning, I was sat in the cabin, the other two lads were asleep in their bunks, this is very strange, the sound of the wind suddenly disappeared, in 13 years at sea I had never experienced this, but I knew that it was a VERY bad thing, about to hit us, and by god it did.

When the sea hit us the water came down the cabin, it was half full, I honestly thought that was it, I ran onto the deck and saw that all the ropes had gone, (3 mile of them), normally they would be down the fish room in this weather, but with the fish we had caught, there was no room for them.

All the top rails had gone, (they were designed to do that), and so if the deck was full of water, they would give way and she could empty herself faster, the top of the mast was lying on the deck, and we now had a wheelhouse with no windows at all, I honestly thought that this was my time.

But the old girl got through it, we rigged up the spare anchor gear, and let it out, when we were back head to the wind, we then started to pump her dry, god what a mess, sat back in the cabin, (about five hours later), having a cup of tea, (wish I carried rum), there was no laughing or joking, we were all very concerned.

Then bang, another one hit us, the anchor gear parted again, and no spare one left, so now it was, stand in the wheelhouse and keep her head into the wind, with the engine, I can tell you that this is a very difficult thing to manage, as if you let her fall off as much as 10%, you were blown broadside to the waves, it was a struggle to get her back head to, even with full power.

All three of us spent the night in the wheelhouse, taking ten minutes each on the wheel, by then you were knackered, all night we promised never to drink, or swear, or fall out with anybody in the world,

I am not a religious man, but I prayed that night, as we all did.

Come daylight the weather had eased away to a force nine, (violent gale), but to us it seamed flat calm, on inspecting all the damage, I found that none of the wheelhouse electronics worked, and I had no idea within 40 or 50 miles, where we were, so I did not have a clue where the ropes were, to be totally honest, I did not give a shit, to me it was get her and the lads home, well we steamed for two days due west, I knew England was that way,(have you noticed I am joking again), that is called relief.

Any way we picked the coast up, and it was off Whitby, GREAT, we never had a radio, radar, or Decca navigator, even my lighter was not working, and that is bad, anyway we followed the coastline down to the Humber river, and docked the next day, all the promises of never drinking again went out of the window.

Yep straight to the bar, and got merrily pissed, Taff always made me smile in the past, if something went wrong, he said, "and they wonder why we drink" well now you know, we made a brilliant £4800.00 that trip, and even the insurance man said to me, "Trevor I am amazed that we are not paying for a total loss", but it did cost them a fortune, but to be fair so were my policy payments.

I was told later by a couple of skippers that there was big concern, with them not hearing us on the radio for three or four days, I told them that we were a tiny bit concerned as well, nice to know others worry about you, I never told the family about those two days, especially mother, but it was over, and you do not dwell on it, if you did you would not go back.

1977

Hi did you have a good new year, I did, but I tell you what, I am only going to give this drinking lark another ten years, if I don't start to enjoy it by then I am going tea total, we never got back to sea until March, as all the jobs on the boat were not finished, but when we did sail, with all new gear, and new windows, (must keep them clean), it was like having a new boat.

Our first trip we went to the NE Bank, the fishing was great, average of twenty baskets a haul, (get in) but sods law on the second day, little Charlie slashed open his hand, while doing a splice in the rope, no big deal, we were only three handed but I let Charlie work the wheelhouse, while I went on deck, to gut the fish, all flats.

I forget the reason, but Taffy was not with us, the third man was a trawler man, called John Lewis, as from now Louie, trawler men in GY were very fast gutting round fish, but when it came to flatfish, well they had a struggle, (GY trawlers were not known for catching flats), as I told you there were lots of them looking for work, with the trawler fleet disappearing, but he was a very good deckhand, also as mad as a hatter, so he fits in perfectly.

The next morning, we got up to shoot the gear, shit, Charlie's hand was as big as a football, so even though the fishing was brilliant he had to go ashore, at the time there was about five boats fishing the stony ground all around us, as luck would have it one was on his way ashore to land, talking to the skipper, I told him about Charlie, and the poison, he offered to take him ashore for me.

That was great, IF I had invested in rope reels, but with just two men left it was not so great, anyway the fishing was that good I did not want to leave, as another boat may arrive and drop on our anchor spot, so after talking to Louie about giving it a try two handed, I dumped Charlie aboard the other boat.

Luckily I had a net drum fitted in the winter, so we did not have to pull that in, see I can be modern, normally we would have four hauls a day, we cut that down to two, that may sound silly, but like I said, I did not want to loose the spot to another boat, also the hauls we did have, the two of us gutted the fish, and put them to bed, out of the heat of the sun.

We sat down to dinner one night, Louie had done a leg of lamb, with a pan of gravity, (gravy to you),

I asked him were the veg was, he said to me "there are only two of us don't be greedy", to be honest I did agree with him, anyway sat there like a couple of Viking's, chewing on the leg, we heard a noise on the deck (it was flat calm so no rolling about) I said to him "who is that?" Louie says "how the fu** do I know I'm down here with you" we both cracked up, what a stupid question to ask.

The good fishing lasted another couple of days, then they were gone, I moved anchor about 20 mile East and tried the deep water, fishing was ok two or three kit per haul, with another man it would have been good, to be honest we found it a struggle, with shooting four hauls, and having to stack all the rope, we done it for two days, one haul the net came up with a small hole in the cod end, (the bag that holds the fish), as I was mending it I said to Louie " hey mate I am fed up, lets go home" he then called me a big baby, so there we go again rolling about laughing.

To be serious the weather was getting a bit rough, not the sort you worked two handed in, so off home, we landed 165 kits and made £3600.00, not a brilliant price, but better than a broken trip, I remember Louie saying it was the biggest wage he had made in all his sea career. His normal share of the catch should have been 13%, but I gave him 25%, it was well worth it, if only for the laughs we had.

After landing day I spoke to Chessy about ordering a set of rope reels, he said "about time you tight sod" so he did not take much persuading, we decided to do two more trips before going to Denmark to get them aboard, strange to stop in mid season, but the makers said that It would be quicker, as the Danish fleet would be at sea, so more men working on our boat.

That trip in I decided to change agents, we moved the boat to a new firm called Danbrit Fish Selling,

Chessy had moved his other boat the Britta, (he had bought her at the start of the season), and to my surprise Mr Moss also moved to them as ships husband, great it will be like the old days, I asked him if he had shifted his filing cabinet as well, his answer? "I sure did Trev, and you are still in it" it was nice to have Peter to work with us again.

Little Charlie was back with us, and I decided to stay three handed, well we did it with two, maybe now Louie would do some veg with the dinner, while we were in dock, I got pally with a skipper owner called Alex Mussel, strange sort of guy, he owned a boat called the Obelisk, a lot of fishermen said it was a wreck, (and it was) but she had a solid hull, the reason they called her a wreck was Alex did all his own jobs, some of them were beyond belief.

But as I was to find out, he saved a fortune on engineering and woodwork bills, he said to me "Trev if I have to get an engineer aboard it will be at the weekend, and pay them cash, also they show me how to fix most things, for the next time they conk out", to be honest I could write a book about Alex and his life and it would be a best seller, (might even do that) if I ever finish this one.

One tale, I had a fuc*** up small engine, and I asked Alex if he would help, if I striped it down, he answered, you do not need help Trev it is common sense, well the crank shaft was fuck**, so I had to strip it down, get the shaft reground, and new big end bearings, Alex told me that each bit I took off the motor, lay it in line in the engine room, when I had got the shaft done and the new bearings in, put it back together in the same order, now why did I not think of that.

Shaft done (on the cheap,) took it down to the boat and started to rebuild the motor, minor problem, Alex had took all the parts, put them in a fish box, (all mixed up), so Trev went mad at him, his answer? "Trevor mate you got to learn that every thing in life is not in order", Bastard.

But I did it, and when the motor started, well I was the proudest man on GY dock, all Alex said was, "nice job mate, I have never striped one of them before" did not know whether to kiss him, or kill him, so I just bought him a pint, it was to go on that way, all the jobs that I could tackle myself I did, and saved a fortune on labour costs.

I don't think the wife was very happy, but to be honest nor was the marriage, most days I would take little Tony down with me, he seemed happy on the boat, he also had a fishing rod, but there was not much to catch in the oily dock, to me he was very funny covered in grease and oil, and he loved playing with Alex's dog Jip, now that dog was a character, he used to go to sea every trip, to be honest he was more of a skipper than Alex was. What I mean there, is if the Jip didn't take to you, no way would you get aboard the Obelisk.

The next trip we made £4000.00, very nice, sat in the office, going through the bills and settling sheets, the owner had to do that, in case there was any bill to query, the office never paid a bill until I had signed it, anyway another skipper was going through his bills, he said to me "how come we made the same money today but you have £800.00 more profit"? I ask him for a look at his, and straight away I saw the silly things he was paying for, one sticks to mind, look you are paying £20.00 every trip for a lad to go on your boat, just to top up the batteries, "why don't you do it yourself"? He told me that he saw enough of the boat at sea, so ashore he kept away from it, my answer? "Stop fu**ing moaning then" he never spoke to me again.

Another money saver was, the boat had to be painted at least once a year, not to look pretty, but for protection from weather and rust, a full paint job was about £1000.00 in those days, and that was for topside only, I told the crew that if they wanted some extra pocket money, they could paint her, £150.00 each, they jumped at it, well that was £700.00 saved, yes I had to buy the paint, but there was a lot of open backed lorries about in them days.

The next two trips we made a brilliant £6000.00, each trip, so that was the reels paid for, and the office were over the moon, at 5% of my earnings, I wonder why, yes that is what all firms charged for selling the fish, and other paper work, think I will start one up myself, saying that worrying about one boat was bad enough, never mind twenty, one last trip to do and then off to Denmark for the reels.

We went to the Nameless Bank, (I am getting sick of this name), us and another six or seven boats were plodding away ok, one of them was Jeff Todd, the Homeward, one morning he came on the VHF to say that he could not start his engine, it was a two cylinder Danish job, and they sometimes used to seize up with carbon, that was not a big problem, as you turned the engine over with the flywheel,

And that cleared it, but this time it did not, the next thing to try, was wrap a wire around the very big flywheel, then let another boat pull it to turn the engine, well I tried three times but sadly no joy, it was a tow in job, Chessy was near the end of his trip, so I let him have the tow, I preferred to fish for another ten days, and then go for the new reels, and a nice drink of Danish lager.

I am very glad I gave the tow to Chessy, as we made a nice trip, £6800.00, sadly I was told that the Homeward had to have a new engine, Jeff had nothing but bad luck since him and Mac had got the boat,
He was a very good skipper, but if things go against you, the harder you try the worse it seems to get.

Well Mac sold his half of Coral Bank, and bought Jeff out, and did him a big favour by paying him what his half originally cost, Mack could have got it a lot cheaper, but they had been mates for years, also Mac did not want Jeff to lose his house to the bank, see there are some decent people in this world.

But that episode made me think, ownership is not all a crest of a wave job, so Trev, while you are earning it, do NOT squander it.

Well off to Denmark, for the new posh reels, no more dragging and stacking ropes, I still say that they should have invented them while I was on the deck, the idea was to fish for three days, and share the money out with the crew, instead of paying them a wage, they were happy with that, (if we caught anything), well we did, a nice 60 kit, all cod, small but very fresh.

Steaming into Esbjerg, we met the Britta, (Chessy) also going in to land, and to keep an eye on us? Well he does own half the boat, by the way Taffy and Paddy, were with him, my crew was little Charlie, and a lad called frank Hanson, (another mad one), after selling the fish, and we got a very good price, I decided not to give the lads all the money, but to give them so much at the end of each days work, I did not want them pissed the first three days, then asking for more.

Chessy was a bit annoyed at me, he said that he was entitled to an equal share of our catch, but I explained to him that he had to pay the crew as well as me, so fu** off Chessy, well he did land fish himself, and I bet he never gave his other partner a share.
Next morning, about 7am, we were woken up by a lot of noise on the deck, when I went up to look, well I was shocked, there was a

wagon on the quay, it was dropping a large working bench, a generator, and welding gear onto the quayside, I asked the driver what it was all about and he told me that every pipe and nut or bolt were done on site, in GY the engineers went back to the workshop about five times a day, to cut or change anything, the English had a lot to learn, about wasted time and money.

After only four days the reels were fitted, not working, but fitted, they now had to do the pumping system, but to me they were flying, I think it was because we were paying a fixed amount for the job, and not by the hour.

Chessy told me that he was sailing that afternoon, so with nothing to do on the boat we went for an afternoon drink, (try morning) but whatever, Chessy told his crew, Taff and Paddy, to be on board at 3PM, bad lads, they were still drinking with us at five, I did warn them that their skipper would go mad, but who am I to give them orders, and he did, go mad that is, well madder than normal.

Chessy walked into the bar we were in and sacked them, well I said to him "calm down Tony, they will be ok in the morning" but I am afraid he was not in the mood to see sense, so I got him a drink, then asked him what he would do, his answer, "get a new lot sent over on the ferry, well to me that was childish, and I told him so.

This answer was funny, he said, "and do not forget I own half the Island, so you cannot give them a lift back, well that really cracked me up, I said "Tony, I own the other half, so they can get a ride home on that" Chessy stared at me for a second or two, and then said "Trev why do we always carry the drunken bastards"? We both knew the answer to that, and we would not change them for anybody.

Well Chessy and his crew kissed and made up and they sailed the next morning, thank fu**, now I will get some work out of my two. And by god I did, I told them to renew every splice in the fleet of rope's, about 40 plus, that will keep them out of trouble for a while.

By now all the work was finished on the reels, so we just had to get the ropes on them, and away we go, onto a very lazy way of life.

Two days before sailing home, we went out for a celebratory drink, (well any excuse), we were in this night club, Charlie was getting the drinks in, all of a sudden there was a row at the bar, (no please not Charlie again), well to be sure it was, but to be fair to him, for once it was not hi fault.

Anyway this English guy decided that Charlie was easy picking's, and of course he was not, but for one time in his life, Charlie walked away from the guy, but I had gone to the bar and told him "no trouble Charlie" well the guy then said to me "hey cu** are you his body guard, I asked him to leave it, as we did not want any bother, I even offered him a drink, he did not bother to refuse one, instead he hit me.

So Trevor waded in, and like I said earlier, I am not a fighting man, but if I do start, then to me it was like no stopping, well after about five or six swift punches, I got a little bit worried, he would not go down,

(got a right hard one here), he had only hit me once and I had given him my best, so I kept punching, I remember saying "fuc* me he will not go down" this Danish lad then said, "how can he, he is on the table" well I stopped, and when the lights came on there was blood all over the show, hey I am not proud of what I had just done to him, but he did start it.

An ambulance came, and took him away, I sat down with the lads, then the doormen came over to our table, I said "ok lads we will leave" the two bouncers then said "no you are ok to stay, he has been trouble all night" they then bought us a drink, I kept my mouth shut, but was thinking, if you guys had done your job earlier, this would not have happened.

Sat drinking our lager, Charlie noticed that my knuckles were bleeding; he put a plaster on them, (what a thoughtful lad), but I did not know he had taken them off the boils he had, well sods law, next morning I woke up with the biggest poison hand you could ever imagine, so hospital for Trev.

As I am allergic to penicillin, they kept me in for a couple of days, anyway the guy in the bed beside mine looked like he had been in a boxing ring for a week, (and came second), and he had a couple of gorillas visiting him, they were his shipmates.

Shit I recognised him, any way I asked him what had happened, he told me that three guys had jumped on him, on his way back to his ship, (lying bar steward) but he was not going to admit to his mates, that it was a one on one, he did not recognise me as both his eyes were swollen badly, but one of his shipmates asked me what I had done, I answered, (fishbone sent my hand poison), well I did not want an all out war, did I?.

Got out of hospital and sailed home, fu** my hand hurts, well the lads took the wheel all the way, (thick sods), arriving at GY the port doctor advised me not to go to sea for at least a month, I told him I never done any work at sea anyway, but he said "no way" and that was that, skipper wanted, to be totally honest with you I can not remember his name, sorry.

Well when he took the boat for ice, the rudder jammed, it happened often with me, all I did was give the steering chain a sharp kick, and that cleared it, always meant to put a new false link in, but never got round to it, like I said, it was not a major problem, but to him it was.

Well he called the engineers down and the whole chain was renewed, £600.00, I went off it, first the office should have rung me before going ahead with the job, also why renew 50 foot of chain if only one link was jamming, anyway it was done, so off they went, (hope the reels work ok, or he will get them renewed).

As it was he landed a nice trip and made £7000.00, what a show up, my best was £6800.00, maybe the steering chain should have been renewed a lot earlier, or maybe I should let him keep the boat, but what mischief would I get up to, could always sail with Alex on the Obelisk, that is if the dog agreed to it.

But no, I took her back myself, and only made a £4000.00, and the last trip of the season, £52000.00, but I never wasted money on new steering chains, O I remember now they called the skipper that took the Island Chinese Ivan, do not know why, he was Danish, or English, or what ever, but he was defiantly not oriental, any way thank you Ivan, nice trip.

I had intended to do one more trip on the anchor, but sadly Chessy and I had a major fall out, I won't go to deep into the reason, let's just say he thought he had a half share in the wife, as well as the boat.

Anyway instead of another trip on the anchor, I changed the boat over to trawling, not permanent, but a winter time job, we would be fishing for King Prawns, and the boat was to fish from North Shields, not a bad job as we sailed each morning, (about 5 AM) and had two tows then back in to land the catch the same evening, (talk about a life of riley), whatever that means.

The pawning gear was very cheap, as Captain Corsak gave me an old prawn trawl, left from the days that one of his boats tried it, another skipper gave me a set of trawl doors, (he was not aware of this), but they were laid doing nothing, so all I had to pay for was the trawl wire, o and an extra drum fitted to the winch,

I got that for £20.00, and two pints of lager, off Alex; I was polite and never asked where he got it.

A new drum fitted to our winch would normally cost over £1000.00, and that is without paying for it to be fitted, no problems we done that our self, Trevor was very proud of himself, all that money he had saved, (WRONG AGAIN), what I should have done,, if I had half a brain, was go up to Shields, and sail with somebody, to see what the best rig up was, for my boat and engine power, also if a job is worth doing, get NEW gear and do it properly.

We sailed for Shields, and by the way, if you are wondering why prawns, instead of sprats, well the sad fact is that they had all gone, either over fished, or they had fell out with the Geordies, to be serious, sadly over fished, on arrival I went to the Dolphin pub, (it is on the quay), so strangely it had a lot of fishermen in, by the way, my crew, little Charlie, and a lad called Chilly Mathews.

Chilly had done a couple of trips with me in the past, but sorry I can't remember you all, anyway in the Dolphin, I got chatting with a few lads that I knew, one of them, Dicky Leighton, was skipper of a prawn boat, and he said that he would let one of his crew, (Ronny Blacklock) sail with me the next day, Ronny had also taken boats on the Prawns, so he would be a great help, and he was, we had two tows the next day, and caught two boxes, something sadly amiss here.

It turned out that the doors were too big, and the net to small, so much for saving money, well remember Nat, I towed him into Shields last year, he was sailing on a boat called the Invader, the skipper was called Digger, (don't ask, never found out his name), well Nat had told him that I would not tell the GY fleet, if there was money to be made on the Prawns, the local lads did not want 50 GY boats working their winter grounds, after the sprats I do not blame them.

  Well Digger lent me a net, to fish with until a new one that I had ordered arrived; I also bought a brand new set of doors, after a week of catching half the amount than the other boats the new gear arrived, so two days on the quay, setting it all up, (with Ronny Blacklocks help thanks' mate), next day we averaged the same as the local boats, so it was well worth the expense.

 Hey this is boring me; let's tell you a few antics, when Chilly sailed with me on the anchor, I found too that he was shit scared of anything to do with electrics, as I was rewiring the fuse box in the wheelhouse ,I had asked him to hold the fuse box door open for me, while I was rewiring it, every time there was a spark he would jump out of his skin, well I told him that we only had a 24 vault system, so there was no danger.

  But no way could I even get him to change a light bulb, anyway one morning we slept in and lost a tow, so only half earnings that day, that night after a few in the Dolphin, back to the boat and Chilly went fast asleep, (drunk), well we taped electric cables to his arms and legs, in the morning Charlie and I got up before Chilly, had a cuppa, then before starting the engine, I woke him up.

  When he started to get out of his bunk, he noticed that he was wired up, "what the fu** is this lot? Well I said to him, "if you cannot hear the alarm mate, I have rigged it so you will feel it", the poor sod just froze, like big time, I realised straight away that the joke had gone a bit far, (a bit far?) as soon as I unplugged him, he got out and started to pack his kitbag, "hold on mate it was only a gag" but it was one to many for him, and that was it, a train home for Chilly, if you are reading this mate I am sorry.

So the Island now needs a cook, (anybody interested?) no, don't blame you, in a way my crews were lucky, they could leave when they wanted, but I had to sail with me for the rest of my life.

  The new lad arrived ,two days later Albert Waddy, very nice chap but a bit too sensible for us, or maybe not, someone had to keep the job going, because to be honest I was not bothered, why?, well I did not go to Shields to earn money for Chessy, exactly the opposite.

Want me to explain that? Well my plan was to run the boat into debt, so Chessy would want out, O the crew saw a good wage, but it was cash in hand, (prove it) but we must keep that quiet, and come November he did, the office told me that Tony had a buyer for his half of the boat, but what amazed me, was the fact that another firm had offered him £13000.00, for it.

Trev was not happy with this, and asked them if I had any say who my partner was, the answer to that, NO, but I did have the choice of buying it myself, as long as I matched their offer, talking to our cashier I asked him why the price of the Island had gone up so much in just 18 month, he smiled at me and said "Trevor they are not paying for a boat, they are trying to buy the skipper".

I was still baffled with that, he went on to explain that with the profit I had made in just one year, they know you will make them money," well I have not got thirteen grand, so that's me fuc*ed, he then told me that if they thought the half share was worth it, then so would the bank, and they did , I got £10,000, loan with no problem, I could have got the whole thirteen, but decided to spend a little bit of my own.

Well Trevor is now a full owner of a fishing boat, hope all my X skippers are proud of me, I know dad will be, and of course mum.

So time to get down to some serious Prawn fishing, we used to fish for the prawns in slack tides, as when the tide was strong, (full moon) the fishing was slack, so when the moon was full we got the train to GY, and had a couple of days with the kids, that is if they had not demolished anything, actually it got so that I did not care if they had, I mean if they were little angels, then they could not be mine.

Alex had decided to go prawning with the Obelisk, a lot of skippers said he was mad, as they knew that the Island, was running in debt, but Alex knew better,

While at home I decided that the train fare for three men, every 10 days was getting a bit steep, so Trev went and bought a car, (old banger) one very small problem, I could not drive, but 175 mile to Shields I would soon learn, and I did, well after a few hairy moments, Albert had a full licence, so with L plates on it was legal, sorry suicide is not legal, but we all have to learn.

But it saved a fortune on train fares, and put years on the crew, it was a Vauxhall viva, bet you all never heard of one, but to me it was like a Rolls Royce, I even washed it the first week, but that soon faded away, well I mentioned a skipper called Dicky Leighton, he invited me up to his house for a bath and a meal, living on the boat that was very nice of him, and his wife Liz.

We were in the house one night, and his wife said to him "Dicky the gas man is due to read the meter; (shit) he had it back to front, if the gas man came he would owe Dicky money, so turning it back to its normal position, we had to sit all night, with every gas appliance going full belt, as it was he got the reading so that he owed the gas board about 50 pence, (for 3 month) I said "tell them you have been away" and he did (PHEW) that was close.

Dicky was telling me that his wife was taking driving lessons, he said that he wished he could afford a little car for her, I said to him drink less, and you could, anyway a couple of days later, sat in the Dolphin having a pint or six, Dicky said he was off home, and silly Trev offered him a lift home, it was not far too his house, but I needed to pick up some clean clothes for the night.

On the way to his house is a VERY steep bank, at the very top of it you joined a main road, so Trev had to give way to the traffic, but being new to this driving lark, (and not passing my skippers ticket) for a car, plus having a few pints, (very bad), I stalled the engine, then we were going back down the bank, shit, I turned the wheel hard over to port (sorry the left), the car kindly stopped, small problem, well two small problems.

One we were in a ditch, and two a police car had stopped beside us, so thinking on my feet, (there I go again thinking), I said to Dicky, so you want a car for the wife?, well mate you have got one, he looked at me in disbelief, "are you sure" I said it is all yours mate, then ran into the trees, well the police got to the car and asked Dicky what was going on, lucky for him, he was not in the drivers seat, they then asked him who owned the car.

Our Dicky three parts pissed, proudly said that he did, the next thing shocked me, they told him not to try and move it, as he had a drink in him, and left it at that, wow, talk about luck.

1978

We went home for Christmas in the car, as I had left the boat to be slipped and repainted, and most important off all, she was to have a new name, Ada Jean, after my mother, I have never felt so proud in my life, not owning the boat, but giving her the name, mum said I should not have done it as she will sink, but I could see deep down how pleased she was, I just wish dad could have seen it.

Time to get back to work, Albert had left, so I had to get another cook, just my luck, Paddy was back, o well, somebody to do the lifting, and shovelling, while I was at home, the skipper of the Invader decided that he had got fed up with nobody speaking to him, (he was not well liked in the fleet), so he started his car in the garage and went to sleep, (very sad) but it was his choice.

Any way a couple of days after the funeral, back at sea, Alex came on the VHF, and said "hey lads Digger is back" when he was asked what he was on about, he said "you all know that us fishermen come back as seagulls, well he is back as one" some silly sod fell for it and said how do you know which seagull is Digger, Alax answered "well there are about 200 gulls around our boat, and one of them is all on its own, the others are not speaking to it" Alex you are sick.

One morning as we were getting ready to sail, one of the local boats came on the VHF, to say that his engine had blown, and that he needed a tow back, he was still in the river, we were just letting go of the ropes, so I said that I would pick him up, which we did, and took him back to the gut, the boat was called St Aden, and the skippers name Stanton Clay, he asked me how much for the tow, I told him no charge mate, well we were passing him on our way out.

When we docked that night, Stan and the owner of the boat came aboard, gave us a case of lager and a bottle of rum, and they kindly helped us to drink it, (always keep in with the locals), sadly St Aden had to have a new engine, so no fishing for at least three months, it did not work out too bad for Stan, as he sailed with us, instead of the boat stopping fishing every ten days, for the crew to have time off, we worked it so that one man was off for a week at a time, and when I went home Stanton took the Ada Jean.

Strange that, because that is when she made the most money, well Stan was a local, he knew the grounds better than me, in other words a better skipper. Well he was about three quarters of a

Chessy, and it was all mussels, so the lads were never late for sailing, to be honest I think they loved it when I was away.

We got up to sail one Sunday morning and it was blowing a gale, so back to bed for an hour or two, when I did get up about 9AM, I went down the cabin for a cuppa, the whole fleet was in, but as I was going forward to the cabin, the whole deck was covered in feathers, blowing about in the wind, strange, I thought a seagull had been fighting, anyway as I went into the cabin, on the bench was an oven ready chicken, or I thought it was.

I said to the lads "have you seen all the feathers on the deck"? Paddy said yep it's the Sunday dinner, a duck, "where the fu** did you get one of them, in the middle of town"? he told me that it just walked up to him, on his way back to the boat, last night, any way I should not have asked him, after a cup of tea I told the lads that I was off to the Dolphin, for a livener, and would see them in there.

Entering the bar and ordering a pint,(it was full) all the fishermen were in the same mind as me, no sea no tea, lager instead, anyway at the bar I could hear a few of the lads on about this duck, it had gone missing, one of the lads who landed the fish, his name was Jackie Harvey, was consoling his mate, who was in a wheel chair, "don't worry Charlie she will turn up" the lads name was Charlie Smith, but everybody called him spacca, (spastic), it did not bother him as it was more an endearment than anything.

Well some prick had pinched his pet duck, and the local lads were saying that if they find out who! they were dead, OOOOOO SHIT, well I said to Stanton that I had left my money on board, and I would be back in five, "no rush Trev I have got money, have a pint first".

Great, how do I get out of this one, " well Stan I have left the engine running, be back in a tic" fu** I ran to the boat and told the other two, get every single feather off the boat, like NOW, if not we are dead men walking. "Paddy dump the duck and do NOT talk about it in the pub", phew they never did find out.

Alex had bought another boat, the Skandeborg, he got it off the same man we bought the Island from, so he decided to leave the Obilisk in Shields, and Dicky as the skipper, Alex went pare trawling, but what I want to know, how can he do all the jobs, if he is at sea in another boat?, yep he asked Trevor to keep an eye on it, thanks for your trust Alex, and the extra work, and worry.

To be fair he did land in Shields, most trips, to keep an eye on me and Dicky, and his pride and joy, Obelisk, I remember one time, the shaft on the Obelisk was faulty, so we had to put her on the beach, you do this at high tide, when the tide goes out you have about four hours to work on the outside, before she starts to float again, any way this job took three days to finish, while I was working with Dicky, and the welder, Barry Moss, Stan took the Ada Jean to sea.

Everybody happy, my boat was earning, and Alex was getting the shaft done for next to nothing, it is great when mates help each other out, the Prawn season was coming to a close, I decided to go home for a week with the kids, and leave the boat with Stanton, on returning we were going anchor bashing, straight from Shields, sat in the Dolphin having a farewell pint with the local lads, then we set off for home.

We were just coming up to the Tyne tunnel, all of a sudden blue lights flashing; yes I was pulled over,
This nice policeman asked us where we were going, "GY officer" he then told me to open the boot, so this I did.
Inside we had two boxes of top quality Prawns, he then ask where I had got them "the north see mate", bet he thought, got a clever one here, he then asked me to blow a balloon up for him, which I did, (that is the old fashioned breathalyser), as it was I had not had any alcohol, as I was on anti biotic, which the dentist had put me on the day before, (PHEW) what luck.
I thought that would be the end of the matter, but no, they took us to the police station, me in the posh car, and another policeman driving mine, on arrival they ask me if anyone could confirm the story about the Prawns, I gave them Danbrits phone number, after half an hour or so, they said all was ok and sorry for the inconvenience, so lets try again, as we were leaving the station, the lad who had driven my car said "hope it makes it to Grimsby mate, it is a fu**ing wreck", and we did make it.
I found out later that my X friend Alex had phoned the police to

report stolen prawns, by someone in a blue Viva.

At home I was telling Mary about how the cost of running a boat from Shields, was about a third of the expense of GY, and that I wanted to sell the house and move up there, she was dead against it, so I then said "ok but I will be landing in Shields every second trip, she was not happy about that, but there you go, the profit from the boat was uppermost, and the expense of running it, I told her that we could buy a house in Tynemouth, or Whitley Bay, both nice areas, but she was not having any of it.

That was the beginning of the end, for the marriage, she said it would unsettle the kids, moving schools, Tony was eight, and the eldest, so how does that unsettle them, plus they never went to school if they could get away with it.

We sailed on the first trip anchor bashing from Shields in march, the first area (NE Bank) is only 45 miles from the Tyne, so I proved my point, it is 180 mile from GY, think of the fuel I saved, to be serious, most anchor fishing grounds were North of GY, so Shields was a far better port, anyway the fishing was very good, but on the third day of the trip, we got up in the morning and found out that we were half full of water, now this is bad, (well not good, I catch on quick), trying to pump her out, with the small motor and hand pumps, I could not start the main engine, it was full of water, well we started to win and very slowly got the engine room empty enough to change the oil and start the main engine.

I had got in touch with the coast guard on the emergency channel, (VHF 16) a Dutch warship was on its way to the Tyne, on a courtesy visit, with luck he was only ten mile from us and called me up, offering assistance, Great, on his arrival he sent three divers down, under our boat, after what seemed ages, one of them came to the surface and climbed aboard us, he told me that one of the main planks near the keel had a bad gap, also the end of another one had lost the corking, (rope put in with tar), they then escorted us back to the Tyne.

On arrival the owner of the slipway was down to meet us, I was not happy with him.

Not happy was an understatement, he had charged £2000.00, for the slip job, and the MOST important part of that is obviously the corking, any way he slipped her free of charge, well it was not a good advert for him, talking to the captain of the warship (Friesland), I told him that I wanted to buy him a drink, but please do not bring your crew, (about 400 of them), to be honest I would have got them all a pint, and charged it to the slip owner.

All jobs done and back to fishing, we had three very good trips, and in the office on the third one, the cashier told me that I was now clear of debt, he also said that his gaffer was a bit concerned about it, well Trevor was not, as that was the plan, god they must have twigged on to that, so now all was well with the world, and the Ada Jean.

That is until we came into the Humber at the end of our next trip, on the way through the lock gates we picked up something in the screw, I could still use her but the vibration was bad, so land the fish and book the slip, again, she has started to spend more time out of the water than in, mind you mum never did like the water.

Talking to Alex that dinner, in the Albion, I was telling him about the slip, "put her on the beach" what beach? There is not one in GY; he then said "true but there is in Cleethorpes" well that meant taking her out of the lock gates and running her ashore, with nothing to tie up to, to keep her upright, well he had done it with the Obelisk, so why not us, and I save on slip charges, now I think that is a great idea, (there he goes again, thinking).

So the next morning, when the gates opened, Trev, Alex, and the dog sailed, as soon as we got clear of the gates Alex told me the spot where he always beached his boat, he did tell me to hit the beach fast, and she would dig her own ditch in the sand, and stand semi upright, and this I did, but when the tide went out she fell over onto the port side, the side the rope reels were on, the harbour master arrived, asking if we were ok, (daft question) Alex told him the dog was on watch, (even dafter answer).

Well we did find a wire in the screw, and cleared it, so far so good, a lot of holiday makers were taking pictures of this stranded boat, god I felt stupid, well the tide started to come in, Alex and I were sat on the wheelhouse wall, which was now the deck, as she was on her side, I said "Alex does the Obelisk lay this far over"? he said yes but I knew he was trying to keep my spirits up, by telling lies, the water was now up to the fish room hatch, (she was half sunk) then all of a sudden, there was a loud hissing noise and a lot of bubbles, whoosh, she came free and was afloat, I said to Alex "hey mate I did not think she was going to make it" he said that he did not think so either.

I was a bit annoyed at that answer, as he had put the Obelisk on the same beach, and I told him so, "yes Trev but she has not got two or three ton of reels on her port side", do you know what it is, why do I work with, and trust this man?, at times I wonder. The office warned me that the insurance would not cover me for beaching the boat purposely. I said how can they prove I did? The dog was on watch, there answer was, Trevor you are a worry at times, funny that's what mum used to say.

By the way I was now taking driving lessons, well got to be legal sometime, and carrying the kids I wanted full insurance, I had scraped the Viva, and bought a mini bus, (with no conductor), that's a ticket collector, in case you had forgotten, no I had not turned posh, it was another wreck, I took the back two seats out, (to carry nets and other fishing gear).

The reason I never went for a new car, if you are at sea for ten month a year, why let a good one lay doing nothing, what with the insurance and all sorts of other expense, I would have invested in one, but Mary could not drive, and to be honest she had no hope of ever learning. I did pass my skippers ticket for a car, but it felt strange ,being legal I mean, the only problem with the bus, Alex thought It was our firms van, so every time he wanted something shifting, ring Trev.

It was ok by me he could borrow the bus whenever he wanted it, but he could not drive, so it was Trev I need a net taken up to Shields, for the Obelisk, when can you do it, ME? O well mates work together but it was a bit one sided, but as you will find out later, Alex was not all take, and no give, he would save me a fortune in the near future. I would make damn sure of that.

We were all stored up and ready for sea, Alex came on the phone, he told me that the Obelisk had a bad problem with her engine, was there any chance of me towing her from Shields to GY, I told him we were sailing at 3AM the next day, but I don't suppose my crew would mind another 24 hours in dock, I tried to ring them, but they were both out, (Charlie and Taffy), so I just sailed that afternoon, me Alex and his schoolboy son Dean, Dean was 14 at the time, silly Trevor did not even tell the office.

We arrived in Shields the next morning, Dicky was not pleased with the fact that I had come to take the Obelisk home, as he was now out of work, strange that, if the engine is fu**ed, how can he work, o well he will work that one out later.

Towing the boat home, (hey we never even went for a pint.) well towing her home to GY, Alex was on the Obelisk, dean and I, well obviously on the Ada Jean, when dean was on watch (with him being a lad) I told him anything at all worrying him, call me or talk to his dad on the VHF.

The tow went without a hitch, but approaching the Spurn Lightship (entrance to river Humber) you are supposed to turn from South to West, I told Dean to keep going South, and when his dad came on the VHF, tell him I was in the engine room,(I was not) and that I told him to hold his course, passing the light ship Alex called me up, Dean told him that I was in the engine room, so Alex said "ok son, you now have to turn to starboard, and hold the course West.

Dean said "no father Trev told me to keep her steady, the two of us were in the wheelhouse in stitches, Alex was going mad, "Dean for fu** sake turn West now, and shout Trevor up, Dean answered "sorry dad, got to do what the skipper told me" well by now Alex was having twins, as he knew that we were headed for a sand bank, "PLEASE son do as dad tells you or we will loose both boats" well Dean and I were now wetting ourselves with laughter, Alex then said "well fu** you son I am going to slip the tow free, and call the lifeboat.

I then turned the Ada Jean hard over, and we were now in the river, I called Alex on the VHF and said "is every thing ok mate" I will not type the answer, but Alex did say that we should both order a coffin when we docked, well all safely home and Alex had calmed down. The office told me that Charlie had thought that I had sailed without him, so he had joined another boat, I was funny in a way, he had gone down dock, walked all round, looking for the Ada Jean, then went to the office to ask them if they knew anything, well they did not, but Mr Moss rung the dock master and he said that we had sailed the previous afternoon.

So doing Alex a small favour had cost me half my crew, o well Frank Hanson was looking for work so problem solved, this time we did sail, to do some fishing, that makes a nice change, so back to the NE Bank, and it was a steady plod, on the third evening as we were on the last haul of the day, a boat called the Border Star came on the VHF, he was asking for a tow into Shields, he was only ten mile off us, and thirty off Shields so we left the anchor gear where it was and towed him in, (I was now thinking about buying a tugboat), but like I said before, all sea men help each other when they can.

Arriving in Shields about 10PM, the skipper asked me to take him to the oil berth, (garage) so I did, laying alongside him I asked what the trouble was, "no trouble we just run out of fuel" is this guy for real. We could have given him fuel at sea, and had a nights sleep, well I let go of the ropes and sailed, no we did not even take up the offer of a drink with him, now I will help anybody in trouble but that was going a bit too far, or am I just too kind for my own good, (try SOFT TOUCH).

Alex was very busy with the Obelisk, so he let Charlie take the Skandreborg, as I said it was pairing with the Tarnborg, a sister ship and the skipper of that was Tommy Scorer, they called him the screaming skull, (cannot imagine why), so Charlie is now a skipper, but no ticket, no problem as with all the spare men off the trawlers, he had a man sign on as skipper for him. And they did well; mind you Tommy had been skipper for years.

Anyway back aboard us, I mean it is my story, (meow) by the way have you noticed that I do not mention the cat lately, can't afford to feed one, so no cat. Maybe I should get a dog,

The next trip I was fishing in an area that I did not know to well, but the skipper of a boat called the Sandringham, she was another sister to the Coral Bank, well the skipper was George Mussel, that's right big brother to Alex, well younger but about one Chessy bigger. Anyway George kept me right about the fishing ground. The fishing was ok but it was the time that the big storm hit England, and even the Q E 2 was having trouble, so George and I decided to shelter in Whitby, while the storm passed us.

We arrived in Whitby but we never had a lot of fish, so instead of landing it we decided to sell it to the local shop each day, it was quite funny, as we were taking large cod to the shop in an Asda trolley, a lot of the locals, and holiday makers started to asked us how much for one large cod, well we had been offered £3.00 per fish, (about a stone in weight) but they were offering up to £5.00, so highest bidder wins.

The local bar we used was called the Jolly Sailors, and they did meals, so we gave the gaffer a full box of fish, a dinner for each of the two crews and a lot left over, for him to make money with in the restaurant, well in the bar, there was a sign up saying, (well reading, it could not talk), No meals served in the bar,

But with the two crews in overalls, Bill (the owner) told the chef to bring seven fish meals in to the bar, and we sat enjoying our dinner when in walked this couple, they ordered a drink, and then smelling the fish ,ordered a meal.

Well they sat with their drink, Bill told them that their meal was ready, and the guy told him that they would have it there, Bill pointed to the sign and said "sorry we are not allowed to serve meals in this room," well looking at us lot he said to Bill "but they are all eating" so Bill said "would you let that scruffy lot into your restaurant" the guy looked at us and agreed with him, then moved into the other room.

After two full nights in the Jolly Sailor we decided to go round the town, we went on the south side of the river and found a nice quiet bar, cannot remember what it was called, well we were sat in the back room (it had a piano) and started to enjoy a sing song, the locals enjoyed this, until we started on the sea shanties, (with extra words) we kept it clean at first, then the drink took over. I went to the bar for another round, the gaffer said to me "these are paid for" how nice "who got them" it was Bill from the Jolly sailor, he was in the other room and told the gaffer to get us a round of drinks then bar us.

And so it was back to Bills bar, o well, his wife was a nice lady, but it is now three nights without any sleep for her, so she told Bill, midnight is last drinks for all, and of course he agreed with her, so off she goes to bed and left us to it. On the stroke of midnight Bill shouts "ok lads last drinks for tonight" and I was in semi agreement with him, well enough IS enough, so drinking up to finish the night off when Bill said to me "Trev I bet you cannot beat me at darts" well the game was go from 1 to 20 in doubles, then finish on the bull.

Two AM, I was after the bull and Bill was on double 18, I did notice that his darts went well wide; strange he is a good player? I said "hey mate you are not trying, and he then told me that he had been upstairs to tell his wife that we were leaving after the game was over, his next words, "if you get the bull you are bared" crafty old sod. The next day after a dinner in the pub, we decided to walk along the sea front, to have an hour or two off the drink, (trying to prove to our self that we were not alcoholics) it is easy to fall into the drink when you are in another port.

We came across a dodgem car ride, and the seven of us decided to have a go, sadly it was shut for dinner (strange) but when we asked the owner if we could have a go, he said ok, normally you get about 5 minutes on a fairground ride, but he said we could have them for an hour, for £10.00. No way there is seven of us, so £7.00, and a bit of fish, this he agreed to and so you can imagine seven drunk fishermen in charge of the dodgems, we had a great laugh, if anybody got tipped over he had to run, as the other six cars were after mowing him down, it got so mad we were getting out of the car and turning someone over, the others tried to run him down, how nobody got hurt that day I will never know.

It was that crazy we drew an audience of holidaymakers; I think that they thought it was a real show, more like a show up. Well the owner did not mind, as we did no damage, it was all in fun.

I say fun, how the fu** we never killed each other, I will never know, well for reasons I cannot print the mate had to go home that night, I told the office to send up a replacement, and that they did, now I do not know if they were taking the piss, or somebody up there hates me, but the next day the mate arrived, three guesses, yep got it in one, Dopy Dave, what the fu** have I done in my past to deserve this.

On the other hand Dave was still alive, so maybe he is not that bad, or thick, or just plain lucky, whatever I had him for a trip. It is now about time we went back to sea, but we still had two kits of cod to sell.

George and I decided to have the last day in and sail on the Monday morning, by now the weather was very nice, flat calm and sunny, also very hot so the lads decided to have an afternoon swim in the river, as you know I am not into water so I sat on the deck watching the others enjoying themselves, Frank was swimming against the tide, he was struggling a bit, but I did not know that, he shouted "Trev throw me a rope" well as it happened we had some spare rope laid on the deck, (about sixty foot of it, so I did as he asked and threw it to him, not the end of it, but all of it.

The next thing I saw was nothing, (strange) two of Georges crew went down, after a while the three of them came up, and we got them on board, the boys were not very happy with me at all, when they asked me what the fu**, was I thinking of I just said "well he was shouting for some rope, and that was the nearest bit".

Now plastic rope floats, but the rope we use for fishing has a lead core to make it hug the seabed. So Trev nearly got done for manslaughter. I would have pleaded insanity, and got off with it, anyway sorry Frank.

Next morning we both sailed, and headed for the NE Bank, the fishing was not very good so George and I decided to finish the day and then steam out into deep water, that is until his last haul, when he got his net in the screw, (dopy sod), but it can happened to the best of us, I tried pulling it clear for him but no joy, it just went tighter, so tow into Shields, and let the diver sort it.

We arrived in Shields about 8PM, the diver was on the quay waiting for us, and it took him over an hour to clear the net from the screw. On finishing we took him for a pint in the Dolphin, small problem, we had spent all the money in Whitby, but in my bunk I kept an old plastic net float, (about the size of a football) it was three quarters full of coins, I always put my change in it on sailing days, but only copper, 5 pence's and ten's, but there was at least £50.00 in it. I made a hole in it with a hammer and carried it to the Dolphin.

Walking in I ordered eight pints, the barmaid, (Margie Ord,) started to pull the drinks, starting at one end of the bar, I tipped the money out of the float, as it came out I walked the length of the bar, can you imagine her face, she had to count it all, but no the gaffer (Joe Lowden) said "give them all two pints each and call it square". I think back on that and know he was the winner, so after TWO PINTS, remember that bit for the coming year or two, we left the pub and sailed. At 1 AM.

I took the first watch, we were heading to a spot East of the bank, all of a sudden the engine started to make choking noises, I went down to look in the engine room, there was more water in her than when the Dutch navy had helped us, looking over the side I could see that the pumps were working, so the problem was bad, after calling the lads out, and getting them on the hand pump, I called George up on the VHF.

He was about four mile ahead of us, but he turned round and came alongside us, the weather was not too bad, so I knew that the water was coming in under the waterline, some times this type of boat can get bad leaks at the point where the deck joins the hull, but that only happens if the boat is rolling badly.

By the time George got to us the water was now half way up the engine, it was entering the air intakes, so I had to stop her, I also shut off the main sea cocks, in case of a broken inlet pipe, but the water was still rising.

George threw us a tow and started hell for leather towards the land, but under tow water was raising a lot faster, I had already called the coast guard, I then informed them that I was putting my crew aboard the Sandringham, the weather was now starting to freshen up, the sea was rising, so my two lads got off.

I still had thoughts of another tow, to save her, but George said that she was so low in the water, I had to get off, and I did.

Standing in the wheelhouse of the Sandringham, we stood and watched the Ada Jean sink slowly, stern first, the only part of her keeping her up was the air in the cabin, then all the corking gave way, and she went under, the air coming out made a very loud screaming noise, a bit like she was CRYING.

I certainly was, nobody spoke for a long time, then George said "Trevor I feel like smacking you" he then went to his cabin, after telling his mate to head for Shields.

It took three hours to get back and the mate and I never said a single word, for the life of me I never want to see that again, in the future I did take a crew off their boat and watch it sink, but I never felt the same sadness, but I bet the skipper did.

On arrival at North Shields the mission man and the coast guard met us, the mission man took my crew to the shops and got them a new set of clothes, and I declined his kind offer, George and I then gave all the details of the event to the coastguard, after that we got the train home, for some strange reason George did not go back to fish, he took his boat home to GY, and had a few days ashore.

This was 22 September, Angie's birthday, which was the only year she did not get a basket of fruit off her dad, when I got home the kids knew something was wrong, but too young to understand.

After a couple of days I went down to the office, and the director said "Trev the first thing you must do is replace the tool of your trade, he called her a tool? But to be honest and looking back, that is what she was, but I do remember the bad storm she had seen us through, and got us home safe.

I had no debt in the office but I did owe the bank £8000.00, she was insured for £36000.00, so pay the bank off and think of getting another boat, so I had, after paying the expense for that trip about enough to buy a semi decent boat, to be honest I was not really ready to look for one, but the bills still have to be paid.

Tell you what, I want to get this year over and go back to having some laughs, and lighten this book up a bit, also writing this page has brought back a lot of sadness for me, no matter what happens at sea if you loose your boat, whether it be, bad weather, a torpedo, an iceberg, or any other act of god, and even a scuttling job, the skipper or captain always blames himself, and you never get over it, but to be really honest, I do Not believe in this going down with your ship crap.

A month passed and I went to Denmark to look at a few anchor boats that were up for sale, and for some strange reason I took a liking to the oldest of the three that I had looked at, she was very slim, long, and the engine was only one year old, also three times the horse power that the Ada Jean had, and as I told you I was thinking of fishing from Shields on a permanent basis, she was called Toledo, and rigged for the trawl.

But it would not break the bank to put reels on her, if I decided that is what I wanted, but to be honest I was thinking of the 300 HP engine, great for trawling from North Shields.

I asked the owner of Toledo to put her on the slip, so I could check the hull, he booked the slip but that time of year there was a two week waiting list, ok back in two.

As it was the office asked me to bring a boat home from Denmark, when I flew over to look at the Toledo on the slip, and if I wanted to I could do a trip fishing, they also said that they would pat for the flight, great that saves me a few quid, but I would need a crew, yep Taffy, and Paddy.

Two days later we flew from Humberside airport, that's ok, but when Paddy saw the plane he said "Trevor no way" it was a very small four man light aircraft, I told him it was safer than a jet airliner, if the engine stops on this one, it will glide down, great five large rums later Paddy was ready to fly, to be honest I wanted a drink to, Dutch courage, so off we go, with eyes shut and holding hands, Paddy said "give me a boat any day" the pilot laughed and told him that we were safer above the wind than we were on the water. When we arrived at the airport in Denmark, there was a very strong wind; on landing (it was very scary) anyway on landing we stopped with about one foot of tarmac to spare, I said to the pilot "hey mate I did not think we were going to stop" he replied "to be honest no did I" PHEW.

After looking at the Toledo, and it was ok, we went to the boat that the office had asked me to take away, she was called Tolana, and had just been in a major refit, she was a small boat but everything had been renewed ,engine, wheelhouse, and rope reels, very posh, that is until we got her to sea, what a horror, after two days of trying to fish I said to the lads "what do you think" they both said "home James" so we did, plus it was very late in the year for anchor bashing.

Steaming home we came across a set of pair trawlers, yes it was Charlie and Tommy, now Charlie knows my sense of humour (warped) so on passing them I told the lads to put the net over the stern of the boat, Tommy came on the VHF and asked me what the fu** I was doing, shooting a net in-between a set of pair trawlers, I never answered him, but we let the net go on two ropes, just below the surface, can you imagine him, he was shouting about killing me and a lot worserrrr, (must be upset), then Charlie told him it was me, but Tommy said that I was still dead, all I said was "sorry Tom I was just cleaning the net".

On arrival into GY I was told that the Toledo would be ready to sail in a week, so I got little Ally, remember him, the Dane who thought swearing was blooming heck, because he knew the type of engine and would be a great help, my third crew member was Mary, the wife, she had never been on a boat, but the insurance said I had to be three handed, (I did not need to pay her).

We went across on the ferry, and spent a week getting her ready for sea, well I did, Alley went to visit family and Mary went sight seeing, ready for sea, five days before Christmas, and the forecast was Westerly storms, o well they would blow us home, so we set sail.

After clearing the river in Denmark, Ally took the first watch, after four hours he called me out, for my watch, he said to me that he thought there was something strange, with our position, according to his chart reading we were doing 13 knots, (M P H) on checking the chart myself I told him that we were.

Now a fast anchor boat may touch eight knots, so this was stupid, the only thing we could put it down to was the wind and tide helping us, he went down to bed and I was checking our speed, every hour, and yes she was doing 13, wow.

Mary was sat in the wheelhouse seat, and ask me if this is what I called bad weather, I said "why?" well she did not think it was bad at all, we were sailing with the wind, that is the most comfortable of all, so I said to her "hold tight I will show you bad" and then I turned her into the weather, hey she was bouncing like a bronco. And Mary was violently sick, I know that is cruel but she had to learn.

We arrived in GY twelve hours earlier than was expected; Mary went to get the kids from Pat and Ray,

And I was busy showing off to Alex, I had tied alongside of the Obelisk, wow what a difference in the boats, Alex said to me "Trevor more power means bigger fuel bills" so more fish kneaded.

How right he was, ok all been a funny year but hopefully the next will be better, and now home to spend a nice time watching the kids have there Christmas.

1979

Hi New Year, new boat, and new fishing, I had decided to take the boat pair trawling, problem with that is we need another boat daft enough to go with me. The office told me that a boat called the Grena Star never had a partner boat, and was already rigged for the job, I asked who the skipper was, but at the time she never had one, well Charlie had done six month skipper on Skanderborg, but Alex was back, he had sold the Obelisk.

Small problem, Charlie never had a skippers ticket, easy to overcome as there is still all them trawler men with tickets, walking about, so the owner of Grena Star agreed, but on a trial basis, fair enough, it cost me £9000.00 for two nets and all the other gear, so off we go on our maiden voyage, Charlie's crew was a Dane called cowboy Jens (do not know why), Taffy, and another lad, can't remember his name.

My crew Frank, from the Ada jean days, and to be honest cannot remember the other two, the first two or three days, when it was Charlie's net, we done ok, not good but a living, that is it would have been if my net was fishing, on this job you take turns shooting your net, but for some reason mine was not taking the fish.

But after a few alterations, we started to equal the Star's fishing, we moved to the Dogger Bank, to try fresh ground, there is a patch of stony ground to the North side of the bank, we shot my net, after towing for three hours we hauled, WOW, the net floated up, and the sea turned white, we took ten lifts of fish from that one haul, 150 kits, hey this job is piss easy, (shit Trev is at it again), the next tow we took one kit, that shows you how mad fishing can be.

We did not fish that night as I still had a deck load to be gutted, with the weather being fine I took two of Charlie's crew on board to help get the fish away, as I was to take the tow in the morning, I went to my bunk and left the lads to it, they would get a sleep the first tow the next day. We landed in Shields that first trip, not a great trip, but we are only beginners at this lark, after landing I gave the lads enough money for a day and night out, I also told them that if anybody was not there for sailing at 10AM the next day, we would sail without them.

Yep guess who was the only one out of eight, not to be there for sailing, (Trevor) what a show up, but I did arrive for mid day, all the lads forgave me and were ready for sea, with the exception of one man, cowboy, well he said that he wanted another night in, and as I was the one to miss sailing time, he was in the right, but I told him that we were sailing there and then, his answer was not without my ticket you cannot.

Wrong no man holds me to ransom, and I told him so, he then said that if I sailed with no ticket for the Star he would report me, also she would not be insured, and he was right, so I told him that he could have as long as he wanted in Shields, we then let go of the ropes and sailed, without him, I rang the office in GY and told them to put me in the logbook as skipper of the Star, they did that but asked about the Toledo, I told them that was a risk I was willing to take, they said Trevor you are mad, if anything goes wrong you are not insured, I replied "fu** it it's a risk worth taking".

But I knew that if I got away with this trip, no man, just because he has a ticket, but no boat will lay the law down to me. Back fishing, this is the first boat I have ever been on with an auto pilot, (it steers the boat), imagine having one in a car, well maybe not, we were towing along and my crew were on the deck gutting fish, I went down the engine room to give her a drink of oil, had to do that every three hours, she drank more than me, (well nearly), on coming back to the wheelhouse the pilot had decided to kill Charlie and his crew, in other words it had conked out and the tow pulled us over to starboard, we also lost the drag of the net so she was flat out.

God we were lucky, I went full astern (reverse) and she stopped about two feet from the Star, another minute and we would have cut her in two, I said to Charlie on the VHF "fu** me that was lucky" and he answered that it was them that were lucky, as they would have been cut in half, after that I always got one of the lads to give the engine her drink, as Paddy says do not do technical, and for once I had to agree with him.

When we got in that trip the office told me that the owner of the Grena Star wanted a more experienced skipper, we were not making a lot of money, but we were not in debt, it reminded me of the Halton, so a lad called Dave Rose was now my partner, on pair trawlers you normally have one skipper in charge, and the other one is called the taxi driver, so Dave was in charge of the fishing and I took the fares again.

Can you remember Derek the chart boffin, from my collage days, well he had a boat called the Gladito, or he did for one trip, well he forgot to turn right at the Humber, and ended up on the beach at Mapplethorpe, (must have had the wrong chart out).

Well she broke her back, so an insurance right off, who bought the wreck? Yes Alex and he got it for next to nothing, she was only two years old, and Alex salvaged every thing off her, and made a very tidy profit. When he sold the engine he got more than the boat cost him, and he still had a new winch, rope reels, wheelhouse, and lots of other goodies to sell. By the way Derek retired from the skipper lark after that, I never saw him again.

Anyway back to us, Dave was a great chap to get on with, only one small problem, he took all the best known tows with his net, he said that he did not think mine was fishing at full strength, that was ok by me, less work for my lads, and less ware and tare on my nets, but one small problem, I have never told the truth about the amount I am catching, well I cannot count, mum always said, if there was a medal for the biggest liar in the world, Trev would win it.

We were towing along one day, Alex was speaking to Dave on the VHF, he had a small problem, (that's what he called it) anyway he said that he had to tell his cook that his father had passed away, so Dave told him to give it to him straight, one small problem replied Alex, "he buried his mother only a month ago". Well I am glad I never had that job. Anyway after a lot of soul searching, Alex dropped the wheelhouse window and shouted to him "hey lad you are now an orphan".

I think even I could have handled that better. When we landed the Star turned out 220 kit, and we landed 260 kit, very nice but Dave went mad at me for the lies, well you have got to be careful, in case anybody is listening, "how the fu** can other boats hear you, we were alongside each other, not on the radio" sorry Dave. Any way in this type of fishing the net is pulled onto the dockside every trip, an overhaul.

   I arrived on the dock the next morning, Dave's crew were busy pulling my spare net onto the Star? My new £3000.00, net that had never been into the water, I went mad, "what the fu** are you up to"? they told me that as our new gear fished better than theirs Dave told them to use it next trip, well I know that we go out there to catch as much fish as we can, but Trev paying for all the gear is a tiny bit over the top, I told them to put it back, and asked were Dave was, "in the office". I told both crews to stop all work and I will sort it out, (hey Trev is now a shop steward).

   Arriving at the office I told Dave that we needed to sort this out, so off we go to the headmasters office, (director), at first they could not see a problem, so explaining to them that it had cost me a small fortune for new gear, (which fished better than the Star's nets) why does the owner of the Star not buy Dave a new one?, to be fair to both of them they agreed with me, after phoning the owner up he told Dave that he was not going into the expense of new gear, and Dave told him to shove the Star, up where the sun does not shine, and left.

   Charlie is now back as skipper of the star, and I kindly lent him my spare net. Alex and I decided to have a code, most mates did, so if you are fishing well and you want to tell him, without all the other teams knowing, you could let them know by just talking about something, ours was, if we were on a good run of 20 kit or more, we talked about his dog Jip, so if the fishing with us was bad and Alex mentioned Jip, I then joined him.

   But sadly even that was a waste of time, with Alex and his warped sense of humour, Charlie and I were on good fishing and I was talking to Alex on the radio, in the conversation I mentioned the dog, Alex came back on and said, "Trev we are on our way home with a trip so talking about Jip, you're good fishing does not help us". My god what a prat, the next morning there were three teams fishing the same stones as us. Of course the fishing did not last very long, well Trevor you will get pally with complete nutter's.

Another trip Frank, asked me if he could bring his son along, Victor Hanson, he was twelve year old, on the school holidays, I agreed as long as Frank kept him from mischief and danger. And he did, Vic was a nice kid and we had a great laugh, like one night whilst towing along his father was on watch, his main job was to keep our boat exactly a quarter of a mile off Charlie, that he did, by looking in the radar, now Frank being new to this job, his eyes were never out of it, (radar).

Vic and I were in my berth playing cards when his father told him to go to the cabin and make him a mug of tea and a cheese sandwich, I whispered to Vic "put mustard in it", when he came back and gave daddy his tea and snack we sat in my cabin watching him, it was so funny, with his eyes glued to the radar, he took a large bite, all of a sudden he was screaming Blue Murder, while he was also choking.

After calming him down and telling him that it was my idea, he decided to let Vic off, with the promise of no birthday presents this year.

Another day we were towing along, with Frank on watch, this time it was our net, so Frank had no worry about the radar, it was the Stars turn to keep the distance, all frank had to do was miss wrecks, on the bottom and the top, we were playing cards again, young Vic and I, I'm sure he was cheating as he now owned half the boat, does that make him his dads gaffer?.

Frank was laid back in the wheelhouse chair, reading a book, to pass the dreary watch away, there was a hole in the bulkhead (wall) the size of a pencil, when you looked through it all you could see was Franks ear, I told Vic to pass me the fire extinguisher, it was one of them that you can turn on and off, without using it all, I held the hose up to the hole in the bulkhead, then opened the valve for a second.

BLUE MURDER, this time there was no talking Frank out of killing his own son, so I had to hold him down until he cooled off, and his ear defrosted, what a stupid prank. Or do I mean stupid Frank, o well whatever.

Now to be totally honest with myself I did not really like this pair trawling lark, as we used too much fuel, the worry was twice as big, and the overall expense was three times that of anchor bashing, so I had a few very serious decisions to make, on top of all that some prick sat in an office in London decided that I had to change the name of the boat, according to him it sounded too much like another boat in England.

Now you cannot just pick a name you like, no you have to submit ten names, the powers that be decide in the end.

Taffy sat down the cabin one tow and played about with names, (Taff is brill at crosswords), well I grudgingly admit that Taffy is a very well educated man, but do not tell him that, after a while he came up with a name for the boat. CARMARAN. It was my two daughters and the wife; anyway the little prick IN London must have had a bad night, because it was accepted.

One fine day we were towing along (Charlie was in his bunk) when this coaster came alongside of us, asking for some fresh fish, as we were busy gutting, we gave him a basket of mixed fish, in return we got four bottles of rum and 600 cigarettes, wow well worth it, as the fish we gave him was just under legal size. Now I do not drink at sea for obvious reasons, but a dram in your tea warms you up. I told the mate on the Star not to tell Charlie, as I would surprise him with a drink when he got up, and some fags.

Well I had two or three cups of tea, before hauling time, when Charlie came on the VHF, he said that if he did not know better he thought I was drunk, "don't be daft Charlie we have been at sea for ten days", he knew I never carried drink on the boat, but said I was slurring a bit.

Going alongside to pass the net over to him, I tied two bottles and 200 fags onto the rope, when he got them aboard he said, "fu** me Trev I thought you were half pissed, well we dropped the anchor early that day, as we had to get rid of the booze, like I said I do not allow drink on the boat.

When we got in that trip, I sat and had a long talk with the office, my bank manager was also there, I told them that I had decided pair trawling was not my thing, we worked out that it would be cheaper to give the Toledo a complete refit, rather than sell her and buy a new boat, the way I looked at it I was only thirty year old, (young enough to take on a bit of debt), so we got the engineers and shipwright,(carpenter) to give me a quote on the whole refit. It was £52000.00, frightening but a new boat would now cost treble that, also Toledo had a very good engine. So I gave the go ahead, (STUPID SOD).

Well it is now October and the refit started, Charlie and I done a lot of the stripping down, to save on labour cost, Frank also helped now and then, why do people love taking things apart?, O well they were happy, and getting a pint or two every day, but can you imagine them two with a set of burning gear?.

I was sat in the Humber pub one dinner, Alex and I got talking about the refit, I said to him "how much do you want for the Gladito's wheelhouse" he told me that he was expecting that question, so I said "well then you must have a price in mind", he was still pondering on that, I mean to have one built the same was £20.000. And that I was not going to do, in my head I had the offer of £5000.00, but do not tell him that.

Anyway he said to me get the round in and I will give you a price when you come back, and being very obedient off I goes to the bar, putting a lager in front of him, I then asked how much, he said "well Trev you have done me a lot of good turns in the past, so that's it, that is what? He said that the wheelhouse had been paid for with a pint, so I went and got him another half, when Alex said what is that for, I told him that I had just bought the mast as well, he just shook his head.

Bet you never see deals like that now, with it coming up to Christmas, the two eldest kids told me that they wanted a bike, so what they get the two young one's want, well I took all four of them to the bike shop and let them pick one each, so no surprise on chrissy day, well there was as I got them a couple of other things, I was thinking about getting them guns, hand grenades and maybe some plastic explosive, but their mum talked me out of it.

I had one VERY strict order for them, that was they were not allowed to ride their bike on the road, (we lived in a very busy street), all I asked of them was to push the bike to the park, and then they could start running other kids down in safety, they promised me that they would do that (push the bikes I mean), it is so nice to have such obedient kids, if I remember well Barry wanted a crossbow fitted to his, but I drew the line at a bell.

By the way I had sold the bus and got an estate car, (to carry the gang) less space for them to fight in, Frank and I had to go up to Shields, as I wanted to do a trip on a fly dragger, I had a very good idea of the job, but the skipper of the Border Maid was to teach me the finer points, and he did, that was to be a great help when the

Carmaran was ready for sea.

Having a couple of nights in Shields, I saw a lass that I had been taking out for a couple of years, she told me that she was pregnant, (I think I could already see that), we did not go into the question if it was mine or not, Frank and I then had a day in Whitby, for old times sake, but Bill had left the Jolly Sailor, and was now living in Scarborough, (thank fu**) now we could get home.

By this time I had decided to give my marriage one last try, Mary had to move up north or I was leaving, but certainly not before Christmas, and her answer, no way. Well to be honest it was the best thing, I had started to drink a lot of rum, and also getting violent towards her, for all my life I have been ashamed of that, so please take that as a warning, never mix drink with your problems, and most of all NEVER hit a woman, no matter what.

We can all make excuses, mine is that I was not a man, try a PRICK, because that is what I was, the kids grew up to understand, but that is still not on, I am glad that bit is over, but remember never hit, always talk. I stayed to see Christmas over and it was one of the hardest times of my life, not for Mary, but watching my children enjoying themselves and not knowing that the family was to split up.

To be totally honest in later years they all said I had done the right thing, but at the time they just lost dad.

I am so sorry about that kids, and I now know that you have all forgiven me.

I was talking to Alex about it, and he said I was doing the right thing leaving, but not moving in with the girlfriend, he said "Trev it will end in tears", and he was right but that comes later.

1980

Come the new year, I was still at home, and working on the refit, one day Charlie and I were pulling the chain from the boat, I had sold it to one of the pair trawlers, any way loading it into the back of the estate car, the weight of it made the back axel lay on the train lines, that ran along the dockside, shit we have now got to unload it all, get off the track, then reload the chain. No we were lucky the crew off another boat were on there way to the office, for their working by money, they asked me for a lift, so being a very kind chap said "ok lads hump the car off the track, then I will run you round", and this they did, as soon as the car was free I shouted "cheers boys, see you" and drove away, I will not type what they were saying as we drove away.

Bet the office was shut for dinner, by the time they got there. O well it will keep them off the drink for an hour. Most of the days we were working on the boat I took young Tony with me, on the dinner break, I would take the lads for a pint or three, Tony had to sit in the car, as there was no kids allowed in the bar, do not get me wrong, every half hour I took him some coke and crisps out.

To this day he tells all that his dad took him to the park, every day, awe how nice, then he tells them the Humber CAR PARK, not so nice, sorry mate. On special days I took little Barry with us, so Tony had somebody to talk to, I wish I could here what they used to call me, second thoughts, no I do not.

Back to the kids bikes, remember how I told them not to ride on the road, well they all take after me, not a blind bit of notice, Taff and I were walking to the house one Sunday, (he was bumming a dinner), as we walked round the corner we nearly got run over by four nutters, flat out across the road, I shit myself, not them killing me, I could have put up with that, but if a car had been coming, well it does not bear thinking about.

I took the four bikes upstairs, removed the pump up gadgets,(too technical) and told them that I was going to sell the bikes, and that I did, years later the four of them said that I had done the right thing, so kids remember your mum and dad does know what's best, for your safety.

I was going to stay in Grimsby until the refit was finished, but the arguments and the violence got a lot worse. I made the hardest move that I had made in my life. Not for Mary, but to leave the kids was horrendous, but to be honest BEST for them in the long run. I drove up to North Shields, and stayed with a mate of mine, Canadian Barry, him and his wife ran a pub at the time, called the Colonel Linskill,

His wife Brenda had a long talk with me, and she was a great help.

The lass I had been seeing for a time had now had the baby, also she was working as a barmaid for Brenda, her name Lynn Petersen. When I told her that I had left home she said that she hoped it was not on her account, so I told her that I would have left anyway, this sounds daft, for the kids sake.

After a lot of talking between us, I moved in with her, I also gave the child my name Robert Potter. I went back down to GY and sorted the divorce out with Mary, the house only had one year left on the mortgage, so I said that I would keep up the payments, but my half had to be given to the kids, that was put in a solicitors agreement.

I got the Carmaran, now £60 000.00 in debt, I know how to make a bad deal, I then went back to Shields and hopefully every thing sorted out, I left the rest of the refit in the hands of the office, (BIG MISTAKE) as they just wanted the boat back at sea, at any cost, well they just gave the go ahead for the engineering firm to do what they thought best. (And that was spending Trevs non existing money), I drove down to GY after a month, as I was told she was almost ready. She looked very good with the new wheelhouse and all the deck machinery in place. But I was then told that the estimate had been a bit low, instead of £50 000 the refit had cost £80 000, nice.

Wish I had bought a brand new one now. I was told that she would be ready for sea in a month; I then told the office that I would be running her from Shields on a permanent basis, they were NOT happy about this, as they would loose their 5% commission. At the end of the day it was still my boat, so fu** their 5%, all they needed to worry about was me, making a profit, and paying off the loan, either that or bankrupt me, so the ball was now in their court . They could see no point in stopping me having a go, so they agreed to let her go to Shields

I was stood in the bar one day and there was a phone call for me, it was the office in GY, the shit had hit the fan, apparently the police wanted to talk to me about the loss of the Ada Jean, WHAT?, well Mary had rung them and told that I had scuttled her, apparently the police had arrested Frank (who was on the boat) and now they were going to arrest me, I did not give them the chance, I got in the car and drove down to GY, entering the police station I said to the desk sergeant "my name is Trevor Potter," he asked me to sit down, while he called somebody.

Two guys arrived (plain clothes) and introduced themselves, they then asked me to follow them into an office, which I did, all I wanted to know was why had they arrested Frank, but I was told to keep quiet while they arrested me and read me my rights, (what the fu**). I spent the next two days and nights in a cell, it reminded me of being in the tank in Vietnam, closed in and trapped.

I was interviewed every two or three hours, you see it on the TV but you do not think it is real. Well it is, it's called the fright tactics, one nice policeman and one nasty one, do not get me wrong, they are only doing their job, but I wish I could get the nasty one to sea for a trip or two, sharp shut him up.

Well I was sent to magistrate's court after two days, and put on bail, pending crown court date, I was not even allowed to see my kids, unless it was under the eyes of their head teacher, it is obvious that the news was in the papers, both in GY and Shields.

Lynn was a bit worried about taking me to her mothers, and telling her that I had moved in, so bit between the teeth I drove her to her mothers house, when we walked in she was sat reading the paper, about this North SHIELDS skipper who had been arrested, so I said to her "hi I'm Trevor living with your daughter, and that is me you are reading about" all she said was that I do not hold punches, best way, we got on straight away.

At last the Carmaran is ready for sea, that is except for us lot to rig the fishing gear, I had a full Geordie crew, on the way down to GY in the car (Trev driving) doing about 80 MPH, as we were passing an airfield, I saw a plane coming in to land, it had no wheels down, strange, so I said to the boys "look lads he has not got his landing gear down" this lad called Daft Johna (Kieth Johnson) yelled "Fu** him get your's down), I was so engrossed watching the plane that I had drifted up the bank at the side of the road, at that speed we were very lucky. Hey I wonder if the pilot on the plane was watching us, so forgot his wheels, you never know.

Arriving at GY (do not know how with my driving) we had three mile of rope to splice, and with fly shooting it was thicker than normal, but this crew were used to that, as most of the lads from north of the Humber were used to that gear. All done and off we go, the very first haul ,Bang, the winch pump collapsed, so back to GY, I was not a happy man, it took two days to replace the pump bedding, OK off we go again.

The first haul was great, about 20 boxes of prime cod, the second haul, bang, the same problem, when I looked at the damage I was now ready to kill some expert engineer, arriving into GY, I went up to the engineers office and ask why the fu**, it was happening, he said that he could not understand it, as they had stuck to the specifications, for the pump bed, it had to be one quarter inch plate, and that is what they used.

I then told the boss to make new bedding, from three quarter inch plate, he said the wrong thing, "Trevor that is very expensive, and also unnecessary" well I blew up, and said that expensive is going to sea twice and not catching fish, also I had a crew to pay, also you are a shit crap engineer, so just do as I tell you and shut the fu** up, so it was renewed with thick plate, and for the next two years, no bother with it at all.

Paddy who did not do technical would have got that right, the reason I have not named the firm of engine queers, is because the gaffer is now dead and buried, if he was still in charge I would name and shame, but there you go, cannot blame the lads who are running the firm thirty years later.

But I will say that this sort of thing went on a lot in the hay days of fishing, and the big trawler firms did not think of the cost, to them it was keep the boats at sea.

At last we managed to get to sea and do an eight day trip without much bother, the fishing was not good but my main worry was to get the boat and the nets working, we stayed in the southern part of the north sea, I knew the fishing was better further north but I was a bit worried about getting too far from GY until I had tested everything, the reason for the short trip was that fishing from Shields, also the type of fish you catch on this job, you had to get it in fresh.

As soon as a fish buyer in Shields saw GY on the bows, it was taken as old fish, so the first thing I let them know was that we were now a local boat, landing fresh fish. We sailed the next day and steamed to the hard ground that Charlie and I had the big haul pair trawling, the fishing was great, on the first day we got 150 boxes for three hauls, mostly large haddock, then one of the crew told me that their was a bad smell coming from the batteries, I went and looked (bad smell and I look) o well, anyway we were over charging them, the cut-out was not working, easily solved turn it off for a while.

It did not cure the problem, but it kept us fishing until we docked, to be on the safe side I had a link call with the electrickery expert in GY, A link call is made on the main long distance radio, to a shore station, and they phone the number you want, other boats waiting in turn can hear every word said, well talking to this expert in electronics, (who did all the work on the refit), I told him the problem, and asked if it was safe to carry on without the cut out working, he answered that it was, as long as I kept an eye on the vault meter, I then told him that it was showing a discharge, and that is not right.

This was his answer. "O THAT'S OK TREV, ALL THAT IS, and THE METER IS WIRED UP BACK TO FRONT" so just ignore it. Now I have just got myself £80 000 in debt, and they cannot even wire a fuc****, vault meter up, worse still they knew that they had but never bothered to correct it.

After the call was over, the shore station asked me if I wanted any more calls, so I said yes please, could you get me in contact with a Mr Benjamin Hill please, he said "the comedian Benny Hill"? I said "yes please, if I have got to talk to one I want a professional on the job" well the radio operator at Cullercoats cracked up. And so did a few boats that were waiting for their turn.

One morning I decided to let the mate, (Keith Johnson) shoot the gear, also I could have a lay in, with four coil to come the cook brought me a cup of tea, and said the net will be up shortly, great every thing had gone ok in Keiths hands, then I fell back to sleep, the next thing I heard was the mate saying to me "Trev will you get up so we can take this fucking net aboard" He had caught a full lift of cod, and we were towing it behind us, they wanted me to work the wheelhouse controls while they took the fish, what a show up, but on the other hand I knew that I had a relief skipper if ever I wanted a trip off.

We fished well that day, and ran out of empty boxes, (we carried 200) so the last haul we had to put the fish down GY style, in the pound with ice, so our first trip as a fly shooter we landed 260 boxes of fish for just two days, what a great start, one small problem, the fish that were not boxed did not sell very well.

I cannot remember how much money we made, but the lads were semi happy.

We only had two nights in dock and sailed again, back to the hard ground we were working the last trip, and the fishing was almost as good, for the first three hauls we put 30 boxes down, on the last haul of the day we had a very nice one 100+ boxes, shit another night with no sleep, we dropped the anchor and started gutting, every one of the lads were in high spirits, (obviously).

There was a set of GY pair trawlers working the same ground as us, and the skipper of one was my old partner Dave Rose, well he asked me if I could help them out with a tank of fuel, that is 300 gallons, as the fishing was so good and I had to do short trips anyway, I told him to come alongside and he could have it, when he arrived I was very surprised to hear that the fishing for them was very bad, how strange is that, they were working the same patch of stones as us, but the trawl was not catching it.

Dave was very surprised to hear how well we were doing, but it has been proven time and time again that different styles of gear took the fish at different times, another day it would be the trawl catching fish and the sea net not. Strange old job fishing, Dave then said that he had five kits in his last haul, we can have it for doing them the favour, I asked if it was gutted, "no" well keep it Dave the lads have enough to do.

My crew all said that if he had put it on our deck, they would have took the diesel back, lazy sods.

The first haul the next day filled the rest of our boxes; we now carried 250, so straight in to land. The first two trips looked like life was going to be ok, but there I go again getting ahead of myself.

We were busy taking ice for our third trip, when Trevor decided to step down a bunker lid, I hit my chest on a metal roller and it was not nice, I could not breathe, so one ambulance needed, and one relief skipper.

So daft Johna had to take the boat to sea, and the deck hand Keith Harvey was promoted to mate.

I say that but on the Shields boats all the lads were on the same money, if they knew their job, and Keith Harvey did,(better than me at fly dragging), by the way a bunker lid is a hole in the deck to put ice in, think of a manhole cover.

I spent three days in hospital as they were a bit concerned about a large bruise on my lung, I was in agony, it hurt that much that I did not even think about how well or how bad the lads were doing at sea, as it was they were having a disaster, Keith had lost a net and most of the rope, not the mate, the skipper, it's awkward having two men with the same name, but remember my first trip in Ling Bank, well at least Johna spent two days grappling and he got it back, thank fu**.

That trip I had to go back to court in GY to have my bail renewed, It was not good news, my solicitor had told me that, if found guilty of the charges, which were sinking a boat and endangering life, and two of insurance fraud, the sentence for the first one was a maximum of 15 years, shit, and that's without the fraud, on the bright side they did renew my bail. On the dark side the firms that I owed money to were now VERY worried that I would sail into the sunset, and never to be seen again.

After a lot of discussions, it was decided that the only way I could keep the boat out of the bailiffs hands, was to bring her back to GY, to be honest they did have a point, plus I was thinking of getting some charts for the Bahamas, the crown court was set for 2/3/1981, and I was told not to be late, or something like that.

Back fishing from GY I decided anchor bashing was the best choice, it is strange how to ports only 170 mile apart, can pay better prices for different types of fish, each trip we landed, I had a hire car waiting on the dockside, as soon as we tied up I drove home to Shields, and left the mate to oversee the landing.

To be completely honest since I had to run her out of GY I had lost interest, and with the court case pending I did not bother to make plans for the future, or lack of it, it did not feel like she was my own boat any more, as being told where to land, I might as well take a firms ship away.

One trip we arrived in GY at about 10pm, and I got straight in the car and drove to Shields, we had just done an 18 day trip, cannot remember how much fish but it was ok, I did not go for a pint with the lads, as I had the three hours drive ahead of me, so that is nineteen days without a single drop of alcohol , (hey that is good), I arrived in Shields about 1am, so I decided to pop into one of the clubs for a pint, it was called the Jungle, very infamous all over the world.

I had two pints and then drove home (and this time it was TWO) well turning into the street where we lived the old blue lights started to flash, so I pulled over, knowing that I was ok, and thought to myself, you are going to be fed up constable, he got out of his car and asked me where I had been, so I told him ,"the Dogger Bank officer" stupid move Trev, he then asked the number plate, which I did not know, I told him it was a hire car and that I had just driven up from GY, well anyway another balloon to blow up, and the result was borderline, so he took me to the station for a blood test, well I failed it, and in the course of time lost my licence for a year.

That was shit, I told the court that I had to drive from Shields to GY every trip, but that did not help, do not get me wrong, as I said earlier I am against drink driving and most days would deserve to loose it, but on this one occasion NO WAY.

I did have one advantage, that was when I left GY and moved to Shields, I had to get a new driving licence, as my other one was still in with most of my gear that I could not get from Mary, but after a while she came round and left all my gear at Rays house, so as long as I was a very good and very lucky lad on the road, I had a clean licence to produce, I know that is criminal but what the fu**, I was facing 15 year anyway. Another thing my solicitor asked me was, am I thinking of getting married, I looked at him with a do not take the piss look and said no.

He then strongly advised me to think about it, as a married man with kids (Lynn was pregnant) would receive a lighter sentence, than a single man; hey did he know something that I did not.

For the rest of the year we fished ok, but to be honest I still never had a lot of heart left in the job, it did not seem to me as a fun job anymore, but the bills have to be paid. One trip Frank's son came with us for another pleasure trip, remember Vic, he made his dad the mustard sandwich last year, his dad was not with us that trip, I wish he was, as they had a bad fire in their home, and sadly Frank was killed.

They told me on the link call not to tell Victor, and that his uncle would meet us in and tell him then, I totally agreed with that, as we were about 18 hours steaming time from GY. I hear now that Vic runs his own building firm, so good on you lad.

Normally the anchor boats did not sail until about February, but all the debt I was in I decided to try a very early trip, and be the first boat to land fish, so I asked the crew if they were up to sailing on boxing day, to my surprise they were, (greedy sods), so that we did, we steamed straight to Helgoland , as that is normally a good fishing area in winter months, now I said that I wanted to be the first boat to land in the new year, well I beat that, after only two hauls the rudder fell off.

Shit no other boats to tow us in, I could still steam along, but with no steering it was a bit hard to do, being a clever sod and remembering tales from the older fishermen, we managed to steer the boat by dropping a fish basket over the stem, on the side I wanted to turn, the drag turned the boat, also we towed a long heavy wire behind us, that helped to keep her from wandering to far off course, god what a clever little Trevor.

We got the hang of it that well, so when I arrived at Esbjerg I managed to go in without getting a tug, and then got a rollicking from the harbour master for trying it. So next day on the slip and they had to make a new rudder for her, by now I was getting big time despondent, (pissed off with it all), and with it being the holidays it would take over a week to sort out.

So a week on the drink for all, the next day I got in with a couple of lads who were working on the north sea ferry, and went aboard for a bottle or two, it was a great party, when I came round I went ashore, to my total amazement I was back in North Shields, o well pop home for a day and make out that I had planned it, on the way home I decided to pop into one of the bars for a livener, (cure for hangover, stay drunk).

Stood in this bar I ordered a pint, small problem, they do not accept Danish money in Shields, one of the lads came to the rescue and paid for it, well after sleeping it off, I had to go to the office and get a ticket on the next ferry back, sailing back over to Denmark I got chatting to two young kids, they were stood at the ships rail beside me, and were chatting about the lightship and coloured buoys, so I began telling them what they meant to the ships.

All of a sudden this woman came over and told them off, for talking to a strange man, I then told her that there was no need to worry about me, but she said that being their teacher, she had to be very careful, and I agree, so all sorted out I asked if I could buy the kids a bottle of pop each, she said there is no need, but dopy Trev insisted, I told her to bring the kids to the bar, and that I would get them one, next thing I knew was she had 20 kids stood beside her, it was a school trip, well I did offer.

On new years eve the lad I got the Toledo off came aboard to look at her, he was amazed at the refit, the total change in his old boat, I asked him if he wanted her back, he was amazed not stupid.

A new year is celebrated different in Denmark, like we were shocked to find out that every single bar in the town closed at 3PM, SHIT what do we do now. Well he kindly invited us to spend the night at his house, and what a night it was, well the bit of it that I can remember, it must have cost him a small fortune for the food and drink, O and fireworks, but he could well afford it, as he had just sold an old boat to some dopy prat in England.

See you next year/ tomorrow, if I wake up that is.

1981

Hi god I have a massive hangover, but it was free, so I cannot complain, the rudder was ready after three days, so away we go, I wanted to be the first boat out, ended up the last, o well, it goes to show you that you can push too hard, and recently that is all I seem to be doing. I think it is coming through in my tale.

Not so many jokes or pranks, but a lot more stress, maybe once the trial is over I can lighten up, or at least relax for 15 year, well we landed a decent trip of small cod, so did the other 150 anchor boats, so the price on the market was crap, as I said the trial was booked for the 2nd of march, so not much fishing time, thank fu**.

I got married to Lynn, as the barrister advised, but if I went down I made her promise me a divorce, who wants to spend time in prison, and worry about a wife, it is bad enough when you are at sea, the next trip I took a pal of mine Mick Overend,, he was to take the boat away while the trial was on, I wanted him to get to know her, and that trip we did well, Mick was not over the moon about me doing the odd fly shooting, but I told him that as he was skipper next trip, well it was his choice but he now knew the job.

His crew were Taffy and Chuck Green, so I knew that she was in safe hands.

By the way Mick was the lad who stopped me killing the tanker skipper, in the Halton collision, Lynn and I stopped at little Charlie's house for the trial, he was at sea, but his wife was good to us, thank you Linda.

I have shown the first newspaper cutting of the trial, I have eight of them, very repetitive, and so I will just show the first and the last one, if it was not so serious it would have been funny. Well to tell the truth at times it was. Remember Dave (the custard) well he was a witness for the prosecution, straight away I thought if he is helping them, well I have got it made. To be honest while he was being questioned, by the prosecutor, even he kept shaking his head, I think Dave was the best defence I had the whole trial.

On the first day, during the mid morning break, I was taken down to the cells, given a cuppa, and they did not bother locking the cell door.

The prison officers from Lincoln prison even sat and chatted with me about boats, and fishing, one of them said that he thought the whole thing was a farce, wish he was on the jury, dinner times I was allowed out, (tight sods, did not want to buy my dinner) so I went for a couple of pints in the bar, opposite the courts. In the afternoon court, every body seemed more relaxed, bet they all went for a pint or two.

After the first day was over I stood at the bus stop, when Dave the custard pulled up in a car, he offered me a lift, (WITH HIM DRIVING), I politely told him to fu** off, also I said "Dave you are not allowed to talk to me" he answered that he had not fell out with me, so why not?.

For fu** sake, did the prosecutor not tell him anything. Also while in the courtroom, I noticed that in the public gallery, there were a lot of fishermen, must have been interesting to keep them out of the pub. Day two was just listening to a load of bull, from so called experts on the amount of water that can pass through a two inch pipe. And another on about how much, and how long it would take a boat to sink if a hosepipe had been put down, depending on the weight of the boat, and the weather, and weather or not it was caught in a certain time, or if I had fish and chips for dinner.

Well come on let's be honest all the real experts were sat in the public gallery, (or a pub). To me it was a total waste of time and money, I mean without anybody else, my barrister alone was charging about £4000.00 a day, and that is without his dinner time pint. They also came up with the argument that we were all drunk on the night; well the gaffer of the Dolphin soon put that right, thank you Joe.

At the end of the second day my barrister asked me why the wife was not in court, and I said that she had a child to look after, he then said, "get a minder, I want her sat in the front seat" when I asked him why, he said "to show that she is pregnant", well what the fu** has that got to do with a boat sinking, he reminded me about the sentence for a single man, "o ok so every thing is looking good then"? he said don't take the piss, just do as he says, so for the next seven days, she was sat in the front row of the court, if my barrister had his way, she would have been sat beside the judge.

Denies seiner charges

THE trial opened in Grimsby today of a seine-net skipper-owner who faces charges alleging misconduct and obtaining insurance money by deception in connection with the sinking of his ship, the Ada Jean, in the North Sea in September, 1978.

Trevor James Potter has pleaded not guilty to endangering the Ada Jean and those on board by failing to take all steps required to preserve the vessel from loss.

He also denies three charges accusing him of obtaining more than £24,000 from the Sunderland Marine Mutual Insurance Company Ltd, by deception.

After Potter (31) of Dorking Avenue, North Shields, had been charged the jury were sent away for Judge Richard Hutchison to hear legal argument in their absence.

The trial is expected to last seven working days and at some point the jury will probably be taken to the docks to see a vessel similar to the Ada Jean.

FROM GRIMSBY TELEGRAPH

On the third day, the jury and other important people were taken down to Grimsby docks; the idea was to let them see the engine room of an anchor boat. I was not very pleased with the choice of boat, (Dover Star) she was half the age of the Ada Jean, but there you go the accused cannot chose, if you see what I mean.

The size of the engine room would only allow half the jury down at one time, so everything had to be explained twice, It was quite funny, on arriving at the boat (in a coach), Mr. Moss was stood at the boats rail, they had made a walkway and a set of steps, for the people to get on board safely, as I passed him I said, "hey Peter why do we not get one of these for sailing".

I could see he wanted to laugh, but he just shook his head, and looked at me with his, behave yourself look, as I said, only half the jury could fit into the engine room at one time, it was very well lit up and the engine was running, (very noisy) so while the experts were shouting to be heard, (I was perched on top of the engine) to me it was daft, so without asking anybody, I reached down and stopped the engine.

I could see the relief in all their faces. Now everybody could hear what was going on, as I said she was a lot younger than the Ada Jean, so had better lighting in the engine room, I said "can we have the lights off" and was told that I could not talk, well fu** it I might as well restart the engine, but my barrister said that if I had a point to make, I should be allowed to put it forward. So the judge asked me why.

So I told them that on the Ada Jean, the lighting system was no way as good as on this boat, they then turned off three of the four lights,(well I did), and said, (in near total darkness), "now this is the light I had that morning, also the water was half way up the engine.

They now looked a bit worried as I might ask for some water to be let in, but no they took my word for it, after that we went to the slipway and looked at a boat out of water, the prosecutor, pointed out the curve of the planks, at the stern of the boat, he said that in the history of fishing, there was never a case of one of those planks springing, and my barrister replied with, " no, true that is because they sink fast".

Well that was a nice day out for all, except me, I missed my dinnertime pint, the next day the prosecutor was to finish, and my guy took over, the first person he called was no other than Mr Moss, well Peter told them that the boat was running well and that it was In profit. He also told them that when I had the rope reels fitted, he advised me to up the insurance and that I told him to leave it until the end of the year. The prosecutor asked him if I was paying Frank's mortgage, he said yes, but most of the owners did, so that the crew had no worries at sea, also it was taken off their money at the end of each trip.

Well that shut him up, I think they were trying to say that I was paying him to keep quiet, like if I was, would I do it through the office. Well for the last two days of the trial Trev was in the box, and the first day they tried every trick in the book, to make me look like some sort of major criminal, but little did they know, my favorite program on telly, was Ironsides. Well not really it was Red Dwarf, but they never had court cases.

On the dinner break, I had more than my two pints, all the lads were buying me a drink, in case it was my last for a few years, I did not go daft, I mean who would go into the box pissed? Not me, but during the afternoon session I had to ask for the toilet three times, (what a show up).

Ok it is the last day, and after giving my answers to my barrister, it was the dinner break again, the jury were sent out, and I was put in a cell, when I asked why, the prison officers told me, that the jury was out, so Trevor had to stay in, and I did, for three hours. While I was sat in the cell, doing a crossword, one of the guards came up and said, "sorry trev but I have got to lock the door", the reason was that some guy in another court room had just been given five years, and they expected trouble from him, when they brought him down to the cells. Now I have heard of being locked up for being naughty, but never for protection, I mean why would the guy have a go at me, well better safe than sorry.

My turn, the jury was back, and the guards took me up to the court room, god I have never felt so alone in my life. I was told to stand, and I did, hope it's not too late to grovel, looking down I could see my solicitor, he had a paper in front of him, it had all the charges written on it, anyway the judge asked the Forman the result of charge 1, NOT GUILTY, my solicitor ticked all four, he knew that if number one was not guilty, the other ones had to be. Well that is British justice for you.

Trevor James Potter   14th march 1981

Seiner owner cleared

ON UNANIMOUS verdicts, the skipper-owner of a fishing boat which sank in the North Sea two and a half years ago without loss of life was at Grimsby Crown Court yesterday afternoon cleared by a jury of all charges alleging misconduct and obtaining insurance money by deception.

Trevor James Potter (32) — who during his nine-day trial insisted there was nothing more he could have done to save his stricken vessel, the 40-ton registered Ada Jean — was discharged.

The jury took about three hours to reach verdicts of not guilty to misconduct endangering the Ada Jean and her crew, and three of obtaining money by deception from the Sunderland Marine Mutual Insurance Co. Ltd.

Potter, of North Shields, had been accused by Mr. Simon Hawksworth, prosecuting, of deliberately letting the vessel sink.

Kept in cell

When the trial opened, he said the prosecution based their case on confessions alleged to have been made to the police by Potter 18 months after the sinking following accusations by the defendant's estranged wife.

But Potter denied that he let the vessel sink and said he could not find the leak.

He maintained that he confessed "to keep the police happy" after being kept in a cell for about seven hours.

After the verdict, the jury was thanked by Judge Richard Hutchinson for their obvious care in what he said had been a long and far from easy case.

Potter was defended by Mr. George Beattie.

After leaving the courts, we went down to the office, the director and I both agreed that now we can concentrate on fishing, thank fu**. But tonight it was time to celebrate; he rang a very posh restaurant and told them to give me a table for four, and to send the bill to him, how kind, well the four of us made him pay, Charlie had three different drinks on the table, well I would hate to see the bill after the end of the evening.

To be honest, we could have drank in there all night, but it was not my sort of bar, even if it was free, (told you trev was nuts). After the meal we went down to Freeman Street, and had a tour of the fisherman's bars, it was still free, as every one we met bought us a celebratory drink, thank you all, in a bar called the Hitching Rail, somebody told me that the Carmaran was being towed in, by the Hatcliffe, (Chessys new boat), She had engine trouble, but even that could not spoil my night.

Well all good things come to an end, the next morning, (with a monster hang over) I went down dock to look at the boat, straight away I lost my temper, with the office, and Mick, there was two engineers just about to go on board, and I asked them who ordered them, one said the office and the other said the skipper.

I said to them that they could go back to their workshop, and that I would ring if I wanted them back, after asking Mick if the engine stopped, or if he could not start it, he told me that he was steaming, all of a sudden it went dead, I then opened the cover for the belts, they drove the air intake, that was needed to help the engine breathe, sure enough the three belts had come loose, after only half an hour I had her running.

Do not get me wrong, anyone could have made the same error, but by now I knew all her little quirks, he never had much of a trip in so I settled the crew on an expense free trip, I saved that on booting the engineers. Well Trev, time to get back to some fishing, I had a new crew, Bob Hopwood, the mate he was twenty years older than me, and a brilliant fisherman. Also a lad from Hartlepool called Peter Green, (chucker). We also had a trainee, but can not remember his name. after two semi decent trips, we all seemed to get on with each other, Bob was a bit of a sea lawyer, but with his long experience we put up with that, and Chucker was, how can I put it? Well as mad as me, so we got on brilliantly.

The office managed to get me a mortgage, and I bought a house in

Blundell Avenue GY, how the hell I got a loan for a house, with my debt, I will never know, unless the bank manager was in the I give up, mood. We decided not to move into the house, until the baby was born, I wanted her to be a Geordie, why? Well if she was daft, she would have an excuse.

Plus I had four Grimmy's, and they were a hand full, Rachael Lynn Potter, was born on the 31/5/1981,

It was very weird, as when I was told over the radio that she arrived at 4.30PM that was the very same time that one of the engine injectors blew up. (SCAREY), anyway welcome to the world kid, she hates that. When I call my grandson Luke a kid she go's mad at me. Anyway we were only 45 mile off Shields, and were a bit short on ice, so we popped in so that I could meet her, that was a waste of fuel, as just like the others she never spoke to me.

A month later we moved in to the house in GY, it was great now my other four kids could come round and stop, whenever they wanted. Also they knew now I was not the bad man, who gave them the monthly rollicking,

I was their escape from home daddy; kids are strange things, no? come July I took little Tony on his first trip to sea, he was now 10 year old, but he was to have his eleventh birthday at sea, well he took to it like a duck to water, (in-between spewing) but to be fair to him, he was not as bad as his father, on his first trip.

We spent most of the trip on the North East bank, and fished very well, Tony had his fishing rod with him, but caught nothing, as the water was too deep also there was only plaice on the ground, after ten days we had about 120 kits, I decided to land them fresh, so for the last day I steamed to a spot 60 mile off the Humber, fishing for small cod, it was our last day fishing, and also Tony's birthday, so I said to him, "son if we do not catch a lot of fish today, you are going to spend your day in the water, tied to the anchor bladder, (it was flat calm) as the net came up, Tony was watching out of the window.

Phew, it was a great haul, about 40 kits of medium size cod, Tony looked at me and I said "happy birthday son", we went on to catch 100 kits that day, so everybody over the moon. To this day on his birthday Tony always say's "X amount of years ago today, we caught one hundred kit of green" it was on a ground called the Cleaver Bank, even after I have gone, he will bore his son with the same story. "Alfie 60 years ago today, I was on the Cleaver Bank and we caught 100 kits".

On that last day fishing Tony did catch a few on the rod and line, and in the evening haul he started to get a lot of Mackerel, with the help of the crew I think he got about two boxes, when we landed the fish, a lot of the buyers said to bob that it was a very nice trip and the fish were very fresh, bad thing to say to Bob, was that we should make at least £14000.00, and what did we make? A scabby £9000.00, do not get me wrong there is nothing wrong with nine grand, but when a buyer tips you for 14000, well that is a kick in the teeth.

Tony had his fish sold separately, as it was line caught, and only one day old, but I thought he had two boxes not five, the lads had added to it, when we went up to the office for the settlings Tony had his own wage packet, imagine that at eleven years old, I cannot remember how much money he got, but it was more than my first years pay on the Wilton Queen, I think he gave a treat to his brother and sisters.

In GY as I told you in the Maxwell days, if you were sailing on an early morning tide, the office organised a taxi to pick up the crew, well it was still the same, anyway I had a night out with Bob McQueen, must have been pissed, well about midnight we ended up in a nightclub, called the Sands, it was on Cleethorpes seafront, sat there with Bob and three other guys, it was turning into a good night, but one of the lads said "sorry I have a crew to pick up for sailing at 4AM, so I must go".

I asked him what boat he was crewing for; he answered "the Carmaran" so I told him to have another drink or two, as the Carmaran had cancelled, he then asked me how I knew that, and Bob told him that I was the skipper. So get them in it is your turn, and he did, I must not make a habit of this, with the debt I am in.

We sailed the day after, Bob had to have a trip off, so Taffy came with us, once again I was fishing with George Mussell, spelt it right this time, I hope, after about ten days, (he had out fished me every day Grrr)

Any way we got up one morning, and she would not start, so now the engine was committing mutiny, after trying it a few times we came to the fact that we needed a spare part, (she was an air start engine), so I rang the office and told them to send the part out on another anchor boat, they told me it would take three days to get one, shit.

So flat calm weather, good fishing, and a five day wait, what the fu** had I done to deserve this, DO NOT ANSWER THAT. Taff and I were looking at the manual for the engine, and I came up with this idea, to bypass the air pipe, with a ten pence piece, we blocked off the damaged pipe, and then had to rig a new pipe to the start valve, small problem, the only pipe we had was rubber reinforced hydraulic pipe.

Sod it, it is worth a try, and that we did.

After connecting every thing up (we only had one chance). I stood by the air bottle and Taff the start valve, I said to him "when I shout pull the start valve" ok here we go, I spun open the air bottle, and shouted, well I saw the two inch hydraulic pipe grow into a massive balloon, then it exploded, the bang it made in the confined space of the engine room was unbelievable, we both staggered out on to the deck. When I looked at Taff, his mouth was moving but no sound.

We were both stone deaf, and then he slapped me on the back and pointed to the exhaust, smoke! Yes get in she was running, but we could not hear it, I ran down the engine room and closed the start valve. She was running but no way must we stop her, Tony Chester was anchored two mile off us, when he saw the smoke he came alongside, and his crew threw us a six pack of lager. Even after the big fall out with the Island, that was his way of saying that we were pals again, thanks Tony Chester.

We had lost two days fishing, but did ok, on landing day we turned out about twenty kits more than George, he went mad at me for the lies, but like I said earlier I can NOT count.

1982

Glad that one is over, I might have been writing about prison life in the eighty's, on the other hand I could have gone to Slade Prison with Fletcher. (Ronny Barker), do you not watch UK Gold? At least it would have been a laugh, which I am not having at the moment.

I was holding my own with the boat, but to be totally honest I was not paying off much of the debt, I know I had the rest of my life to do that, but it was not as enjoyable as it used to be. Also when you are in a worry situation, everything seems to go against you, well that was how I felt. One trip we were fishing very well and then a storm hit us, we lay at the anchor with the storm gear out for five days.

That is a very long time for one gale to last, when the weather eased a bit I shot the gear and it came up empty, with a northerly storm the fish go into deep water, so I decided to move, and try again.

While we were steaming we came across this yacht, for some reason it did not look right, for a start why was it this far out in the kind of weather we had for the last five days?, also I noticed that her boom was moving from side to side, as she was rolling in the swell, very strange, I decided to go along side and check that they were ok.

When we got along side of her I shouted out for the crew, but no answer, by now I was really concerned so even though the swell was still massive, I told Bob to get a life jacket on and try to jump aboard her, and he did (must be mad). After about ten minutes he came up on to her deck and told me that she was empty.

I then got on the radio to the coast guard and told them what was going on, after telling them the yachts name, (Fleet) they told me that she was reported as capsized four days ago, well no way had this boat been over, as Bob told me that she was bone dry, and that there was things still on the cabin table, wow talk about a ghost ship, well this was certainly one.

I asked Bob if her engine would start, but after trying, there was no power, also he could not get the VHF to work, I then decided to tow her to GY and told Bob to stay on board, I do not think he was very happy about that, but there you go. It was now salvage, and no way was I going to loose her. The coast guard asked me to take her into Hartlepool but I told them that I was going to GY and leave it in the hands of the receiver of wrecks.

When we arrived at GY the office told me that they would send a small boat out into the river, to tow the yacht into the royal dock, I told them not to bother, I had read somewhere that if you hand over a salvage at sea, you could then loose it, and no way was that going to happen, when the lock gates opened I towed the Fleet into the royal dock, on arrival this chap jumped on board, it surprised me that he had a policeman with him, (and no I did not ask if he had his tights on).

 The reason for the police was that there had been loss of life, so the yacht had to be sealed off, for obvious reasons; the guy then told me that I could sign the boat over to him, and that I did, the office were not pleased about this as they were thinking of the lump of money that could come off my debt, but I told the receiver that I wanted all transactions to be done through my solicitor. Now I was very unpopular with the office, but do you know what? Fu** them, this time me and my crew were going to come first.

 I was a bit disappointed with the outcome, as instead of getting all of the Fleet, I was told that I could only claim one quarter of the insurance value, the reason for this was that the crew did not abandon her, they were washed overboard.

Do not ask me how they knew that but there you go, she was insured for £17000.00, so we were to get

£4250.00, still not a bad catch, but this time (not like the days of the Island) I took half for the owner, and settled the crew on their percentage, to me that was very fair, well they did not complain, when the money came through, well I was talking to the cook and his wife about 25 years later, and she thanked me for making her children's Christmas a good one, apparently it took eight months for the money to get to them.

   Is it not nice when somebody you have not seen for 25 years, remembers you as Father Christmas, and I still have not gone grey. Even at 62 years old, I must take after dad. On second thoughts he would never have got in debt like this. He had a lot more sense.

Here is a copy of the Grimsby Telegraph write up of the yacht.

A 25 foot yacht, whose crew were lost overboard in a race off Hartlepool on Monday, was towed into Grimsby this morning by the seiner Carmaran. The Hartlepool based Fleet was found drifting 45 miles NE of Whitby yesterday. Still under full sail and in high seas. Skipper of the Grimsby seiner, Mr Trevor Potter, sent one of his crew on board to bring down the sails, seal the cabin and prepare the vessel to be taken under tow, for the steam back to port.

After delivering his charge to the Grimsby yacht club at the Alexandra dock today, the Lowestoft born skipper, who now lives in Blundell av, Cleethorpes, found it difficult to understand why the yacht had been to sea in conditions that made even fishing impossible. "We found the yacht about 45 miles NE of Whitby, we were steaming to another fishing ground when I saw her" she was in full sail, but the main sail was yawing a bit. I thought it was a long way off land to be sailing in this type of weather, he explained. Forty year old Dave Nicholls and his forty year old fiancée, Joyce Meason, who were to be married soon, had put to sea for a race organised by Hartlepool yacht club on Monday morning.

The Tees coastguard had advised against running the event, but the organisers went ahead with their plans, which were to keep the racing yachts in view of the shore. Despite the assurances from the organisers that their members vessels, which were of an ocean going nature, were able to cope with conditions, the couple were soon in trouble, and lost overboard. The woman's body was recovered by lifeboat, but they are still looking for the other body. Skipper Potter said that when they went alongside the conditions were still bad, "it had been blowing force 8-9 northerly; I decided to see if the crew were ok, and when we got along side we found that there was nobody on board. I put a man aboard to take the sail down, and then took her in tow. I called Humber radio, and was told that the crew had been lost of a capsized yacht; he said that this one had not been capsized, and was in perfect condition.

As the Carmaran slipped into dock this morning, with crewman Robert Hopwood aboard the yacht, she was met by customs, and police, after handing over the yacht, the Carmaran went in to the fish dock, to land a more routine catch. With his crew Robert Hopwood, and Geoff Reedon.

The yacht, with the Carmasan behind, being berthed in the Alexandra Dock today.

Seiner finds 'ghost' yacht

That summer little Tony came for another trip, I hope he is as lucky as last year, we also had Bobs son with us. I think I should start school trips, would make more money, but on second thoughts no thank you. After about five days fishing (the boys were doing my head in), we had a very large and heavy Oil Rig cable hung on the net, it was one hell of a job getting it in, we had the net in the power hauler, but it was not powerful enough.

I told the two lads to stay in the wheel house, and went to get the Gilson, (heavy lifting gear), while I was dragging it aft to put round the net, I heard Chucker screaming "hold on Bob" I dropped the Gilson and ran aft, Bob was busy leaving the boat through the power block, but Chucker was very fast and thinking straight, he slacked away on the block and Bob went through it, he then dragged him clear of the net.

Most men would have tried to hold on to him, but by slacking the block he saved his life.

Twenty eight years later, I was sat in a bar with Bob (now in his eighty's) when In walks Chucker and Dean Mussell, Bob did not recognise Chucker, when the lads spoke to us, Bob said "hey lad do not but in when we are talking" so I then said to Bob, "that is no way to speak to the man who saved your life".

Bob then remembered him, and it was drinks all round; we had a great laugh about it. Well back to the past, or do I mean the present, I'm getting a bit confused now, O I know back to 1982, after getting him clear of the net he was in a lot of pain, mostly in his upper leg and his chest, after getting the net on board, I decided to run into Shields, to get him checked out, better safe than sorry.

We arrived in Shields at about 7PM, when we tied up there was an ambulance waiting to take Bob to the hospital. Chucka and I decided to go for a couple of pints, in the Dolphin, before we left the boat I told the two boys not to leave the boat, as Shields is not a dock like GY, an open harbour has a very large rise and fall with the tide.

A lot of fishermen have been lost in Shields, trying to get on their boats at low tide, at high tide the boats rail is level with the quay, at low the top of the mast is level, that tells you how much rise and fall you get,

And I told Tony and young Bob that, with Tony thinking about being hung over the Saxon Kings stem, I think it sank in, plus with pride I can say that our Tony was a very sensible lad.

Bob came to the Dolphin at nearly closing time, he was badly bruised but nothing broken, so I asked him if he wanted to go home, he said no, well a couple of pints for him and a nights sleep, then back to fishing. At about one in the morning we went back to the boat, funny Bob said he had no pain now, I thought to myself; wait till you wake up sober mate.

When we got on board the two kids were sat with tears in their eyes, I asked them what was wrong, well they thought that we had fell in the harbour, this time I felt REALY guilty. But little Bob was over the moon to see his dad was safe and drunk. We turned in for the night and sailed the next morning. We finished the trip with no more mishaps, but there was more to come, I am getting used to it now, my mother always said (God does not pay debts with money), work it out for your self.

The next trip we were hauling up the anchor, Chucker was stowing the net and Bob was guiding the wire and chain on to the winch, normally the mate is stood by the stop/start handle for safety, but on the Carmaran, I had one inside the wheel house, thank god, all of a sudden Bob passed out and lay over the anchor chain, within two turns of the winch, he would have been cut in two, but I was able to stop the winch in a split second, I went out on deck, put Bob in the recovery position and he slowly came round.

After asking him if he had any chest pains, or shortness of breath, he said that he had not, but he was very dizzy, well even more than usual, must be bad, I told him to get in his bunk for an hour or two, and we would see how he felt then.

Taking no chances I got in touch with the shore station, they put me on to a doctor, I gave him Bobs symptoms and he said that it sounded like a fit, fu** off, I have seen men have them, and this was nothing like, I asked him if I should get him air lifted, and he told me that there was no need for that.

I was not happy with the doctor so I took the boat home to GY.

And it was a very good job I did, when we arrived at GY Bob was taken up to the hospital, while he was in the waiting room he took another bad turn. It was his heart, apparently it started to pump the blood in the wrong direction, (he never was any good with pumps), and so Bob never went to sea again.

So that means I have got to take Taffy back, o well better the devil you know, and by now I knew him very well, he can mend now, but still would not let him sail as cook.

Well little did I know at the time but the next trip was to be my last one on Carmaran, we were fishing north of Hartlepool about 70 mile off, it was a bright, hot, summer day, and as I remember I had a splitting head ache all morning, I put it down to the sun, any way we were out shooting the first rope and I had to turn 90% to drop the net, when I put my hand on the auto pilot control I could not feel it.

And then I felt myself going, luckily I had the mind to stop the boat. When I came round I was in a hospital bed, Taffy and Chucker had hauled the gear back, lifted the anchor, and Taff took her into Hartlepool, the doctors told me that I had a trapped nerve, I did feel a lot better and by the end of the day they let me out.

Chucker took us to his mother's house for a bath and a meal, very kind of her thank you Mrs. Green, but she did say to Chucker "Trevor is looking very ill, and no way is it a trapped nerve". That evening the three of us went into town for a pint or three, in those days the pubs shut at 3PM and opened at 7 PM. Well it was about 6.30 when we arrived at the first bar, Stood outside were four skinheads, that was the trend in the early eighties, they had number one haircuts, bother boots, (steel toecaps), and braces holding their jeans up, when you saw a couple of them, you were supposed to be afraid of them, as they were the tough guys.

Chucker was very polite to them, and asked what time the pub opened, they said seven mate, Chucker answered "you are wrong lads, it is open now" with that he gave the door a sharp kick, and the pub was now open, the hard guys ran away, we went in, the gaffer said, "hi Chuck long time no see" well Taffy and I looked at each other and shrugged our shoulders, by the way mine is a lager.

I did not have more than three pints that night as I had started to feel lousy again, Taff walked me down to the boat, and tucked me up for the night, (he never read me a bedtime story), I told him to go back for a drink, and that I would see how I felt in the morning, he said "Trev for fu** sake go home", and that was when I knew that I was far from ok.

When I got up the next morning I felt as if the four skinheads had kicked the shit out of me, I rang the office and told them that I needed a skipper to take the boat, or a man with a ticket, so Taffy could take her, to be honest I felt that bad, I did not care which, they drove up a skipper called Frankie Josephson.

Well I was over the moon, as Frank was one of the best skippers in GY, but he had one small problem, he drank three times as much as me, but when you got him to sea, to me there was no better fisherman.

When he arrived, in a car with the engineer from the office, I told him that Taffy knew the engine and all her little quirks, so I had nothing to show him, Taff had sailed with him in the past, and they got on well.

Frank then asked me if there was any fish on board, I told him only about ten kits, he said "well Trev I do not take another man's fish, so we will sell it and then sail, if that is ok" so I told him that he is now the skipper, so do what you think best, and he did, bet they had a big hangover the next day.

When I got to GY, I saw the port doctor, and he made arrangements for me to go to Hull, for an MRI test.

They found out that I had a mild stroke, the vain in my neck had a small clot in it, but it had cleared it self

My now wife Pat had the same, but here's was a lot worse, I except that the medical profession are not infallible, but when we sit and watch the government advice advert, about acting fast with any sign of a stroke, it really annoys us how we were diagnosed in the past.

In the next part I must come to the present, and tell the true story of my wife's suffering at the hands of the North Tyneside medical profession, to be honest I think it will shock you.

Pat had the stroke in November2005, I have a copy of the letter that her daughter wrote, and feel very strongly about it. So here it is.

How bad is this letter from Patricia's daughter?

SUNDAY 20 NOVEMBER 2005

Mum took a funny turn whilst out in North Shields, an ambulance was called and she was taken to North Tyneside General, A&E, symptoms were, flashing lights, loss of speech, head ache and numbness.

She was much disorientated.

The examining doctor diagnosed migraine, and advised her to take paracetamol for 48 hours. When asked if there was a prescription, as mum had an exemption certificate, we were told that this medication was available at any shop, we left and bought tablets, then returned home.

MONDAY 21 NOVEMBER.

I contacted the GP as both headache and her speech had worsened. On the telephone we were told to continue medication.

Over the next few days we remained in touch with the GP, as her symptoms continued.

We told him that there was a strong family history of stroke, but were told that this was not the diagnosis that had been given, and that she needed to follow the instructions given. By this point mum was unable to sustain any conversation, she could only nod yes or no, but this was not always correctly.

The headache was continual, she was lethargic, and had no real concept of time/ awareness of those of us around her.

FRIDAY 25 NOVEMBER

We again contacted the GP, and requested an emergency visit from a GP, as mum was now unable to answer simple questions, the GP who visited was very sympathetic but concluded that I was certainly not a stroke, and told us we should return to A&E. the doctor rang the department, arranged a time for us to go and we duly attended, when we arrived at 1PM, we had to wait for 5 hours before she was seen.

The doctor advised that things did not look good, and that he "feared something sinister".

He arranged an MRI scan, but told us to be prepared for bad news.

Mum was oblivious to all this, she was admitted to a ward to await the scan, on MONDAY.

I arrived on Monday for the scan, I was booked for 9AM and by 5PM, and she had still not been seen

It was postponed until the next day. This continued for days, with doctors advising not to tell mum anything. We did not know how much she understood. By this time the doctors were mentioning possible brain tumours.

While visiting mum I had to shower her and wash her hair, brush her teeth, and change her cloths, as she smelt really bad, I would ask her if she had been washed, and she would nod.

But was still wearing clothes from the previous day. The staff were unable to confirm if she had in fact been showered or bathed, as shifts had been changed.

I was also heartbroken to come in twice to find my mum had food in front of her, it had not been cut up

And nobody was trying to feed her.

At this point she could not hold a fork or spoon, also one day she did not have a meal, as she could not fill in a menu card.

Before the MRI scan was taken, I found that a doctor had told her what they suspected was wrong with her, she was alone, unable to ask questions, and very frightened, as she thought she had a terminal illness

After being told not to tell her anything, by other consultants I was devastated that she had been given this kind of information, with no support, or way to communicate.

The MRI scan finally took place days later, (on the Thursday), I had been at the hospital constantly waiting for a vital scan, that took days to take place.

Eventually a diagnosis was given that mum had suffered a series of strokes.

This was a welcome relief as we had been told to expect bad news - at least we now knew she could recover, though not to what extent, her transferral to the stroke unit was helpful,

With staff who genuinely cared, and helped her recovery immensely.

By the time she was released, there was again a distinct lack of input from social care regarding preparing her for life at home.

Each of us has only one mother, and the devastating catastrophe of events I believe could have and should have been handled better.

      Sorry folks I had to put that letter in, as like I said with my minor stroke at sea and the fact

That I was told it was a trapped nerve it makes you wonder.

BY the way Jamie if you ever read this book, please think back, on the fact that you only ever have one MOTHER.

The main reason I put that bit in, is because when I told Pat about the stroke, she showed me the letter, and how lucky was I, that mine was only a minor stroke, but any stroke is bad and at 32, well.

The amusing side of it, when I went to the GY port of health doctor, he told me to sit down, then gave me a Park Drive, (cigarette with no tip) and a glass of whisky, he then informed me that I had to give up smoking, yes true, he knew that he was wasting his breath.

When the Carmaran landed she made £9000.00, I was over the moon with the trip, the crew came round my house on landing day, and they took me out for a drink, thank you Taff and Chucker, strangely the office phoned me and said they wanted to see me, about the boats future, I told the two directors that if they wanted to talk, then they could come to the house and do it.

Deep down, I knew what it was about, and to be honest I did not give a fu**. They came round the next day; they said that they were not happy with Frank taking the boat, my answer to that was "what after nine grand"? But Frank did have a bad name for getting to sea on a regular basis; they then told me that the firms I owed money to were getting edgy about the fact that I was not fit.

By now I was really rock bottom, and said to them "well I will just go bankrupt, and you can all fight it out" but to be honest that was not the best plan, they then said to me that if I signed the boat over to them, they would let me keep the house, and when I felt up to it, there would be a skippers job at any time I wanted one, REMEMBER what mum used to say, "god does not pay debts with money".

And I was now paying the debt. Any way I let them have the boat, and I was clear of debt, and worry, well I thought I was clear of worry, but the feeling of all the years it took to be an owner, and now I was back to square one, after a couple of days brooding, as I told you I had been on valium since the tanker episode. One afternoon Lynn was out, and I took them all, maybe it was a cry for help, as after taking them I rang my sister Jean, in Beccles, to say goodbye.

Jean did not know my address, but she kept ringing our number, Lynn came in from work and answered the phone. I woke up the next day in a hospital bed, I then had to see a trick cyclist, but I knew that it was a down side thing to do, but after loosing every thing you work for all your life, well it is very hard to explain.

I sold the house but not much profit as I had only had it for one year, and the price of houses had not risen by much, we went back to Shields, and stopped at Lynn's mothers for a while, because I had taken an overdose they stopped the valium, I was in a right mess, I began to think that I was back in the tank, and that all around me was not real.

I never left the house for over a month, even going to the corner shop was too much for me to put up with, I was in my own eyes a vegetable, one day Alex Mussell came round the house, he told me that he had a run job for me, all I had to do was take a yacht down to Lowestoft, from the Tyne, (300 mile), I would get £500.00 in my hand, before I sailed, and that is VERY easy money, but I turned him down.

Later on I realised that he had the job, but was trying to get me out and about again, I do not know how I got through the rest of that year, but at some point I knew that I must pull myself together, a man I had met in Shields a few years earlier Alfie Walker, came round to the house and told me that he needed a crewman, I told him about my problem, but obviously he already knew.

He said he was in the shit for a crew, and also that if I felt bad at sea I could go to my bunk, Alfie knew that I had been a skipper/owner, and that I had always done ok. Well I bit my lip, and told him that I would be there for him in the morning, for sailing, that was the hardest thing I have done in my life, walk down the harbour, and climb aboard his boat, I went straight to a bunk, and let the other lad let go of the ropes.

When the boat stopped to shoot the gear, I fought it and got up too help; I was shaking like a leaf, it was worse than my first trip back in 1963.

When I got on deck I saw that he had three other men on the deck, I said "why do you want me"? His answer was. "You're back now Trev, so it is up to you", Thank you for my life back Alfie. I am just sad that you will never read this, RIP.

I did a couple of weeks with Alfie, he had an ex Dutch beam trawler, but now she has towing hard ground gear (Rock Hoppers), and no way did he need the extra man. So I left, it was costing the other lads money to carry me, after a week or so mending nets on the quay, for £10.00 per day, (please do not tell the job centre).

One day a mate of mine John Geddes, who was skipper of an X GY anchor boat called the Danbrit, it was now on the prawn trawling lark, asked me if I would take her away for him, as he had to do six weeks at college, for his skippers ticket, and to this I agreed, I had sailed with one of the crew before, Ronny Blaclock, the other lad was from Holland, his name was Yuppie, hope that is spelt right mate?.

We were day fishing for Prawns, and if I say so myself we done ok, one small problem with the Danbrit, was that we had to pull the net in by hand, but with Yuppie being built like a brick shithouse that was no problem.

One evening after the second tow, and the weather being flat calm, I said to the lads "we are not going in, I am going to try a night haul" and to my surprise they both agreed, it did not pay off, as when we hauled there was only two boxes in it, but on the plus side ,we were on the Prawn grounds earlier than all the other day boats, well I did three weeks as skipper of the Danbrit, and like I said we did ok. Well the crew were happy, and there was a profit in the office, so every thing great, (Wrong again TREV).

Sat in the house one Sunday morning, there was a knock at the door, when I opened it a lad called Jimmy Cullum, was stood there, he said that he wanted the keys to the boat, as I had been sacked, "and why had I been sacked"? He told me it was for selling fish for cash, in other words, robbing the owner (and the tax man) but he does not count in the fishing industry.

I then asked him what it had to do with him, as he was not the owner, NO he was the new skipper, in our job it is called being stabbed in the back, (if you are reading this Mr Cullum, and you do not agree, well ask the fleet), I did hear later that Yuppie found out that he was being robbed, and well I will leave the outcome for you to imagine.

So Trevor is out of a job again, this is getting to be a habit of mine, but to be totally honest, I had now started to enjoy fishing again, and no worries about anything going wrong, if it did it was the owners problem, do not get me wrong, I still had the pride of keeping the crew in money, or if I sailed with anybody, I knew that I could do my job on the deck.

It was now coming up to Christmas, I had met a skipper from LT, he was born in Shields, but spent most of his life in LT, when I first met him, he was skipper of a large beam trawler, but just like me and hundreds of other fishermen, his marriage broke up, and he also moved in with a North Shields lass,

Well his name is John Ord, and he was now skipper of a very small steel trawler called Gallant Venture.

He sailed just two handed, the other guy was from Holland, but when he spoke to me, he had a broader Suffolk accent, than I did, it turned out that he was Yuppie's brother.

Well they got there heads together and decided to ask me if I wanted to sail with them, and thank you lads, I did, we did not go to sea each day, three handed, John worked it so there was always one of us ashore, so it was two days at sea and one ashore, this way we all got time off, except for the poor little Gallent boat, one day John asked me if I would take the boat, with the owners son, as my crew, he told me that I would get £50.00 for the day, no matter what we caught, so not being a complete nutter, I said "ok".

In the morning there was a large northerly swell running, a lot of the fleet did not bother sailing, but with that offer I let go, the wind was very light, but the swell always made the Prawns dig in to the sand, we shot the gear and towed south for five hour's , when we hauled there was only two baskets, but I said to the lad," your father is paying me for a day at sea, so we will tow back North, when we hauled there was about 30 boxes of Whiting in the net, they are a very poor price, but we took them in, arriving in the evening John was stood on the quayside to meet us, we sold the fish straight to a buyer for cash, and I got £100.00, put in my hand, great wish we could do that every day, then on top of that John Ord sent me to the office, to get the £50.00, for taking the boat. Wow thank you mate, you made my Christmas.

1983

Hi again, god this prawning lark is cold, stood on an open deck, sorting the little buggers into different baskets, to be honest I would rather have the D Ts, (that is a massive hangover). I went back with Alfie Walker, on the Fillia Maris, this time he did need a crewman, and at least there were no prawns on this boat, as I said she was trawling on hard ground for cod and haddock.

The mate was called John Duff, he was about twenty years older than me, a typical old salt, he used to frighten me with sea stories, well John always took a bottle of rum to sea, do not get me wrong he was no alcoholic, but it was a lifelong thing, with the old trawler men, under the cabin table we always had a grate of fizzy pop, very refreshing when you are seasick, or hung-over, well Trev was both, I got out of my bunk, it was dark in the cabin, and I had a mouth like a toilet, and that is being polite, I reached under the table and got a bottle of pop, took off the top and took a massive swig.

It took me about an hour to get my breath back, yup John had put his bottle of rum in the crate, and I do not think I have had rum to this day. And John said to me "Trevor, I do not mind you having the odd dram, but make it last" the old sod had a smile on his face when he said it, Alfie was saying that he did not feel too well that trip, so we landed after only two days, and not much fish.

While at home, Alfie rang me and asked if I would take the boat away for him, and I never had a problem with that, but to be honest, even after pair trawling, I was crap at hard ground fishing, so we sailed the next day, and I went on one of Alfies charts, we had three tows and only caught two boxes of fish, John Duff said to me, "Trevor you are from Lowestoft, try flat fishing" I knew he was taking the pi**, or to put it in a polite way, extracting the urine, but we were close to some of the best flat fish grounds I knew, and luckily I had my own charts with me.

The boat never had a fine ground fish net, but there was an old prawn trawl on the after deck, god knows when it was last used, but I added some chain, (to make it dig in the sand) and towed through my anchor chart. After two days towing, we landed 60 boxes of mixed flatfish, there was 20 boxes of Lemon Sole amongst that, so we got a very good price.

We sailed again the same night, after three days fishing, we landed 80 boxes, and a good price again, so it was time to have the weekend off. I was talking to Alfie, and he was still under the weather, but he made me laugh by saying, "Trev stop showing off or I will get the sack" he had worked for that owner for over 10 years, so no way could that happened.

Wrong again, sat in the house on the Saturday, the owner rang me, he lived in London, anyway he asked me if I wanted a permanent job as skipper of the boat, I then asked him if Alfie had left, he told me "no but the week you have done, is the best since I got her" I told him that I would ring back with my answer.

Lynn said that I should take the job, as the family came first, I nearly bit her head off, and told her to remember how she felt when I was stabbed in the back with the Danbrit, I then rang Alfie and asked him if he had finished in the boat; he said "no why"? so I told him about the phone call off the owner, Alfie called him a pr***, but told me to take it, as after ten years with him, he could have had the decency to tell him first, that he was sacked.

I did ring the owner back, and I told him to stick his boat where the sun never shines, Trevor Potter has still got a little bit of pride, AND NO JOB. But to me if a man could do it to one skipper, then I was the next out of a job, after a couple of bad trips, I have always been told that a skipper is only as good as his LAST trip, and that is very true.

To be totally honest I can still remember Alfie getting me back to sea. As it was, the boat was given to another skipper, and after only two trips at sea her gearbox blew, and then after it was fixed, the main engine blew, do not get me wrong, it was by no means the skippers fault, just age.

She was scrapped after that, and as Mother used to say "God does not pat debts with money.

I was told one day that this Polish guy was looking for a skipper to take his boat to sea, I was berthed up the Tyne, in what they called the Ranger dock, called that because that was where the freezer trawlers used to land, and they were al called the Ranger Ajax, Apollo, or some other name, all beginning with Ranger, any way that is how the dock got its name, and with having lock gates, there was no tidal rise and fall.

The lad who told me about the job, was James Purdy Cullen, from now on Jimmy, do not get him confused with the infamous Jimmy Cullum. Now Jimmy had skippered a few boats, and done well, so I asked him why he had put me up for the job, and not taken it himself, and like a lot of other men before him said, "Trev you do the worrying and I will spend the money, the owner said to me, "I want a skipper that goes to sea, and not let a little weather worry him.

His last skipper was a bit, shall we say, over careful, Jimmy said to him, "no worry there mate, he is a stormy bustard, thank you James. The name of the boat was Meva, she was an old Polish trawler, it had 12 bunks aboard, the owner told me that in her day she did six month trips, and landed her fish on to a mother ship every two or three days, the reason for so many bunks, was that they carried borstal boys, teenage lads in Poland, instead of going to a young offenders prison, the government sent them to sea.

We should do that now, I can remember seeing the Polish fleet fishing, in the sixty's and seventy's, and the mother ship was as big as the tanker that I was on, she had about 20 trawlers, landing there catch on to her, then they were refuelled, and stocked up with food, the mother ship then processed, and froze the fish.

To me that is what you call fishing, without wasting time. We sailed on the Prawns two days later, there was me, Jimmy, Ronny Blacklock, and the owner, so no shortage of bunks, towing along, I was stood in the wheelhouse thinking what a waste of a good boat, but to be fair, I did have to get to know her, before tripping it.

After two days on the Prawns, and not doing that well, I talked the owner into letting me go for fish, and do a 5 day trip, he agreed to that, we sailed the next morning, and I headed to the same spot that we caught the flat fish in the Fillia Maris, the fishing was a slow plod but good fish, after two days I had 22 boxes in my book, I asked Ronny what we had down the fish room, and he said 16 boxes, strange for me to over count, but I thought that we should shift grounds, George Mussell was fishing well on the NE Bank, so I went and joined him, it was an all night steam to get there.

After the first tow, we had a full lift of fish, 20 boxes, and great? Not so great, it was all Dabs, unwanted in them days, I moved a bit to deeper water, while we were towing, the bogey man arrived, (fishery protection), he asked me when I was going to haul, as he wanted to measure my net, and check the catch.

When I did haul, they came aboard and did just that, the net was legal, then he looked at my fish log book, it had 22 boxes, but I told him that the fish room man said 16, the fisheries officer smiled and said "you both want to learn to count, as you have a total of 36 boxes down the fish room, luckily the rules were not as strict in those days, so all was ok, when they left the boat, Jimmy and I went mad at Ronny,

As we had left a living of top class fish, shit, and too late to steam all the way back north.

Even to this day Jimmy always ribs Ron about that, if we had stayed put, and plodded away, we would have had a decent landing, to be honest it was all my fault, as I had always under counted, and was surprised when Ronny had less than me. Well there is always next trip, or so I thought.

When we landed we were told by the wives that the office refused to give them any money while we were at sea. Normally the wife could get an advance of £50.00 a week, while their men were at sea, but the office told me that the owner was in a bit if debt to them, so no advances, well we solved that problem right away, we packed our bags. And started looking for new jobs, I will give the office in GY their due, even when I was all that money in debt to them, they still gave the crews ladies their wage.

Tell you what it is only the start of a new year and Trev has had two skippers' jobs, and watch this space,

As I had more boats in this year, than my entire career put together.

As it was I was not walking about for long, a friend of Jimmy Cullen, who was a welder Barry Moss, no relation to Mr Peter Moss, was looking for a skipper, Jimmy had sailed skipper for him in the past, not only fishing, but diving, and salvage work. Barry was a keen diver, again I asked Jim why he did not take the job, he told me that he was doing ok with his new net mending job, and Jim was very good with the old mending needle.

Come sailing day, by the way trawling for fish, thank fu**, I hate the Prawns, Barry told me that I had to be back in 3 days, as he had booked the boat out to a wreck fishing party, so that gave me 48 hours fishing, well not going to break the port record then, plus he told me that the winch, (it was a hydraulic one), would not heave a big weight, as there was a leak inside, and he was waiting for a spare part from Denmark.

No pressure on me then? In the two days I fished, we got 45 boxes, of top class flats, brilliant, the makings of a very good trip, and I had to go home for a dopey angling party, o well he is the gaffer, so off we went, we arrived in Shields at 9 am, missed the market, but the angling party was on the quay, Barry came with us that day, and I am glad he did, as he knew the inshore wrecks better than any fisherman.

It was quite clever, as he told me to steam north, and when I had the two land marks in line I had to head inshore, and when the north and south pier were in line drop the anchor.

He even knew the name of the wreck, as he had dived on it a few times, Easton. After three hours, and nobody catching anything that was too big to fit into a sardine tin they started to moan, well can you blame them. They had travelled over 100 mile, to catch zero, or next to zero.

A couple of the fishing party even said that we were not near a wreck, I said to them "do you not trust a fisherman to find a wreck, to be honest, I was beginning to have my doubts, I decided to lift the anchor and shift further out to the stony ground, maybe that would put a smile on their faces, if that was possible after all morning catching nothing.

We heaved up the anchor, and this is unbelievable, but on the anchor was about 20 feet of a ships side, with a brass porthole in it, I felt great, and Barry said, "shit I thought I had taken them all off her, well I cracked up, and shouted out of the wheelhouse window, "is that close enough for you all" but that is fishing, another day they would have been reeling the cod in.

Luckily enough when I moved to the stones, they started to catch a few fish, so everyone happy, that is except for me, as I had lost two days good fishing. We landed the next day, and sailed again that night, steaming back out to the ground we had left two days ago, BANG, the engine blew up, so another one, Trev is beginning to think that he is either a very unlucky man, or a crap engineer. We got towed back in; Barry said it was not me, as he had been expecting it to go. Now where have I heard that before, um yes the Ling Bank. That is now 3 skippers, jobs so far this year, I think I better sail cook on the next boat, but I would most likely blow the oven up.

George Mussell landed in Shields, a few days later, as he had to go home to GY, for some reason or other, we got talking and he asked me if I fancied taking his boat for a trip on the anchor, so to help him out I said yes. "But only if the engine is not ready for renewal" he gave me a strange look and said, "Trev let the mate look after it". Thank you mate.

I let his crew have two days in dock, and then we sailed, as I was fishing for a GY landing, we took extra ice, I was thinking of 16 days tops, as Shields ice does not last as long as GY ice, bet you are thinking that ice is ice. Well you are wrong, in shields the ice is made not to go solid, it is called flake ice, made to keep the fish in boxes, for short trips. GY ice Is made to go solid, as the fish is kept in large pounds, so it will last up to three weeks. So you learn something new every day, I wonder how they make the ice for the pubs, well that only lasts a few minutes, so there you go, I bet you never look at a lump of ice in the same way again.

George's boat was called the Sandringham, another sister to the coral bank, built in Scotland, and very good boats they were.

We sailed at 5PM the next day, which was a bit dopy, as I was only going to the south side of the N E Bank, and we would arrive at mid night, but not as dopy as you think, it would let the other two lads get some sleep, and sober up a wee bit, I intended to drop the anchor on a wreck called the Paravane, I say on it, but you always put your anchor a quarter of a mile off it, that way you have no chance of catching the wreck with the anchor, with it being night time the radio navigator was not spot on.

The first haul, normally the best one, on this anchor was very bad, one box, but I decided to fish the day out, as five hauls = five boxes, sounds bad but it is better to steam in the dark, and not lose daylight fishing, any way the second haul gave us two boxes, and a little gift left over from the war.

Yup there was a small bomb in the net, one of the lads, for some stupid reason of his own, decided to bang the nose of it on the rail, shit it started to hiss, in shock he dropped it back on the deck, and then ran behind the wheelhouse, why the fu** did he not drop it over the side, into the water.

To be honest, I think he got such a fright, that he froze, any way It was still laid on the deck, and still hissing away, I went and picked it up and dropped it into the sea, and it did not go bang. Well you must have gathered that, as I am still here typing. When I held the bomb in my hands, it was so strange, my arms were tingling and my head was spinning; now that is true fear.

On the bright side George still had a boat, on the third haul, again only one box, by now I had given up on this spot, as the next haul would be up on to a shallow bank, and for years Nat, and I had never caught fish on it.

Put it this way ,if you got ten boxes in each of the other hauls the one to the NE, was at the most, two boxes,

Also at the Paravane, it was a one day job, and then the ground needed a few days rest, as the fish were feeding on worms, not sand eels, the eels move in fast, and the fish follow them, so I decided to call it a day and steam east for fifty miles, heaving up the anchor, the winch came to a grinding halt, and on the echo sounder I was marking the wreck, shit I had dropped the anchor right in the middle of it.

After a couple of hours trying to free it, I realised that there was no hope. Normally the next thing to do is cut your losses, and cut the anchor away.

But for some strange reason, there was no spare anchor on the boat, now they call us anchor bashers as that is the MOST important part of the fishing gear, without an anchor you are fuc***, big time, now this was bad, as if I cut it away, we then had to go back into Shields to get a new one, any way I said to the lads "we will fish the next day, and with luck the anchor might work loose of the wreck, more wishful thinking than anything.

I was very shocked the next day as the haul that gave 1 box the day before, came up with 3, see I do not know it all, and never will, the next two hauls also gave 3 boxes apiece, and Trev being a stubborn sod decided to shoot the bank haul, thinking another one box and it is a small days pay, SHOCK time it had ten boxes of top class flats in it.

Well I give up trying to work out this fishing lark, we spent the next ten days, on the same spot and landed 160 kits of fish, but still ended up having to cut the anchor away.

That trip made me think, how many times me and other skippers had left a particular spot, with no fish, and the next day here they are, or maybe with all the years of men fishing, the fish were a lot cleverer than us, well it does not take much to out think Trev, but when a fish does it, it makes me wonder if I am in the right job.

When we landed the fish, it did not look too good, as I said the ice was not made for long trips, it was not off, but it could have and should have looked a lot better. Anyway we made £4000.00, not good but not a complete disaster. I did give George a rollicking for not having a spare anchor, and he gave me a 5% bonus, £200.00, on top of my settling, thanks mate, I do not know if he saw a profit out of the trip, after buying a new anchor, and chain, but he seemed happy enough.

Back in Shields, I went down to see how the MA Fleming was getting on, the engine was out, and the winch had been taken off, so I said to Barry that I would find another boat, until she was ready. But he told me that if I wanted to hang around, he would put me on the books as one of his staff, in the meantime I could paint the boat, that sounded ok to me, so I agreed, for the next four weeks I was now a painter. And for the first time since my days on the bus's I had a proper wage packet, on a Friday.

It was very amusing, as Friday dinner Barry would bring the wage packets to the lads that worked for him, 10 welders, and when he gave me mine, he would then ask me to go to the club with him for a drink.

A lot of the lads were a bit surprised at this, as Barry was the owner, and they could not understand, how the new boy, (who could not weld), was taken for a drink by the gaffer, one of them did ask him and Barry said, "Trevor does not work for me, he is my skipper", so that shut him up.

A lad who was lodging at Lynn's mothers had just left the Merchant navy, he was an engineer, apparently he had an accident on board a ship, and was now unfit for the engine room, with his money he got from the firm, he bought a small boat, his idea was to take out angling parties, at weekends.

He asked me if I would sail with him, and help out with the seaman ship side, until he got his bearings, the offer was £20.00 for each day that I did at sea.

My job was to show him the spots to fish, and help him to drink the lager that he took with him, and I had no problem with that, so all week I was a painter, and on the week end I was an angling expert, to be honest I loved doing that as I have always been into angling myself. So I was getting paid to do my hobby, after two weeks the lad decided that the job was not for him, so he put the boat up for sale.

I said to him, "while you are waiting for a buyer, "can I take her away" and we agreed on a straight split of the takings, we were by law, allowed ten passengers, and two crew. So Trev being a tight sod took eleven anglers, at £20.00 per man, and no crew, so that was me on £100.00, per day.

Wish I could afford to buy it. Well I got four weeks out of the boat before it was sold, so that was a handy £800.00, on top of my wages off Barry, and the cost of fuel was zero, as we had about 600 gallon, aboard the M A Fleming, that was not theft as I had paid my share of it in the one trip I had done.

Well I have lost count, hold on, got it , with this boat it is now 4 different skippers jobs, so far this year,

Please keep count for me.

Back to the MA Fleming, she was now fully painted, and I started to put a new compass table in her, but one day two guys arrived, and told me to get all my personal gear off the boat, where have I herad that before? O yes Saxon King.

They then slapped a writ on her mast, Barry had gone bankrupt, all that work painting, and now we had lost her, o well, back to looking for another job, but this time I decided to go back on the deck, or to be honest, back in to the galley, can you remember the ships cat? Well I had now come full circle, and got a job on the Frem, with my old mate Nat, he was anchor bashing, but the only job going was the cooks, so I took it, loading the stores aboard for my first trip in her, reminded me of the Maxwell.

The deck hand was Nats stepson, Paul wenn, another guy built like Rambo, and he had not long finished school, what the fu** would he be like when he had finished growing, as he passed the food down to me, I said "hey Paul there is no cat food" he looked at me, shook his head, and then got on with his other jobs. I did two trips with Nat and we did well, one funny incident comes to mind, the mate, (Alan somebody) cannot remember his last name, but he had a dislike for me, I do not understand why, maybe he thought I was after his job. Nothing was further from my mind.

I was enjoying the cooks life, and having a laugh, with out a worry in the world, except for breaking the lads eggs, in the mornings, one evening Nat had gone to his bunk, and the three of us were gutting the last haul, about six boxes, for some reason the mate was giving Paul a hard time, and Paul lost his temper with him, and took a swing with his fist.

I pushed the mate aside, and told Paul to go down the cabin, to cool down, which he did, I then told the mate that he should know better than to argue at sea, to be honest I think Paul gave him a fright, leaving the mate gutting the last box, I went down the cabin and had a talk with Paul, he had now calmed down a bit, I said to him, "lad if you want to fight, do it in the dock, when we land" great he agreed to that.

Paul came back on the deck, and the fish was washed and ready for the fish room, nothing was said between the two of them, but sometimes silence is golden, well that is what the pop band the Searchers said in the 1960s.

A couple of days passed, with no more arguments, that is until one haul we were approaching the anchor gear, I had passed down three out of four baskets, to the mate in the fish room, I then asked him to take the last one, as we were at the dhan, he told me to hold on, and I said "come on take it, so I can help Paul", the basket was already hanging over the fish room hatch, he stood under it and told me to take it back up to the deck, now Trev Is really pissed off with this attitude, so I gave him the fish, yep I dropped it on to his head, then went and helped to clip up to the anchor.

The mate was going mad, and he shouted about how I was a dead man, when he got out of the fish room,

Well I think I need a bit of an advantage here, so when we were all finished and heaving away, I went down the cabin, took off my wellies, and put on my shoes that I wore ashore, I then returned to the deck, as the mate came out of the fish room, I said ready when you are dick head.

He, by now had calmed down a bit, and said to me that it would be sorted on the quay, fair dues, and wellies back on. Paul then cracked me up, he stood beside me and said, "never fight at sea, you should know better" we fell about laughing, through all this Nat the skipper never said a word, he knew that it would sort itself out. On arrival at Shields, the mate said to me "shall we forget it all" and I agreed, so alls well, except for the two of us getting the sack, off Nat. and I would have done the same.

Can you remember Alex Musell, (OBELISK), of Course you can, who could forget him, well he still had the Skanderborg, but also he had bought a very large trawler, sorry can not remember the name, but his plan was to take her to South Africa, and make his fortune, so he said to me "Trev if you take the Skanderborg, and earn a profit, I will give you a half share in her".

Well that is how I started in the Island, so give it a go, but I did tell him that I would be fitting rope reels, and spending a lot of money, bringing her up to scratch, he agreed and told the office, Caley Fish, that as far as they were concerned Trevor was the owner of the boat, maybe not on paper, (yet) but what I said goes, they told Alex that it was ok with them, as long as I was not too deep in the red.

So Alex sailed for Africa, and Trev started to get ready for anchor bashing, again. One very tiny problem, getting a crew, there was only two anchor bashers in Shields, and the lads who knew the job, went down to GY.

On the plus side I had the rope reels, so to try the boat out, I only needed men who could gut fish, and cook the odd egg, or two, so my first crew was Lynn's brother Michael, who had never been on a fishing boat in his life, and a lad called , Eddie woods, who had done a bit of fly shooting, plus Eddie was a very good worker, a lot like paddy, nothing technical, but will work himself to the ground for you.

To try the gear out I went to the NE Bank, as it was the closest ground I had off the Tyne, things went ok, the first haul had two boxes in, not great, but I was happy to see that the boat was working ok.

But the first haul was also the last of the day; this did not bother me as I was thinking that the trip starts tomorrow.

While the lads were putting the fish to bed, and then dinner, I got talking to Nat on the VHF, he asked me if I had listened to the weather forecast, and I told him no, well Trev if you can get the fu** back into Shields now, Nat was not the type of skipper to over react on anything, but he told me that they had given out SE storm 10 to violent storm 11. Shit, normally I would have put the storm chain out, but being only 45 mile from the Tyne, I decided to head in. the weird thing was that it was flat calm, but I have seen that often and also I could feel the pressure, not by looking at the barometer, but some times you can feel it.

After stowing all the gear away, for bad weather, we heaved up the anchor and started for Shields. After only half an hour steaming the storm hit us, and by god did it hit, the wind was on our port bow so we were taking one hell of a beating. Also it was snowing heavily and visibility was only about a quarter of a mile.

All the Shields were already in the harbour, with the exception of two other boats, Nat in the Frem, and Ray Morse in the Conduan, Ray was first to get to Shields and on the vhf he was telling Nat that the swell in the harbour mouth was horrific, we still had thirty mile to go, and now had a violent storm, talking to Nat on the vhf I told him to let me know when he got to the harbour mouth. When he did hi informed me that in all his years out of Shields he had never seen it so bad.

I then lost contact with him, when I looked at the vhf and the radar they had both gone dead. We still had lights but had lost all power to the navigation equipment. Enough of this I decided to drop the anchor and ride it out, as she was taking a very bad beating, and at anchor she would ride the waves a lot better.

I told the lads to let the anchor go but as they were dropping the wire on the drum jammed, on trying to heave it back and clear the snag the winch for some reason would not heave, now this normally is only the drive belt slipping off and no major problem, but when I went into the engine room to fix it I found that she was half full of water. Also all the main batteries had broken free and were now being washed all over the deck.

This was enough for me, I turned on the main radio and thank god it had life, it was on the lighting system so as long as the engine was running I could use it. Gave out a May Day call and thank god it was answered first time, I could only give them a rough position but I told them that I would leave the radio on auto alarm, and that as long as she was afloat the signal would give them a fix on us, I was then told that the RAF rescue chopper was on its way.

Not knowing how long she would stay afloat I told the lads to stand by to launch the life raft.

It did not take the chopper long to get to us, but it felt like hours. It was still snowing, and it was having a job finding us. I fired a distress rocket but with the strength of wind it blew well away from us, I then fired one straight into the wind and when it landed, wow lucky right beside the boat.

Well a man was lowered down to the boat, when he saw the state of the engine room; he told me that we would be winched up two at a time. Then another miner hiccup the wire from the chopper got wrapped around the after mast, and that was only tubular steel, but it had to be cleared, so not thinking of any danger I climbed up and got it clear.

They had a very powerful light shining down and while I was clearing it I felt and saw a snag in the cable, by the time I got back on deck the RAF lad had my crew in the harness, and signalled for them to go, he then pushed them clear of the boat, at that very moment we were hit by an extra large wave and I saw the lads go under it. My thoughts were shit the cable has snapped, but they then came clear of the water, phew.

It is very strange that while all this was going on I felt calm and relaxed, I think it is the mind taking over, like some sort of safety valve. Well it is now our turn to get lifted and while we were hanging on the cable we saw the old girl turn over, wow talk about timing.

On the flight home they gave us a cigarette and told us to hold it in a cup with a bit of water in for safety reasons, now this amazed me but there you go.

Can you remember when I sent the fish to the RAF lads, with my brother Ivan, well they dipped the wrong one, thank fu**, on arrival at RAF Bulmer, I was told that the pilot was very new, and the pilot is the man who says yes or no, to take off, if the wind is at a certain speed, it is left to his discretion.

Well that guy took off in winds ten knots stronger than the limit, so thank you, if you ever read this, I would love to meet up for a pint, on ME. After landing, the RAF gave us a bottle of whisky, and it did not last long.

To be honest, while all this was going on, I was as relaxed, as if I was watching it on the telly, but the next day, well it hit me, I cried like a baby, and did not want to talk to anybody, the local newspaper reporter came round the house, and I told him to fu** off, I know that sounds bad, but it is called after shock.

It still to this day amazes me how calm I was during the incident, and how bad I was after it was all over,

I had a couple of days in, then Peter Scapp, a local skipper owner came round, and asked me to do a couple of days on the prawns with him, I realised that he was getting me back on the horse, (if you fall off get back on), so I said ok, we sailed the next morning at 5AM, as we were leaving the piers I said to him, "hey Peter I have no baccy with me, can I have some of yours"? And he then told me that he did not smoke.

So not only did I have to get my nerve back, I had to do it without a fag. O well. I did two days on the Vertrowen with Peter, then his other lad came back, so out of work again, I then heard from the office, that the insurance company were not happy about paying out for the loss of the Skanderborg, Alex had flown home to have a meeting with them, and they kindly invited me, aw how nice.

In the meeting they were asking me some funny questions, about the loss, and Trev was getting a little bit pissed off, with the insinuations that one of the guys was coming out with, he must have read about the Ada Jean, so I lost it a little bit, well to be honest I lost it big time, I told them to stop the meeting, and then turned to this guy and said, "if you think I sank the boat, in that weather, then you had better call in the police". Alex and the other guy looked in total shock.

I then said, either pay the owner out, or openly accuse me, the second insurance man said "Trevor we are not accusing you of anything, but we want to know how she sank" I said "that is easy to sort out, write down, force 11 violent storm, and a broken boat". I then stood up and left. To be honest, I had to leave, as I was coming close to smacking the stiff collard prick.

An hour later Alex came into the Dolphin and told me that they had passed the claim, I was still shaking with temper, he then said, "it did look bad trev as you have been to court once for sinking a boat", so I asked him if I was to get half the insurance money, of coarse not, then why the fu** would I sink her?.

Alex and I were never as close after that. Still good mates, but we used to be more like brothers. I spent the next week or two helping Jimmy Cullen, with his net mending, and to be honest it was a nice change from blowing up engines and sinking boats, the only thing I could sink on this job, was a few pints at the end of the day.

Stood on the quay one day, this lad called John Hedridge came up to me and said that he had bought a boat, she was called the May Queen, and was laid in Bangor North Wales, and was I interested in bringing her round to Shields, well I knew John, as he was an engineer, and had done a lot of jobs for me in the past. Jim Cullen turned round and said to him, "why Trevor as skipper, don't you like the boat"? Cheeky sod.

It was now November, and John said that he wanted her in Shields before Christmas.

Well that would be pushing it, as the Caledonian Canal closes for the December, plus I had not even seen the state of the boat yet. So we decided to drive down to Taffy Land, with a crewman, and Michael, (Skanderborg) bringing the van back. He said that was preferable to bringing the boat, as vans do not sink,

Well not often, at least I was not skipper of the van, so it should be safe. The other crewman was named Billy Bones, well he was on the thin side, sorry bill, he was a young lad, so daft enough to trust me to get him home safe.

We set off a couple of days later, and arrived in Bangor, with only two weeks to go before the Canal closed, I took one look at the boat, and thought, well to be honest, if John had not been a friend of mine, I would have got back in the van, I said to him "how much did you pay for this", he told me £19000.00, I said don't you mean £1900.00?, nope. But the engine is only two year old, um where have I heard that before? O yes Toledo.

The May Queen was laid up on the river bank, high and dry, she only went afloat for three hours, when the tide was in, I say float, but when the tide did come in, there was about two foot of water, above the cabin deck; well at least I now know what my first job is. Find the leak and stop it. So Trev spent the next two days caulking and tarring the cabin. That done, when she floated again, it was dry, do not be extra cited, as that was only job one.

Walking round the boat at low water, I saw that the planking round the stern tube was split; now that is the first sign of a bent shaft. I said to John "when you bought this wreck, was she floating, or dry". He said, "Floating" right, ok, and "is there any chance of cancelling the deal?" No" right mate you are in the shit.

I spent most of the day caulking around the shaft, but to be honest, I thought that I was pissing into the wind, that night we went to the local pub, the other two had washed and changed, but Trev working till dark, went as I was, black, and in overalls. The locals were great, and one old lady was talking to us about fishing, (her husband used to be a skipper); she asked John if he was the skipper, and he told her that I was.

This baffled her a bit as she assumed I was the engineer, well at least I was in uniform, we had a great night, playing darts, and chatting to the locals, I say night, it was 3AM when we left the bar, in the morning Trev did not feel like playing with tar and old rope, but there you go, self inflicted, so get on with it. When she did float, we decided to start the engine and with strong ropes ashore, try her in gear.

Very bad news, the stern gland, (the bit the shaft goes through) was moving about, John, being an engineer, knew that we had problems, but I said to him "tomorrow we will take her for a run, and see if it gets any worsera. As I told you earlier, than is a lot worse than bad.

So the next day we ran the boat up and down the river, there was a wobble on the shaft, but banging in a couple of wooden wedges on each side of it seemed to lessen the wobble, a bit, we both decided that it was no danger, but I did tell John that there was no way that we could make the Canal, in time for closure.

The plan was to take her up to Whitehaven, a short drive from Shields, and get the shaft out, so that he could renew it over the holidays, so this we agreed on, and set sail the next day, it was very nice weather on the run north, except for the last thirty mile, then the weather started to freshen up, from the North West, worse possible direction for Whitehaven.

We only had eight miles to go, I was talking to the harbour master on the VHF and asked him if the lock gates would still be open in one hour. He told me that we were pushing it, but given the weather he would hold them open as long as possible. It had to happen, I mean things were going a bit too well, with five miles to go the engine blew up, if I was reading this, well I would find it a bit hard to believe, come on 3 or 4 engines blown, in the space of one year.

Well it is true, anyway I told the harbour master and he said that he must close the lock gates, we then had only one choice, drop the anchor, I am glad I had one rigged up to the winch, well anyone with my luck would have took the same precaution, what I really mean is that any proper sailor, with half a brain, is ready for all incidents.

One tiny problem did arise, I saw that we were dragging the anchor, and with no power to heave it back up, to see if it was clear, well we were knackered, the wind was blowing us onto the shore, now I could have put up with that, if it had been a sandy beach, but no, it was a very rocky shore.

They had two spotlights on the boat, from the top of the cliff, as they knew that she was going to end up on the rocks, the coast guard ordered out the lifeboat, actually they had two of them on the way, one from Mary port, and the big one from the Isle of Man.

The smaller one, from Mary port reached us first, I say smaller, and she was almost as big as the May Queen, we slipped the anchor and they got us under tow. She towed us head to wind, and into deeper water, so far I could see no problems, then the tow parted, (broke), the lifeboat renewed the tow, and off we go again, twice more the tow parted, and the lifeboat crew had to tie knots in it, to me It was a bit short for this type of weather, but he is in charge of the tow.

All of a sudden, to my horror and amazement, he told me that we were getting too far out to sea, and that he was to tow us in a bit, and he then turned around, like I said, I thought the tow was a bit short, but turning to go with the swell was madness, yep BANG a large wave lifted us up and dropped us on top of the lifeboat, Billy came out of the cabin and told me that we were taking in a lot of water.

I ran forward and looked into the cabin, ok we now had two rudders, ours and the lifeboats, his rudder had came straight through the bow, and it brought a massive amount of water with it.

I told him that we were sinking, and could we please have a ride on his boat, when he told me that he had lost his rudder, I told him it is not lost we have got it, anyway a line was fired and the two boats were pulled together, then we three jumped aboard. Shit, forgot my fags again, I must start keeping a spare packet in a waterproof bag, in my top pocket. And they wonder why fishermen drink?

So now we are on a lifeboat with no rudder, but at least we had an engine, but one very large problem arose, only two of the life boat crew smoked and they didn't have many ciggys with them.

The powers that be, decided to send the RAF helicopter, to take the three of us, and two of the lifeboat crew off, so the five of us were winched off.

The Isle of Man lifeboat took the other one in tow, and when we landed ashore, I said to the coast guard man, "where is the nearest shop, for fags," he passed me a packet of twenty and I shared them out.

The next morning the Isle of Man lifeboat towed the other one in, so every body happy and safe. The BBC sent reporters and cameras down; I declined to be interviewed, and told them that John was the skipper. It was a little bit embarrassing, as John not being a sailor, when they asked the skipper what the conditions were like, he answered "very bumpy" even the reporter looked at him with a strange frown.

Ok that is 1983 over, and thank god, how I am sat here is beyond belief.

THE MAY QUEEN.

1984

Hi, by fu** I am glad that year is over, if this one is half as bad I will get a job as a road sweeper, saying that I would loose the brush down a drain, any way one day in Febuary, John Ord and I were walking home, along the fish quay, and I noticed that the Hatcliffe was in to land, so we went on board, Taffy was one of the crew, and we sat catching up on old times.

Tony Chester was in the wheelhouse, but things were still strained between us. But he did (after a while) ask if I would go up and talk with him, in the wheelhouse, he said to me that he had heard of my bad luck,

And making light of it, I said to him "not luck Tony just a crap skipper". He smiled and said "come on trev, we both know better than that.

To my surprise, he then asked me if I would take the skippers job on the Hatcliffe, and I said "sorry Tony, but I will not sail from GY again". He then said that I could run her out of Shields, that surprised me,

Then he went on to tell me that she was £5000.00, in the red, and if I did not clear it by the end of the year, he was going to sell her. So up for a challenge, and a decent boat at last, I agreed.

Tony went along to Richard Irvin's office, to ask if they would be the boats agents, and they happily agreed, that is until he told them who the skipper was to be. They told him that they thought it was a bad choice, as not only was I a bit of a rebel, but also they did not trust my fishing commitment.

Tony told them that they did not know the real Trevor, and as far as he was concerned, I was the skipper for him, thanks Tony.

He then told me that the port rail had some damage, so he would carry on down to GY, and have the jobs put right, when she was ready for sea he would ring me, and I could get the train down to pick her up, ok, Taffy would not be sailing with me, as he had another job lined up in GY, so it was up to me to get a local crew, witch for anchor bashing was not easy.

Luck was on my side, for once, a young man named Kevin Caffrey was looking for a job, he had been on a boat called the Mimosa, (it was a very successful anchor boat from Shields) and Kev had been in her for nine years. The office rang him up, told him about the mate's job, and was he interested.

He drove down to the quay, looked the boat over, and then said to me, "Trev I was going down to GY to look for a berth, but I will give you two trips, and if we get on, and earn money, I will stay".

Very nice of him, but to be fair he knew my recent past, BUT he did not know about my real capability as a fisherman.

We went down to pick the boat up two weeks later, just the two of us, as we were not going fishing, just running her to Shields, when we arrived, at about midday, I told Kev that we would start to sort her out the next day. To my amazement, he wanted to scrub out the fish room, there and then, now that is what I call keen, so Kev scrubbed the fish room, and I had to wash all the pound boards, 100 of the things, I was starting to wonder who the skipper was, but it was very nice to have a man dedicated to the job.

I decided to work the boat three handed, and a lad named Tom Bailey was looking for a berth, so great off we go, the Hatcliffe was rather small, for an anchor boat, 300 boxes max, but with doing short trips from shields, (10 days at most) that would be plenty big enough.

The first trip we made £6000.00, and all happy, or so I thought, but both the lads were not happy, we settled the boat GY style, and they were not used to that, I will explain.

GY the boat gets 55% and the crew 45%, skipper 17% mate 15% cook 13%. Now in Shields, the boat settles on 50% each, so it is 18% for the skipper and the crew decide how to split the other 32%.

Some boats split equal and some not, depending how they get along, and how they work together. Any way I rang Tony and told him what was going on, he then spoke to the cashier, and they decided to run her on the same style as the Mimosa. So all happy, and a nice trip to start off with, the next trip we made £8000.00, so Kevin said that he would not be going to GY, very nice of him. I think the office were a bit shocked at the two trips, but they should have had more faith in me from the off.

I was very surprised when Kev told me that we had broken the record for an anchor boat.

But to be honest every time the Mimosa had a large shot of flatfish, the skipper Ronny Jenson, would either land it in GY or send it down by lorry, Shields has never been a flat fish market.

But in the very near future it was to become one, as more anchor boats arrived and the fish buyers started to find outlets for them, to be honest if they had done that a lot earlier the port of North Shields would have been thriving, as a hell of a lot of the anchor fleet would have landed there, as it was a lot cheaper than GY, and also a lot closer to the fishing grounds.

O well I am getting too political now, so I will tell you a couple of adventures from 1984, I say adventures, more like daft stunts.

Alex had now bought another boat from Scotland, Good Tidings; he was doing well fishing for prawns,

Any way one day as we were sat in the Dolphin, with a nice afternoon pint his dog walked into the bar, (Rocky) it was a little terrier, or I should say TERROR, it lived on the boat, and was a very good guard dog, any way the dog walked in and he had a red paint mark on his back, and we could see that it was not an accident.

Well this boat from LT, (can you remember that one), called the Quiet Waters, were busy painting their boat, and a small give away was the fact that she was the only red boat in Shields, talk about red rag to a bull? Alex never said a word, I told him to go to the boat and sort them out, but he just smiled, and said "no worry Trev I will bide my time", when Alex says that watch out.

We did an eight day trip, another good one, I think I am more relaxed with not having to worry about the boat, so I have more time for the fishing side, after landing; I was shifting the boat into the gut, that's where we lay, for time ashore. As I turned into the gut I saw a bright yellow van, parked on the quay, now when we sailed it was a red one, but now it was yellow, with blue windows, red wheels and tyres,

And on the side, in red, was painted Rockys Revenge, I knew the van belonged to the owner of the Quiet Waters, and it was quite new. O well Alex said he would bide his time. The Quiet Waters was on a five day trip, so the paint had plenty of time to dry hard.

When it did land, the skipper came into the Dolphin, screaming blue murder, (I think he meant yellow murder) but there you go, he shouted to Alex that there was no need to go that far, as it was only a little bit of paint on the dog, Alex stared him out, then said "well he is only a little dog".

The skipper decided to leave it at that, and I do not blame him, even though Alex was always a happy go lucky man, he was also one of those men you do not cross.

After six month, we had not only cleared all the debt that Tony was in, but he bought a small wooden stern trawler, something for him to play with, while we were making the money, o well It keeps him out of our way, Tom Baily had left, and in his place was my old pal Ron Blacklock, but Ronnie's first trip was very nearly his last. When we came down to sail, we found that the engine room had a very large amount of water in, and that was with all the sea cocks closed.

I went to Tony and told him that I was a bit concerned about how the water got in, we may have had a bump off another boat, causing the leak, but after pumping her dry, we saw that the stern tube was leaking badly, the strange thing about this is that when I turned the shaft a bit, the leek stopped, I repacked the gland, but she still leaked when the shaft was in a certain position.

This was very strange, Tony booked the slip, and we were taken on that same day, when we steamed up the Tyne to the slips in Wallsend, Tony followed us in his new boat the Winaway, and said that he would take us back to Shields, after the Hatcliffe was out of the water.

At the entrance to the ship yard, there is a pub, so instead of standing about we went for a pint or three, after a couple of hours, the slip owner came in and had a pint, he told me that the engineer was busy drawing the shaft, and that would take another hour.

Tony did not come in the pub, as he had to steam the small boat back to Shields, but for some reason of his own he decided not to hang about and take three half pissed crew back with him, this little tantrum annoyed me a bit, I got on the VHF and told him to come back for us. His answer was Fu** off, strange?

So having a drink in me, I told him to shove the Hatcliffe, and get a new skipper.

Kev did advise me not to be rash, and talk to Tony when we were in a sober frame of mind, but when Trevor is annoyed, well he is also daft, I told the crew to take all the stores off the boat, about £300.00 Worth, and then we got a taxi home.

The next morning when I came round, Lynn was going mad, and saying that I had threw the best job I had away, and to be honest she was for once right, so Trev swallow your pride, even though Tony was wrong to leave us stranded, I rang him, he told me to go round to his flat, (that was in the next street to me), and so off I goes.

But I knew that Tony knew that Trev would not grovel; anyway I walked into his flat, and attacked "why did you leave us"? "Because you all had a drink" this was going to be a very strange meeting, so I sat down on a chair, looked at him, then said "have you got a new skipper yet"? He opened a bottle of whisky, and answered "yes you, so grow up", I thought to myself, ME, and what about you? But decided to keep my mouth shut.

She came off the slip the next day, all repaired and ready for sea, well except for the fact that there was no food aboard. The grocer was over the moon when we told him to repeat the order from three days ago.

The rest of the year went with no major hiccups, and we plodded away ok, in October we changed over to Prawn trawling, she had never been trawling before, so the cost was steep, a gantry built over the wheel house, (that is for stern trawling) two new nets, doors, and new wires, as usual Tony was moaning about the outlay, but if he never moaned, he would be dead.

As it was, it turned out to be a very good Prawn season, and all the new gear was paid for in the first month, so then it was profit all the way, up to the end of the year. Just before Christmas, I was sat in the office, going through the bills, (checking up that no one was robbing us), the cashier said to me, "would you like a cup of tea Trev", I turned to him and said that he had never offered me one in the past, why now? He then said to me" Trevor if you think we were against you, you are wrong, it was the manager.

And the salesman backed him up by saying, "we know from the Filia Maris, that you can catch fish, and at last you have proved them upstairs to be wrong".

Tony walked into the office, as I was getting my tea, and said to me "with this week Trev you have made £110.000.00 for the year, "thank you".

I cannot begin to tell you how good that felt, so time for the celebrations in the Dolphin, ON Chessy of course.

WINAWAY

1985

Hi all hope this year is as good as the last one, or better, now I am getting greedy, but if you loose the greed, you lose the fish, this year we took a trainee with us. I say trainee, he would never make a fisherman as long as he had a hole up his bum, but again he was a very hard worker, his name? well it was Joe????????, some lads called him banjo Joe, and others Junkshop Joe, a very strange guy, he lived on the boat while we were in dock, and his hobby was going round the charity shops, looking for what he called bargains, after about two months we had hardly any space on the boat for stores, as he had filled all the lockers with his so called bargains.

The reason for the other name (banjo Joe) was because he was always playing one, or trying to. He also had a guitar and a piano accordion, in the end I had to stop him practising at sea, as the lads wanted to dump them over board, and him with them. Also he was not the sort of guy you would put your faith in, well not in the wheelhouse, as one day we were steaming out to the fishing ground, flat calm weather, Joe came down the cabin to make a cuppa, we were all sat yarning away, as she had an auto pilot I knew that she was on course, but I did ask him if there was any ships within three mile of us, and he said no, so all ok.

He went back up, but two minutes later he came back into the cabin and told me that he was locked out, how the fu** can you be locked out?, well the wheelhouse door had two locks, one dead lock, and one Yale, but the Yale was only off the snick when we were in dock. So I said to him "Joe why is the Yale lock on?" and he replied, "You told me to make sure everything was locked when I left".

Do I really deserve this, or is he taking the piss, any way Kev managed to open the window at the back of my cabin, I climbed in and opened the door.

So on to the fishing ground, we dropped the anchor on a spot that I had got out of Mac's book, I had used it a few times, and always got a couple of decent days off them, there were two anchor spots about one mile apart, and in the book it said 10 coil of rope only, so that meant that the ground around them was stony.

To be honest I do not think that Mac had ever tried them, and I was right, as I did ask him in later years,

But when I did lay on them after the two days I always moved to another spot. While we were fishing the same spot, it was given out on the radio that the Decca, was to be turned off for repairs the next day.

Now the Decca is a radio receiver that gives you your position, it had different channels for different areas, where I was fishing all my info was on channel 3B, but there was a new one on channel 2A,

Hope I am not getting too technical for you?

Anyway with having to fish blind on the Sunday, I decided to make a new chart for the 2A, obviously it was empty, but shit or bust we moved along the haul, that always gave the best fishing, Mac always told me, if you do not know the area, follow your best haul, and hope for the clear ground, one way or the other you will learn something.

I dropped the anchor in the same depth of water as the fish was laid in, then went to bed, thinking Trev tomorrow you will do well or loose all the gear, at least this time I did not have to pay for it. Tell you what I'm glad Tony Chester is not on board; I was gambling a lot of his money on the next day.

As it was LUCK was on my side, and you need a lot of that in fishing, we had 4 hauls and put about 80 boxes down, and all top class flats, I moved to where I dropped the net in the best haul, and dropped the anchor in the same depth of water.

The next day we had the same, "hey this fishing lark is a piece of piss" now Trev do not get carried away, you have been lucky so far, the third day I was brought down to earth, the first haul had a bag of stones in, and no fish, the second, 20 boxes, same in the third, so still a great days work, and the last haul of the day, we snagged the rope on something, but knowing that I would be back in this trench of deep water again, I picked up the rope ,and got a position of the obstacle, when I was over it, I saw that we were marking a wreck, on the echo sounder, now I have it's position I will not catch it again.

We landed the next day and made £12000.00, WOW my best ever trip, and all LUCK, but like I said fishing is 80% luck.

The next trip I obviously went back to the deep gully, the fishing was not as big, but still very good, we averaged 10 boxes a haul, to be honest that is great but when we shot those hauls a week ago, they gave twice as many, but like Fred Sayers said years ago, on the Ling Bank, ("you have landed them Trev".

After three days we had about 120 boxes, then bang, the rope reels blew up, normally that would have not been a major problem.

Being a Friday, and a bank holiday, so no market, and no engineer, well: if I was a German boat, I would have been in shiten strasser. But we are not so back to Shields, we docked on the Friday evening, and Tony told me that there was no way of getting them fixed before Tuesday; also we could not land the fish.

On the bright side, I was pretty sure of the part that was causing the failure.

Speaking to the GY engineers on the phone, they were in agreement with me, or they hoped that they were, it cost Tony £200.00 to have the part sent up by car, and on the Saturday I went on to replace it, I told the crew that if I got them going, we would sail that same night, to finish off what was the beginning of another great trip.

As it was I did get them going, (with the new part fitted), Tony and I got to the Dolphin, at about 3PM and I said to the lads that we would let go at 5PM, two of them said ok, but the third man (full of drink) decided that he wanted the night in. I said to him that if we did not sail the fish in the fish room, were going to start to go off.

He said that was a daft thing to say, as the fish was in ice, but the water in dock is a lot warmer than at sea, anyway there was no talking him round, and he got a taxi home. The next morning I went round to his house, had a long talk to him, about how he was throwing a good trip away, and also his good name in Shields, but as we all are in the same boat, lets forget it, and finish the trip, now he was sober, he agreed and we sailed that afternoon, we fished for another three days and landed another great trip. I had to stop myself telling him how much he had lost us.

Did you notice that I did not name him; well all I will say "it was not Kevin".

The next trip I went back to the gully and it was empty, So we

steamed north 100 mile, as it was the time of year for this bit of ground, now that was a daft thing to say, as fish do not have calendars, after a couple of days plodding along on about three boxes a haul, I could not believe my ears,
Tony was calling me on the VHF, normally a 30 mile range, now and again you get freak reception on the VHF, but that is if there is a high pressure over you, anyway I answered him, and he told me that he was steaming up to us. What? We are 100 mile off the land and he was ten mile from us, in the Winaway?

It he mad or what? He had Lewie (John Lewis) with him.

I asked Tony what he would do if a freak storm came, and he said, "jump aboard your boat" anyway he had one tow, lost his net, and no spare, so he had to go all the way back home, and I thought I was daft.

Nearing the end of the anchor season, you know how I hate prawn trawling, I decided to try another trip on the anchor, as the NE Bank is only 45 mile off Shields, instead of taking a lot of ice and stores, if there was no fish, then we did not have a big expense, so off we go, it's now mid November, and after 4 days we landed about 100 boxes.

So this looks great, better than sorting the little pink Beatles, (small Prawns), I said to Kev, "with a bit of luck we can work the anchor all winter" he was happy with that, so after a couple of days off we sailed again, Trevor and his gob again, first haul, 1 box, same in the next two hauls, I told the lads that we were to have one more, then in to change over to the Prawn Trawl, I was really pissed off, as my stupid idea of no Prawning, had gone out of the window, o well cannot be right all the time, but just one time would be nice, I nearly never bothered with the last haul, but I thought to myself, it is a drink for the boys.

So we did shoot the last haul, by the time the net came up it was dark, not the net, it was night time, (sorry), heaving it up in the power hauler it was very heavy, and I said to the lads that we must have a wire or a big stone in the cod end.

To my total shock it was fish, all flats and all top quality, WOW where did they come from, another suicide pact?, we heaved the anchor and steamed into Shields, the lads were still gutting the fish along side the landing quay, as they gutted them, and threw them into the water, the shore workers were taking them out and putting them on the market, now that is what you call fresh.

When the sale started (7 AM) the fish were still flapping about in the boxes, Chessy was leaving the Tyne on the Winawy, and saw us alongside the fish quay, so he came alongside to find out why we were in, he thought we had some trouble with the engine, or deck gear.

Any way he said to me "what is wrong", and I told him that we had just landed 120 boxes, and then he asked me why I did not stay out and fill the boat. Is there no pleasing this guy? No typical owner, greedy.

With the fish being so fresh we got a good price £50.00 a box, so for that one haul we made £5400.00.

We sailed again that same evening, and after 4 hauls we landed 120 boxes, we will never be poor again, (famous fisherman's words), on landing the next morning we made £5600.00.

Now while the fish is on the ground, you have to keep at it, as it never last's long, we did have one night ashore, (well we were ready for a bath), then off we go again, sadly it took us 4 days to get 140 boxes,

Landed them and another £5000.00, and this time we did have the weekend off.

Well nearly all fishermen read the Fishing News; it prints the top landings from every port in the U K,

Taffy was fishing the west coast at the time, he said to his skipper, "look at this, Trev has made three big trips in ten days" his skippers reply was that the tax man reads that as well, then Taff said to him, "Trevor knows that, he is not daft, you can add a couple of grand to them earnings, cheeky sod, as if I would do that.

I was over the moon, not just about the earnings, but the fact that we did not have to go Prawn trawling,

Wrong again, will I ever learn to stop thinking. After a couple of days off, we sailed back to the bank,
Guess what? After two days fishing we caught the total of five boxes, so back in and Prawn trawl on, god I was fed up, as I have told you I would rather have a mega hangover, than sort Prawns all day.
Coming up to Christmas Kevins car would not start, so he had to get a taxi to the boat, well that is expensive, as he lives nine mile from Shields, so as we are now day fishing, I gave him my car, until his was fixed, as it was his car was in the garage for a week, no problem, I lived five minutes walk from the quay, and now I could go for a pint or three each evening, after landing.

I got a surprise on Christmas morning, as Robert and Rachael were opening their pressys, daddy had one, and that was a pair of socks, why did she not wrap them up separately, and then I would have had two.

Anyway Kev arrived at the house about nine in the morning, to return the car, with him having no kids to him Christmas was just another day, we had a couple of drinks, and then I drove him home.

One small problem, when we got to his house we decided to have another couple of drinks, and then more, well his wife was getting a bit concerned about the amount we were putting down our necks, and also have you ever tried to get a taxi on Christmas day? Well no chance, so trying to sober me up, she gave me a turkey dinner, but NO wine.

After the meal I felt ok to drive home, I may have felt ok, but if I had been stopped I would still be inside to this day, and to be honest I deserved to be.
When I got home Lynn was going mad, I told her to calm down as all I had done was take Kev home,

When she did calm down, she put a full dinner in front of me, Shit! And no way was I going to tell her that I had already eaten one. WELL would you?

1986

Hi again and a happy new year, but I tell you what, if I see another turkey I will scream, this is a really happy year for me, as my son Tony decided to come and live with us, I just hope he behaves himself,

Any way Prawn trawling over (thank fu**), don't get me wrong we did earn money at it, but I still hated it with a vengeance.

I still had the same crew, Kev, Ronnie, and Banjo Joe, so I must be doing something right, that is unless they cannot get another berth, after a couple of trips on the anchor, Chessy told me that he was going to buy another anchor boat, she was called the Mark Nielson, and was fishing from GY.

He said that he was going to take her away, as he had sold the Winaway, to be honest I thought to myself that the new boat would not be under his command for long.

Anyway he asked me to go down to GY and look the boat over, so I told Kev that he would be taking the Hatcliffe for a trip, if that was ok with him, and he agreed, I remember that the new boat was £47000.00, not bad, so Chessy said that before we go, he had to go to his bank, to get a bankers draught, well they did want the money before letting the boat leave GY.

I was sat in his car, for what seemed like hours, and then he came out and threw a bag onto my lap, I asked him what was going on, as I could tell he was in a bad mood, he told me that the bank wanted to charge him £100.00 to give him the draught, so he closed his account, and I was sat with £98000.00 in a bag, I was thinking of doing away with him, but with my luck I would get caught.

We went into the office in Shields, and they put the money in their safe, phew, well we drove down to GY and went to the boat, Chessy never even got out of his car, he asked me to go aboard and check her out, well he was buying the thing, so why ask me?, I started the engine and all the wheelhouse gear, every thing seemed ok, but after the Toledo I asked him if he had seen her out of water, he replied, "Trevor this is the first time I have seen her in the water, well I just shook my head and said that as far as I could see it was a decent buy.

Then he told me that he wanted me to take her as skipper, and give Kevin the Hatcliffe, he got a shock with my answer, "no thank you I want to keep the Hatcliffe" now this boat had twice the power, she was a lot bigger, and also had a shelter deck, so he said to me, "why Trev this is a much better boat", and I told him that two years in the Hatcliffe, with good earnings, and very little trouble, and the fact that she was a very good sea boat, (I could trust her in a storm), so why change a winning team?.

Well he did buy her, but said that he would skipper her for the first year, fu** off Chessy I will give you two trips.

Back in Shields, Chessy got a crew together to go and pick the boat up, from GY. He had renamed her to the David Chester, after his younger brother who had died, I spent a lazy week with the three kids, and to be honest it was nice to be away from fishing boats for a while.

The office rang me and told me that Kevin was landing the next day; he had reported 180 boxes, so let's hope the market is good for him. I went down to the quay the next morning, about 10AM, had a pint in the Dolphin, then walked to the office, on the way I saw the skipper of the Mimosa, I asked him if he knew how Kevin had done, and he told me £7800.00, (get in there Kev, well done), then he said "well anybody can make a trip if they are told where to go" Fu** I was so annoyed, the lad took the boat to sea and made a good trip, at least he could have given him some credit.

But sod him I was happy, and so were the crew, you would think after nine years his X skipper would have been happy for him, but there is nothing stranger than folk.

When I told Kevin what he said his reply was no bother Trev, he thinks I went to sea under sealed orders, which made me laugh big time. I told Kev about the new boat, and that Chessy was to skipper it for the rest of the year, and then I said to him "you will have it within three trips" he then asked me why him?

And I told him that I was happy with the little Hatcliffe, and he agreed with me, but I think deep down he was hoping that I would take the new one, and leave the Hatcliffe to him. NO WAY.

We sailed the next trip, and on arrival at the NE Bank I saw Chessy on one of the anchor spots, in his new boat, he had iced and stored up for a trip before he left GY, the fishing was not very good so I carried on to the East for another 30 miles, Chessy decided to stay put, until he got used to the boat, as all boats have there own little quirks, some of them worse than others.

After a couple of days fishing, not catching a lot, I was talking to Chessy on the VHF he told me that the fishing was better, and advised me to join him, now you do not often hear another skipper telling you that they are on the fish, but with him being the owner of my boat, and wanting it to earn money, well thanks mate, we both made a decent trip, so everybody happy.

The next trip was a different story, we were plodding away on 3 or 4 boxes a haul, but my lord and master (Chessy) was one of those skippers that had to be on big fishing, he hated a plod, so he kept moving grounds, looking for that big haul, and as Mac told me years ago, "Trev you cannot steam them aboard".

Half way through the trip Chessy asked me when I was going in to land, and I told him that I was doing another weeks fishing, he then said that he was sick of catching nothing, so Kevin can have the David Chester, so will I land early so that she would not be laid up waiting for him. Is this guy for real?

I then told Kev that this was his last trip, and also Chessy wanted me to cut the trip short, Kev replied to me "tell him to fu** off, we have a trip to finish". And that is what I knew he would say.

But when we do land, and Kevin takes the new boat, he will be a big miss, as he is one of the best crew man I have ever sailed with, in two and a half year, I never heard him complain once.

Well we landed and Kevin left, so now I need a mate, my luck was in, as Taffy had arrived in Shields, looking for a job, when I asked him to sail with me again, he said, "well there is no decent jobs going, so I will have to" cheers mate.

My son Tony had done a couple of trips with me, and to be honest I expected too much of him, so Kev took him as trainee, and to be honest I was very happy about that, as I do not believe in family sailing together, if the boat goes down with all hands, it must be hard to loose a husband and a son, in one go.

I know that the Scottish boats are family boats, but like I said it is better to loose one of the family than two or three.

The next trip Ronnie left, and Alfie Walker (Filia Maris) took his berth, now Alfie is an old trawler hand, so nothing bothers him, or so I thought, but one day we were fishing in a NW gale and as I told you earlier that is the type of weather that brings the large plaice, I did not have to use the anchor, as with one rope shot each side of the wind, and having a main sail up, the weather kept us stationary, we got about 15 boxes the first haul, but I made an error by shooting the gear again, before the lads had put the fish away.

Shooting the first rope she dipped her nose into a very large wave, I could only see water, and the mast, when the water cleared Alfie was under the winch and Banjo Joe was hugging the mast.

I could not see Taffy, and thought FU** I have lost him, and that is a feeling no skipper wants to go through, well with luck Taff was down the engine room starting the deck hose, we never lost any of the fish, (I don't know how) but I did decide to call it a day, and drop the anchor to ride the gale out.

The HATCLIFFE a brilliant boat in a storm.

1987

Hi we are back fishing for the wee pink beasties, and I still hate them, I wish I could find a skipper for the Prawn season. Chessy has bought another small stern trawler, Fiberglas this time, she is called the Kingfisher, about 30 feet long, and more gear in the wheelhouse than I have seen on an ocean going liner.

She was used as a show boat, and was owned by an electrician, he had all the gear in her wheelhouse and then he could show a buyer while they were working. (Good idea) she even had sonar.
That is a machine that tells you that you are going to hit a wreck, before you get to it, well it gives you time to fill the mending needles, she had 4 echo sounders, and one of them even talked, true!
I did your head in, as when you were entering the harbour, it kept saying TOO LOW/ TOO LOW,
WE ALLREADY KNOW THAT SO SHUT THE fU** UP. Sorry all but it did get on your tits, I am just glad I was not skipper of her.

Alfie had left to take another boat skipper, to be honest he said I was mental, don't know why he thinks that, I mean I did not make the wave that washed him, I just hit it a bit too fast, so the crew was now Taffy/ Joe/ and the head, (Mick McGinty), remember him, Joe said he was a cretin, I had to look that one up in the dictionary, I am glad Mick didn't bother.

Anyway we were shooting the Prawn trawl one fine morning, Kevin was about two mile east of me, and already towing, he came on the VHF and told me that Tony my son, had got tangled up in the small motor fly wheel, I went ice cold, I told the lads to let the gear go, as I wanted to get aboard Kevs boat, I know that there was nothing I could do, but I had to be with him, then to my utter relief Kev told me that he was ok, a bad fright but ok. My mind went back to the engineer on the Wilton Queen, the one who lost his son in a winch.
I then realised how quickly your life can be changed, when we docked that evening I tied up along side the David Chester, Tony was stood at the tray sorting Prawns, I jumped aboard and said to him "are you ok mate"? He answered that he was and he said that he was lucky that he had one of my old work tops on, as if it had been his normal leather one it would not have torn free of the flywheel.

I went into the wheelhouse and asked Kev how it had happened, he told me that the motor never had a guard over the flywheel, but said that it would have before the boat went to sea again; he also told me that Tony was badly bruised, but he did not want to go back for a check up as he felt ok.

Climbing back aboard my boat I said to Tony, "hey mate you owe me a new top" he just shook his head, but we both knew the relief that we felt.

After the Prawns were landed we always went for a pint, as you know I used the Dolphin, but over the road was another bar called the Low Lights Tavern, and as it was Taffy was lodging there, so I went with him for a pint, while sat there in walks Kev and Tony, now Tony at 16, had decided to have a lager, but when he saw his dad sat there he ordered a coke, but to his shock I went to the bar to pay for their drinks, and when he said coke please, I answered, "hey son you do a mans job, so you have a mans drink", and then told the barmaid to give them what they wanted.

Tony told me years later that he did not enjoy the lager, as it felt strange drinking it with me. And that reminded me of the first fag my mother gave me when I was 13, I told her that I did not smoke, she said "well who is taking them from my packet then".

Also that Prawn season our Barry came up to Shields for a visit he was only 11, but when I took him to sea for the day, I could see that he was in no way going to follow in his brothers footsteps, and to be honest I was over the moon about that. So after that day Baz stayed ashore while his big brother went to sea, I was told years later that he went into Tony's bedroom and gave himself some pocket money from his draw, it is quite funny as Tony always blamed Robert.

Well Prawn season over and back on the anchor, (thank fu**) if any man in this world says that he likes Prawning, well you are either drunk, or mad. But then you like whatever is earning you the most money.

I do know by reading his book (Trawlerman) that Jimmy Buchan does earn a lot of it, and long may it continue Jimmy.

While we were putting the anchor on board, I noticed that the Prawn trawlers were all landing a few boxes off small and medium size cod, it was March, and I knew that for the months of March and April, there was always cod on the prawn grounds, but this year it was better fishing for the inshore boats.

So Trevor, not to let a good thing pass, decided to drop his anchor 4 mile off the Tyne, and with about 40 trawlers working the same ground, well one or two were not very happy about that, too be fair I did drop my anchor on or tight beside a wreck, so to me I was helping them, by marking it.

But it was not the anchor they were worried about, it was the fact that my ropes covered over a mile,

And their trawls were only a quarter of a mile behind them, the first day they were on the VHF asking me if they were clear of my ropes, and I told then to ignore my gear, as they could tow over the rope, with no damage to them or me.

One skipper asked me "what about your net"? and I told him if he caught it, then it was my fault, after that we all got on great, in 11 days fishing I only had two mishaps with another boat.

The first was a boat called the Castle Dawn, skipper Ollie Allcock, she was a small boat, about half the length of the Hatcliffe, well he caught my anchor in his net, I told him not to haul it, as the anchor would rip his net to shreds, so I heaved the anchor up, and cleared his gear, all he said to me was "that will cost you a pint".

A lot of skippers would have gone mad, but to be honest, he did catch the anchor, I did not know Ollie that well, but we ended up very good friends, the other little mishap was with a boat called the Silver Echo, to be fair to him I was shot in a very tight spot, and he had no room to get clear, Ken Foster the skipper, asked me if he was ok, I told him where I had dropped the net and he tried to miss it.

When we had hauled all the ropes in we had half a net, o well, I got on the VHF and said to him "when you haul, you will have the other half of my net on your starboard door, will you bring it in for me"/

It was more hope than anything.

But when he did haul his gear, there it was, hanging on his starboard door, he was amazed, and it did not harm his fishing, so we were both over the moon. One thing I did notice, after a couple of days, was that the first haul in the morning was very bad, so I started to sail each day, after the market had ended, also it gave the other trawlers time to tow away, to the North or the South, so when we arrived it was clear of most of the trawlers.

That is except for the lazy sods who slept in, another great thing about this day fishing was the fact that we had our dinner at home each night, and also we never carried ice, and at £20.00 a ton that was a saving, Kevin was fishing the NE Bank at the time, and doing ok, I think he wondered what I was piss farting about at, but there you go, I was making a profit and spending every night at home, also Mac always said to me, "if you are earning a living, never worry what the rest of the fleet are doing" thanks for that mate.

Now is the time I get really daft, I dropped the anchor one mile off the beach, in a little bay off newbiggin, as I had found out that there was cod going, with the local cobble's, it is against the law for me to fish inside the three mile limit, that is if I was Trawling, but it was ok to use the ropes.

So there I am anchored one mile from the land, (yes mad), while we were hauling on the first haul of the day, the fishery officer came out in a small launch, I bet he thought he had me.

When he arrived alongside he said that he thought I was trawling, he also told me that it was over 20 years since he had seen the ropes used in the bay, he was still tied up to us when the net came to the surface, I do not know who was more shocked, him or me, but we took 80 boxes out of that one haul.

Sometimes it pays to be daft, and this time it did, we did not go ashore that night, and the next day we caught nothing, zero, fu** all, how mad is fishing?

Any way Nat in the Frem was trawling about 15 mile off the land, and told me that he had a good haul, the wind was off the land and only about force five, I said to him that I did not want to run off in this weather, well he cracked up. "Trev you are used to fishing 200 miles off". Then we both cracked. He never let me live that down.

After eleven days fishing we made £12000.00, kev did a twelve day trip on the NE Bank, and made £13000.00, so to me we averaged the same, but I had a pint every night, nice trip Kev.

The Hatcliffe had to go on the slip, as we were having trouble with the shaft again, it needed a brand new one, so while she was out of the water Chessy decided to get the hull fully overhauled and painted.

So that is me out of work for at least two weeks, not that I minded, but wrong again, Chessy rang to ask me If I would skipper the Kingfisher while the Hatcliffe was dry.

Shit back on the little pink beetles again, he told me that he had some business to attend to in GY, to be honest I knew that he wanted to stop ashore and watch the football, world cup. And as I told you earlier in the book, I was not into football, so Trev is now the proud skipper of a boat, with an echo sounder that talked to me, at least I might get a sensible conversation with it.

My son Tony had left Kevin, for whatever reason, I did not ask, and he was already one of the Kingfishers crew, the other lad was called Norman Goldie, a very nice chap, another guy that never moaned, well I hate sailing with people who are always groaning about some thing or other, it seemed to drag the days out, I mean if I wanted to sail with a moaner I would take the wife to sea, let an expert do it. After three or four days decent fishing, after landing the Prawns, I was taking the boat into the gut, for the night, on the way in I brushed against a wooden stern trawler, it was not a collision, more a touch, so I carried on to the end of the gut and tied up.

All of a sudden I heard this mad voice, shouting at my crew, (Blue Murder). The skipper then came into my wheelhouse, he was ranting on about me wrecking his boat, now he must have thought that I was going to deny contact, but he got a shock, all I said to him was "skipper if I hit you and there is damage, then get your insurance man down, and it will be sorted" I think he expected me to deny hitting him, and was taken aback when I said that to him.

To be honest the way he was ranting, I did think about hitting him, (with my fist not the boat) but every body acts different in a crash, we could call it road rage, but this was more like water rage, or whatever you want to call it.

So the next day the two boats were kept in dock, so that both insurance assessors could look at the damage, now the skipper owner of the other boat was saying that we had cracked one of the ribs in the stem of his boat, but when his insurance man looked at it, he told him that the crack was years old, also that the most damage we had done was a small scratch on his paintwork, he was advised not to try a claim against us, and he did not, well I could not help myself, I went up the town and bought one of those spray paint match pots, and had it delivered to his boat, he never spoke to me again, but nice try mate.

So we had a day in, but the next day back on the prawns, when we hauled, and as the cod end came up to the back of the boat, Norman was about to put the lifting gear on, then he said "O SHIT look at this".

In the cod end was a massive war time mine, well it was mine now, and before I go on I will explain about fishing boats catching wartime memorabilia.

If you caught a bomb or mine, the German government paid us for the damaged gear, and any loss of fishing time, that is if it did not blow up, then they never bothered, as there was no proof. Anyway, well this one was ginormus, and for some strange reason, looked new, I hope they have not started again?

Any way we are told not to lift them aboard the boat, so I slacked the net away a bit, then we tied a rope around it, and started to tow it inshore, after telling the coastguard, I was told to cut it away off Tynemouth beach. I was also told to drop it in 4 fathoms of water, and that I did, or I thought I did, with having four echo sounders arguing with each other, and doing my head in, I turned three of them off.

I should have left the talking one on, as it would have told me what a dick head I was, but no I knew best. So I dropped the mine, and then cut the net away, when we got into Shields the police launch was waiting for us, and they had the bomb disposal squad aboard. By the way as we were towing it behind us our Tony said to me "are you worried dad"? I told him that I was, as if the net gave way we would loose three days earnings, he said "no dad what if it explodes" my answer was "you will never know about it son". He shook his head and put the kettle on.

The lads went for a pint (lucky sods) and I went to sea on the police launch, I had given the skipper the position, and he asked me to check it, now that annoyed me a bit, but there you go, so I did, and told him that it was spot on.

When we arrived at the mine, that had a buoy marking it, he said to me, "were you not told to drop it in 4 fathoms of water"? I replied that I was and that is what I did, do they think us fishermen are thick?

Well they are right as I had the stupid echo sounder that was in feet, not fathoms, any way the navy lads blew it up, and a few windows on Tynemouth rattled a bit, sorry all.

That was my skipper's job on the Kingfisher over, but we did get a new net from the German government, and three days loss of earnings, so everybody was happy. Great I have the Hatcliffe back so let's get to sea and earn some real money, and for the rest of the year we did ok, well my crew seemed happy. Chessy then decided to add another boat to his fleet, I say add, but what he did was buy another anchor boat, and part of the deal was to give the owner £40000.00, and the Kingfisher, in exchange for a boat called the Bennison, to be fair I think that was a good deal.

He then asked me to take the new boat skipper, and again I said "no way" and now I am beginning to think that he wants the Hatcliffe for himself, well he may own it, but the only way he will get her back is to sack me.

This swapping and changing is hard to keep up with, a Dutch lad Whillum, was now skipper of the Kingfisher, so with her being sold he is now skipper of the Bennison, I think, o well as long as I know what boat I have, that's all that counts. I say a Dutchman, but he fished from LT, with John Ord for a long time, and his English was broader Suffolk, than mine, I wonder if that is why they call it the broads.

Well how lucky is this, I came down to sail, and in the gut there was the Kingfisher, but all I could see of her was the top of her mast, yep she had sunk during the night, glad nobody was asleep aboard her.

Anyway she was refloated, and found to have a leek in her stern gland.

I had to feel sorry for the new owner, but I wonder if the echo sounder that talked was shouting HELP at the time. The rest of the anchor season passed without any problems, and we had a very good year, we grossed £150,000.00, for the year, but I was sat up Chessys flat, having a drink, when he put his computer on, and told me that the David Chester had beaten us by £20,000.00.

I said "great I knew kev had it in him" then Chessy asked me if I was sick, because a beginner had beaten my earnings? Sick? I was over the moon for him. The only time I worry about another boats earnings is if she is paying my bills. And she was not, so get in there Kev.

One thing was concerning me a bit, was the fact that the government had introduced new laws on, log books, mesh size and a lot more Bullshit; it had now come to the point that we needed an auditor to look after the paperwork. I mean the Prawn boats had been told that they had to tail small Prawns, and also the by catch of fish was reduced.

Has the fun, and the fight gone out of the UK fishing, also the boats now needed a fishing licence? It was a long time before I got a driving licence, but I still had a car. Also the DTI were getting stricter, on safety I agree with that, but the power in each port was put into one mans hands, if you upset him in any way, or if he was in his wife's bad books, then we suffered.

Sorry I am getting a bit political now, so back to fishing. And Trev got conned big time, Chessy told me that he was in the shit with the insurance company, as Whillem never had a skippers ticket, so would I pull him out of the shit by taking over the Bennison, after a lot of thinking, sorry I meant drinking, (he was filling me full of whisky) I agreed.

So now trev has finally left his beloved Hatcliffe, and was skipper of one of the worst boats ever to come out of Scotland, actually she was built on the plans of Saxon King, but smaller, there was only two built of her class, and the first went down with all hands. Have a relaxing Christmas Trevor.

1988

Well a new year, and a new boat, lets hope she is as lucky as the Hatcliffe, and Chessy getting carried away with the earnings had bought another GY anchor boat, she was the Mary Ronn, on the other hand he sold the David Chester to Kevin, and kev renamed her the Apollo, and the skipper of the Mary Ronn was no other than Taffy.

I wish he would not keep pinching my crew, and giving them a boat, so the new mate was Davy Butterfield, I knew him, but never sailed with him, to be honest I must be a lucky man, as Davy turned out to be a very good hand, and also a good friend. We also had a young lad called Norman, to be honest that was not his real name, but Davy said he looked like Norman Wisdom, so from that day on, he was known as Norman. I seem to remember his name was Andy, he was in the fishing college, and they asked me to take him. God that brings back some memories from 1963.

I did tell Norman about my college days, and the brass I had to clean, he looked around the boat, and saw no brass, I bet he thought thank god, there was some brass, but over the years it was now a nice shade of green, so why spoil it?.

Our very first trip was trawling for the dreaded pink beasties, but I had been given a chart for a spot just to the west of the NE Bank, and it was mostly night fishing, also the Prawns were a lot bigger, not many but a better price, for one box of the large Prawns, you needed 4 or 5 boxes of the crap that we caught off the Tyne, to make the same money.

Well our first tow the net came up in two, so that is a great start, we never had a spare Prawn trawl, so I put a small cod end onto the fish net, and hoped for the best, the first tow was ok, not great but if I plodded along on this much I would have a trip, after a month towing. No seriously it did not seem a lot, but it was top quality. While we were towing along the second time, the weather got a lot worse, from the NW, and by the time we hauled the trawl it was a full gale.

On hauling the wires in I told Davy to drop the doors inboard, and we would call it a day. (even though it was night) but you know what I mean, when we hauled the cod end in ,WOW about 10 boxes of large plaice and 3 of prawns. So I said to the lads, fancy another try? Davy said yes, and the other two did not count, so we shot away again. The bad weather lasted for two days, and the good fishing lasted the same, but on our last day the weather fined away, and the flat fish disappeared. I wonder why I can only catch fish in a gale; maybe they come out to play in bad weather, thinking all sane men are in the harbour.

O I forgot to tell you about one small point, during the gale, as we were hauling the bilge alarm went off, going down the engine room we found that the main pipe from the deck pump had broken, I hammered a large rag into it and stopped the flow of water, Davy then turned off the sea cock, hardly worth mentioning, but it was nice to see or hear the bilge alarm was in order.

Steaming into the Tyne to land a very good catch, and plus the whole fleet had been in dock for the weather, I passed one of the local boats on his way out, he spoke to me on the VHF and asked me how I had done, so I told him, 80 boxes of fish, and 25 of prawns, he then said "where have you been fishing Trev"?

And I told him. The cliff, now that is 20 mile SE of the Tyne, and I had been 35 mile NE of the Tyne, when he left the piers I saw him turn to the SE, well I know I should not tell lies but he was a guy that never gave me the time of day, when we were ashore. So fu** him.

When we did land, and got a great price, we had the weekend off. We tried another trip at the same spot, this time it was flat calm, we did ok, but no where as good as the first one. Maybe I should only go to sea in a NW gale, and stop ashore for the nice weather.

Well back on the anchor, and after last year I fished the inside grounds, we did ok, not as good but ok, and to me that is ok, hey I am learning to spell ok, with out looking it up, or using the spell check, and I bet my dear wife does not find fault with it.

Well she is my editor, so any mistakes in this book are your fault Pat, my Princess; I will stop grovelling now and get on with the book.

Well Joe had now taken over most of the lockers and cupboards on the boat, also his new name is Junk Shop Joe, as his hobby is buying anything going, all I get out of him is, "well it was a bargain" true Joe but do you need another jumper, as you have about twenty of them already, plus the lads had started to complain about his bathing habits, (or lack of them).

Anyway as it happens we were fishing the next trip, and Joe got pulled over the rail by the gear, but luckily he got clear of it, and was now doing the doggy paddle to keep afloat, I shouted "throw him a life belt, which they already had, then a voice shouted, "while he is in the water throw him a bar of soap".

I was just relieved to get him back, but as I said he would never make a fisherman, and after three years I decided he had to go. For his safety, and my sanity, sorry Joe.

At least now we had room in the lockers for the stores, and spare parts.

Every year in Shields they hold the blessing of the fleet, and all the boats dress up, and take the kids up the river to Newcastle quayside, and then back to shields, last year in the Hatcliffe we came second.

The Condowen got first, this year we had the theme of the wizard of oz, and came first. Big head.

We all dressed up in costumes, Davy was the tin man, and I was given the privilege of being the scare crow, the lads said it would save me hiring a costume. Cheeky sods.

But it was a great day for the kids, sadly the North Tyneside Council took it over, and it changed from a fun day out, into a money making racket. I then vowed that next year we would be fishing while the festival was on.

Chessy has done it again, Taffy decided that the wheelhouse was no place for him; I cannot understand that, as he did ok, and landed a decent trip, each time. He did tell me later that the worry of it all, was not worth it, I know what he means, and you have to be daft to be a skipper, which is why I have done it for so long.

Any way Davy Butterfield took over the Mary Ronn, and Trev got a new mate, but I seem to be a lucky sod when it comes to crews, the new mate, Davy Phillips, was in my eyes, another great bloke, and I could trust him with his job. The other man was called Mickey Dolton, a very strange lad, if he was moaning and groaning I knew that he was happy, but if he went quiet that meant I was in his bad books.

Lucky as I am he moaned most of the time, plus Mickey did the cooking, and not bad at all, remember I told you years ago, never upset the cook, well if Mickey was in a quiet mood, I lived on a cheese sandwich, and corn flakes.

The next trip we went to the deep water gully, the one I had discovered in the Hatcliffe, the fishing was great, strange as it was nice weather, and as I said the fish normally only come out to play in a gale, o well why moan, well Mickey Dalton did, he said that there was too much, and that I should slow down a bit, and if I did slow down he would have gone quiet on me, I just cannot win.

We only did six days fishing and then in to land, after landing the fish, taking ice and oil to sail again the next day, I called the office up on the VHF to find out what we had made for the trip of fish, they told me £13960, well I was over the moon, but a little bit sick that we never cracked the £14000, then I asked what the king crab legs made, and they said £70.00, now let me explain, ever since Norman had been with us I had let him keep the crab legs, and depending on the type of ground I was fishing on he got between £50 and £100 for them, as the lad was only on a trainees wage, and the odd treat off the lads, it made his money up a bit.

A bit?, wish I was keeping them, any way I told the office to add the lads money on to the trip, so now we made , £14000.30. Great my best single landing ever, I wonder what the rest of the fleet thought about that move, as they could all hear what was being said on the VHF. Hey do not get me wrong I gave Norman £100.00 out of my own wages. Now I know that I am the daftest man ever to take a boat to sea.

After the next trip I was told that the boat had to go on the slip for her DTI, that is like an MOT for your car, if I remember it was every four years, also Chessy had booked the slip in GY, so we had to take her down, when we arrived the crew went home to Shields, as the DTI inspection took about a week.

She had to have the shaft drawn, and x amount of spikes drawn, and a roll test, to see if she was stable,

Well I could have told them that she was NOT, and saved them the trouble.

Actually she was the only boat I had heard of that had to have a book, it was about her stability problems,

It gave the skipper instructions on how much ice and oil she was allowed to carry. When I gave it to the DTI man he said, "Ok I remember this one I made the book out myself", and I then told him that we only did eight days at the most, so I did not fill up with ice. He was happy with that, and passed her fit for sea.

Well they also found that she needed a new shaft, that meant another week out of water, and I stayed in GY, to do a lot of odd jobs on her, I rang Chessy and told him that I was coming home to Shields for the weekend, and would he OK it with the office for me to hire a car, on the boats expense.

He was not happy, but said "ok but not an expensive one" tight sod. So when I arrived at Chessys house in Shields, he looked out of his window, and there stood a top of the range Rover, plus I put the petrol on his account. He smiled and said "Trev if I had told you to get a good one, you would have got a wreck" and I agreed.

But he was happy when I told him that the insurance was paying for the new shaft, on the boat, he said "how did you manage that"? "Well there was this old bit of wire lying on the quay, and I told them that it came out of her screw" he shook his head and then told me that we would both end up inside. (Prison?).

"No way, if they had asked me, I would have told them that I was under your orders".

So he opened a bottle of whisky, and I got a taxi home. One of the great things about spending a couple of weeks in GY was the fact that I got to see the kids. Our Barry was down on the boat nearly every day, and I popped round to take Angie and Caz, for a treat or two. It was a brilliant feeling to have the girls chatting to me, and of course moaning about their step father, that they all hated, and I can be totally honest, by saying that I had tears in my eyes, with the guilt of leaving them.

Years later when they were grown up and had kids of their own, they both told me that I had done the right thing by leaving. Thank you girls.

HERE IS THE BENNISON SHE LOOKS OK BUT TO ME A FLOATING DEATH TRAP.

1989

Chessy has done it again, another anchor boat from GY, this time she is the Foursome, and I told you Shields would end up as a flat fish market. But for once he did not pinch one of my crew, as George Mussell had sold the Sandringham, and came up to take the Foursome away.

We now had six anchor boats based at Shields, and sadly the GY fleet were dwindling, a lot of owners decommissioned their boats, as the expense to run a boat was now out of hand.

I found that there was not a lot of fish on my normal fishing grounds. But I did here a whisper that there was fish at Helgoland, it may be 300 mile away, but there you go, or there we go.

I decided to give it a try, but no way was I going 300 miles just for one trip. The plan was to fish over there for as long as the fish lasted. So I told the lads, Davy and Taffy, that we would be landing in Denmark or Holland for the next two month or so.

I did not want to get all the way over there and have one of the lads saying that they missed home. Well I knew Taff was ok, but had to check with Davy, as he was married. It was ok with him, as long as we were earning money.

So we said good bye to our wives, and I told Lynn that I might be away for up to three months, wow three month without any moaning. I will think that I have gone deaf.

Steaming over took us two days, the weather was great, but too hot, actually at the time there was a heat wave over the north sea. When we arrived at the ground Davy told me that I had to catch fish fast, as half of the 5 ton of ice had melted, O shit, so that gives me two days to fill the 150 boxes that we had taken.

We had two hauls, for eight boxes, great only another 112 to go, the next haul was into stony ground, I had shot it years ago, and parted the rope, but who dares wins, as Dell boy would say, (only fools and horses). I never had any horses, but there was a fool on hand, doing the skippers job.

I was using 12 coil of rope a side, so that was shorter gear than the last time I was there, we did come fast on the stones, but luckily the rope pulled clear, with about 4 coil to come, one of the ropes came out of the water, and it was stranded. (Now a rope is made up of three strands, coiled round) but two of the strands had broken, while we pulled it over the stones.

I knew that when it came to the roller it would break, and any fish gathered lost. I put the clutch for the engine into astern, (reverse to you) to take the strain off the gear, luckily It came in and did not break.

When the net came up, it was a massive haul, at least 200 boxes, but a lot of the fish was under the legal limit. 12" so we had to dump it, and watch the gulls eat them, as the fish were now full of air, and could not swim back down, they would be eaten by the gulls.

Where is the sense in this stupid law, to me I agree with a legal size to sell, but why cannot the smaller fish, be given to the hospitals, and other needy places, I mean 2 year ago they were legal, and the buyers paid for them, but some dick head said that we now had to put them back, but I can promise you that none of the fish we returned to the sea lived.

And to be honest I was now thinking about giving it all up. My dreams as a young lad, was to fish until I was fifty. Then buy a pub on the Norfolk Broads, to live my life out in peace and tranquillity. But there you go dreams do not always work out as you want.

Back to that haul of fish, we had time for another haul, but with the heat I decided to call it a day, and head to Holland to land them, it took the three of us a long time to clear the deck, but at least they were fresh.

As I said it was extra hot, and when we were clear of fish, we went down the cabin for a sandwich, even 50 miles of the land we were plagued with flies, and that is not seen often. Well not that far off.

When we arrived in Holland, I went up to the office, told them that we had 120 boxes of small cod, but I only wanted 100, on the market. (Cash for the other 20) they told me that they had to ring GY and check that it was ok. "We may have GY on the bows, but we are a North Shields boat" so they rang the office in Shields, after Chessy told them to treat me as the owner, every thing was different, they could not do enough for us. (Phoney pricks). I told them that the fish was boxed.

They had landed about five GY boats in the last two days, and their fish was in bulk. They then asked me if I wanted shore labour to land the fish, I said no, as it was boxed we always landed our own fish.

With it being mid afternoon, we decided to go for a pint, on arrival at the bar I saw a few of my mates from the GY boats, Bob from the Ashvill days, was in, (that cheered Taffy up).

As we had to be up for 1AM, to land the fish, I said to the lads that we had better get some sleep, so we left the bar at 8 PM. Now the lager in Holland is very strong, also a lot more acid in it. When the alarm went off at midnight, well I thought I was dead, or wished that I was, Davy and Taffy felt the same.

I crawled along the quay, to find the man in charge of landing, and then told him that I wanted men to land the boat, he looked at his duty sheet, and said that I had told the office that my crew were to land the fish; I told him there must have been some mistake.

He got three lads to do it, I could have kissed him, then I went straight back to bed. Davy was not happy when I told him to keep his eye on the landing, but in my defence it is the mate's job, and to this day I feel bad about it, as Davy was suffering more than me. If that was possible.

In the morning I went up to the office, to find out what price we had got for the fish, also to pick the money up for the 20 boxes, that did not exist on paper. Well the price on the market was crap, well £10 a box lower than Shields, on that day.

When I asked for the cash, they told me that we had a lot of undersize fish, so they used that for the cash, fiddling sods, they knew that I could not complain, so they took their cut. Well I should not fiddle, as everybody jumps on the wagon. If I remember right we got £600 cash, £30 per box, piss off.

Anyway we then took on ice ready for the next trip, after storing up the harbour master told me to go and tie up with the other GY boats, I informed him that I was sailing in two hours, he was gob smacked, and told me that all the GY boats had two or three days in. I replied "not this one mate".

Before sailing we got the bond aboard. BOND? Well that is tobacco, drink, and things like coffee sugar and other things. Now fishing boats, working outside the three mile limit got the said things tax free, and that is a massive saving.

But in England this only applies to boats over 60 feet, so if your boat is say 59.9, then we are not allowed bond, and have to pay full tax. But if I an in Denmark or Holland, I then get it, no matter what the length of the boat is.

To me there is something wrong, when I have to land over seas to get a tax cut, so thank you to the English government, pricks.

Sorry getting political again, the book was a lot more fun when I was younger, but now I am old and cynical. Any way fu** that, we did sail that afternoon, to the surprise of the GY lads, and the harbour master, and ME, but I knew that we would be landing in a week.

I went back to the same anchor spot that we got the big haul off, and again it gave us 80 boxes, but the other hauls were down, big time. So I decided to land back in Shields, as we were on our last haul, the bogey man arrived, (fishery patrol boat), he said that he wanted to come aboard to check my nets, and catch.

Well I could not really say no, so I told him that he was welcome, as they arrived on board I was surprised to see that it was an English ship, so Trev is 60 mile off Denmark, and the same off Holland, and I have the English police on the boat, the first thing I said to him was "is there no foreign boats off the UK" so you have to come over here to check on us. I do not think he was very happy with that, but I did offer the boarding party a can of lager, but they turned it down.

I bet the three seaman would have had one, but the officer said no first, after checking the fish, and nets, they were ok, he then asked me for the ships papers, well the log book and other papers were kept in a water tight case, so I opened it for him, after going through them he asked me where our fishing licence was. I did not had a clue, so I said in the office in Shields.

He then told me that it was the law to carry it on the boat, I said I was sorry about that, and would make sure that it was on the boat as soon as we got in.

To my utter horror he then read me my rights, and told me that I would be hearing from the fishery office about this offence. Now where the fu** am I going to find a decent solicitor in the middle of the North Sea but he did say that I would only get a warning, as it was my first offence. Good job he never had my past record with him, or I would have been put in the brig. (A ships prison).

Great we then set off, back to my local waters, safer there as the bogey man was too busy looking after other waters. Steaming back across the North Sea, Taff called me for a meal, so when I went down to the cabin, Davy and I were sat across the table looking at each other, you will not believe this, there were no flies. Well no live ones, but hanging down from the deck head were 4 fly papers, and they were full of dead flies, if that does not put you off eating, then nothing will.

Fly papers are illegal in the UK, but not in Holland, and Taff had got some because he was fed up with the flies pinching his dinner, what a put off, I made a cheese sandwich, and then went back to the wheelhouse.

Taff had the cheek to ask me why I had a sandwich in my hand; I did not even bother to answer him.

Back in home waters, we had one day's fishing in the gully, and got 20 boxes for the day.

So Trev had just steamed 600 mile, and there was fish on the doorstep. But they only came out to play because they thought I was in Holland, but I fooled them, god I am clever, well lucky.

Well festival time again, but this year I was going fishing, away from all the bull, Taff stayed ashore to help out in the Tavern, (help out?) O well that was his excuse, we did not go far off, as there was a living at the cliff, (30 mile SE of the Tyne, Micky Dalton was with us, so I had to put the ear plugs in, sorry Micky, only joking.

The first day was not great, but with most of the fleet being in for the festival, it was a plod, on the second day, on the last haul, Micky decided to get a fish bone down the back of his thumb nail, I tried to get it out, but no chance, and for some stupid reason, he would not let me cut it off, at the wrist.

So sadly I had to take him ashore, for medical help. We got in to

Shields, about midnight, the mission man ran him to the hospital, I told him if he was fit for sea, we would be in the Dolphin,

As the Dolphin had been so busy, with the festival, there was no chance of an after time drink, but as we had just come in from sea, with a man on deaths door, they did give us a pint.

Anyway Micky came back, with his thumb all bandaged up, so I asked him if he was ok to sail, he said yes, I then told him to have a pint before we let go. But sadly, they had put him on antibiotics, so he had an orange, and then we sailed again, like I said, we were not catching a lot of fish, but we got a great price for them, as most of the fleet were in on the piss. I must apologise about the language, but if a fisherman reads this, he would not know what I was on about.

One morning I got a call from this lad, he told me that he was a free lance photographer, and he was interested in sailing on a fishing boat, so I said that I would meet him in the Dolphin, that dinner, well what he wanted was to sail with us for two or three trips, and take photos of us as a working crew.

I had no problem with this and after asking Davy and Taffy, we all agreed.

His name was Peter Fryer, and I found out later, that he had travelled the world, doing photo shoots, on what he thought interesting. He did tell me that the first week with us he would not use the photos in his gallery. The reason for this was that he wanted us to get used to him, and start to forget he was there.

Now to me that is a man who knows his job, wish I did.

Peter did three trips with us on the anchor, and I think he got a bit of a shock, what with our way of life, and the hours we worked. But credit to him, if we were at work, so was he, even more so, as he had to be up taking photos of us waking up in the morning. Pete did tell me that Amber Films were thinking of making a film about fishing. And most of all they were interested in anchor bashing.

So the crew was Davy Phillips, Taffy, and young Norman. To be honest the first week was a bit strange, with a guy taking photos, from the time we got up, until the end of the day, but like he told me, we got to not even notice him. And to me that is an artist at work.

Peter was a very genial guy, and I had a few yarns with him, while in the wheelhouse, and I could not believe the things that I was telling him. But he knew how to open a man up.

As I said, there was a local based film company, (Amber Films) and in with channel 4, they were going to make a film, based around the life of anchor fishing. They did approach Chessy about hiring one of his boats, to do the shots at sea, At the time we were averaging about £1000, per days at sea, so that is what he told them he wanted.

But to me that was being greedy, as the other boats were not averaging that. So Amber decided to go to Denmark, and buy a boat that had been decomissioned, which they did, and got a working boat for £6000. It was not allowed to land any fish that she caught, but that was the least of their problems.

So anyway back to sea, we fished the NE Bank that trip and it was good, now Davy Butterfield was skipper of the Mary Ronn, it's hard to keep up with Chessy and his skippers.

Any way we had a decent trip in and were ready for home, Davy was anchored about one mile from us, also doing ok, but he said to me that he needed a bottle of gas, and would I drop one off to him before I left. The lads had already scrubbed the boat down, ready for home, but when we got alongside of him, his crew decided to give us some spare eggs, they were thrown, and splattered all over our nice clean wheelhouse. Now Trevor not amused at this decided to return fire, and we did, with jam jars full of paint.

Well the Mary Ronns wheelhouse was grained wood, or it was, but it now had a very nice colour tone to it.

They do say if you start a war, some body else will finish it, and I thought we had, but no, my wheelhouse changed from white to dark blue blotches, yep they had done the same and made some paint bombs, not to be out done I decided to shut them up with a distress flair, now that would make them surrender.

One small problem, the flair I used was out of date; instead of going over to them it decided to blow up in my hand.

After the initial shock I looked at my hand, and was minus a thumb, or to be honest, it was still there, but hanging from a peace of skin. The mate looked at it, and then wrapped a towel around my hand.

Now I know why dad said "never play with fire" sorry dad forgot.

The next thing I knew was getting lifted off by a helicopter. Well as we were flying over the entrance to the Tyne, one of the crew of the chopper asked me if I wanted gas and air. I said "no way, if this thing goes down, I want to be all there" he said to me "mate if this thing goes down, I will be taking the gas not you" what a happy lad. At the time they were doing some work on the helipad, at the hospital, so we landed on the centre spot, at Newcastle Football ground. That is the only time in my life I had gone to Saint James's Park. Good job they never had a game on. I woke up the next day, and was shocked to see that I still had a thumb. Some clever sod decided to cut off the top of my hip, and rebuild the thumb, very clever really, except that my hip gave me more pain than the new thumb. But when I thought about it, I need a thumb to pick up a pint but the hip was not a miss. So thank you doctor, I wonder if he was thinking that when he did the operation.

I spent three weeks in hospital, as the hip went poisonous, but at least we could smoke then, when I got out Chessy told me that the relief skipper was fed up with the job, on the Bennison, so would I take her to sea?. Me with my hand still in a sling, and a metal rod down the length of the thumb, to hold it in place, so I said "ok" now that confirms my mental state. As it was I was bored, and ready to go back, also no deck work for me, not that I did much when I was healthy.

The boat was back on the prawns, as the relief did not do anchor bashing, but as it was nearing the end of the year I kept her on the trawling lark. It was great watching the lads sort prawns, and not feel guilty about not helping. O well my hand is still hurting with all this typing so see you all in 1990.

1990

I carried on with the Prawn trawling, as the hand was still not ready, (my hand, not the deck hand.) anyway one day Peter Fryer, (the photographer) rang me and told me that the Independent Newspaper were interested in doing a story of fishing from Shields.

As they had seen his photo gallery, (let go) on the Amber Film website, I told him it was ok and to set a date for the writer to come up, and sail with us, which he did, I cannot remember the chaps name, but no matter, as we were still day fishing, it was no bother. As we were towing along the first one of the day, I got chatting to the man, he told me that he did a lot of sailing, and as a part time job he delivered boats to other ports for the owners.

So great I have a second skipper on board, my son Tony was with us that day, as one of the lads had to stay ashore, and I never shouted at him once. (Mind you he was getting bigger now).

The first haul was very good, and the second and last of the day was even better; well I had to show off with a reporter aboard. Steaming back to Shields, the weather became very bad, and we were heading into it. I asked the guy to watch the wheel and the radar, so I could go out on deck, to help the lads sort the prawns.

No problem, I mean he had taken boats all around the world, so getting us to Shields was a piece of piss to him, or at least I thought so, after half an hour, feeling cold and wet, with Peter clicking away on his camera, I think he is as daft as me. I had to be out in this gale, he did it through choice, and yep Pete you are mad.

When the Independent magazine came out, it had a good write up, and the pics from Peter were great, that is except for one. He had taken a photo of us the next morning, as it was still a gale of wind; we all went to the Low Lights Tavern. It was 7AM, but that was normal, for the two fish quay pubs, they catered for the men who were up all night landing fish, and the fishermen, on a bad weather day.

When the gaffer of the Tavern saw the picture, and the quote under it. (The Tavern at 7 AM) she said to Taff "that will be my licence gone", sorry Rubel.

George Mussell, (Foresome) came into Shields with a very large catch of flatfish; they were all top class, off the Dogger Bank. Before he landed, I went on board to find out where he had been fishing, and he told me the spot, also the depth that the best hauls were in. as I was changing the Bennison back to the anchor, he had given me a great starting point.

We all got a shock at the price George got for his fish, it was very poor, and he vowed never to land in Shields again. Chessy told him that it was now a Shields boat. Also he did not want her landing in GY, both the skipper and the owner were now at loggerheads, (not timber merchants), but they were not happy with each other.

The next trip George did land in GY, Chessy being childish about this, decided to take the boat off him. As he never had another skipper for her, he tied her up, in the Ranger dock, until he could find one. And to me that was extra childish, George has always had it in his head that the reason he got the sack, was because I wanted the Foresome, well nothing could be further from my mind.

Hey I have just remembered an amusing incident. As I told you Chessy was a very big guy, he could eat for England, one day he and my son Tony were working on the Hatcliffe, doing a job on the rope reels, any way when they had finished he gave Tony a lift to the office, to get his money, on the way Chessy stopped at the fish shop, gave Tony some money and told him to get fish and chips twice, Tony got out of the car, as he was about to go into the shop Chessy shouted to him, "Tony if you want get your self some" when Tony told me that, I cracked up. Another day Tony and Norman Goldey were doing a job, on the Hatcliffs winch, I went on board for a yarn, while they were finishing off. When they did finish I asked if they were going to the Dolphin, they both said that they had no money on them.

Well I said "you get paid for doing the work on the winch". No it is part of the job, WHAT?

So I told them that they were share fishermen, not engineers, so if they work in dock, they should get paid. They were a bit wary about this, so I went in to the office with them and told the cashier to give them £20 each, and charge it to the owner. Well he shook his head and gave them the money; I think he just wanted to keep the peace, sensible man.

My younger son Barry who was 16 at the time, came up to Shields for a holiday, and asked me to take him to sea. Problem was I was doing ten day trips at the time, and as I remember he hated the one day on the prawns, I did warn him that once at sea there was no going back.

His answer "hey dad I am grown up now" o well we will see. We were to sail at 7PM, and we spent all day playing computer games, so I did not see the evening forecast, anyway off we go, when I was steaming out of the Tyne, Taffy came up to the wheel house and asked me if I had seen the forecast, I told him no. in 28 years of sailing together Taff had never questioned me about the weather, but this time he told me that they had forecast storm force winds.

The only reason he told me, was because my 16 year old son was on board, I turned round and tied her up, thank you Taff. And that night we got a violent storm in Shields, I was so glad that I came back in, as I said earlier, I do not believe in family sailing on the same boat.

After a couple of days it dropped away, so off we go, the fishing in my usual spots was very poor, so I went another 100 mile off, there were a few GY anchor boats plodding away, so I joined them, the first day fishing was ok, not great but a plod. That evening I moved the anchor to a wreck I had on my chart, and remembering the Sandringham, (lost anchor) tried to mark the wreck before I dropped it.

After an hour I could not mark it on the sounder, so dopy Trev dropped the anchor by the Decca readings.

The next day we had a decent days fishing, mostly cod, but when I came to lift the anchor, yes I have done it again, in the wreck.

I decided to give it another days fishing, but sadly there was nothing on the same ground, so I tried again to lift the anchor, but it was stuck fast, talking to another skipper, I told him that I was snagged in a wreck,

When I gave him the position, he told me that it was a well head, which I was caught up in.

O shit you do not mess with them, if it is a gas well and you damage it, the gas takes the buoyancy out of the water and down you go. So after three hours tugging and pulling I gave up, to my crews delight, (and young Barrys) and cut the anchor away. One tiny problem, I never had a spare one. Now that is very bad, for an anchor boat to go to sea with no spare anchor, I did have one but it was ashore, having new mud plates welded on.

I asked the GY boats in the area if they had one I could use, but for some reason they all said sorry no, so it was back to Shields for the Bennison, much to our Barrys relief. To this day Barry tells me that I was mad to try and get the anchor back, as the crew were saying how dangerous it was.

After two more trips it was time to change over to the wee pink beasties again. (Prawns). But as luck would have it another skipper, Alan Jenkins, who owned a boat called the Janet Jenson, asked me if I fancied going pair trawling for the winter months, well I went for that straight away, I did not even ask Chessy if it was ok. I told him, and he knew from past years not to argue with me.

The cost of the change over was very cheep, as Alan had a hard ground net; also Dicky let us use his fine ground one. So off we go, the first tow we shot the fine ground net, and towed over the ground about 15 mile off Hartlepool, Alan knew that spot well, so he was the skipper, and I just sat back and let him do the worrying, on hauling we had a great catch of flats, also about 4 boxes of lemon sole, (big money fish).

I was very surprised when Alan shot the hard ground net for the next tow.

But he told me that there was not much fine ground in that area, and who am I to argue with him. We did three days fishing, and made £7800.00. That will do me, better than sorting prawns.

The main thing is we got on well with each other, and with pair trawling that is VERY important. There can only be one skipper, and on those grounds he was the expert, big head. Thank you Alan. Well it is Christmas again, god it comes round quicker the older you get.

1991

Well all it is nearly the end of my days at sea, bet you all guessed that, as you are near the end of the book,

And I promise not to write Grand dad Boats 2. Over the Christmas holidays I was asked by Chessy if I wanted a half share in the Foresome, on the same terms as the Island, to be honest, he was sick of it being laid up. But I did agree and took her pair trawling with Alan.

To be honest, even after 4 years in the Bennison, I still did not feel safe in her, where as the Foresome was a very good sea ship. We did a couple of trips pair trawling, but not as good, to be honest I wanted to be anchor bashing, as it was a lot less expense. But until I got her running, I took her on the prawns. A mate of mine Davy Noon took the Bennison.

Little Charlie and Taff was now my crew, can you remember Charlie? From the days in the Ada Jean. Well he was still a little fireball in drink, you would have thought he had grown up by now, but he seemed worserer than ever, but still a great fisherman. One evening while we were taking the last haul on board, one of the alarms went off, at first I thought it was the bilge alarm, but when I looked aft I saw smoke coming from the engine room hatch.

When I looked down, it was an inferno, no way was anyone going down there, well I was thinking of sending Charlie, but even Trev cannot be that cruel. As luck would have it, the Foresome was very up to date, thank you Board of Trade. We closed the engine room hatch, then opened the two bottles of gas, that took away all the oxygen, I think it was co2, but lets not get technical, as long as it put the fire out, who gives a fu**. And it did.

Any way we got towed into Shields, and on inspection it was the wiring that had caught fire, and so the whole engine room had to be rewired. Hey do I really want half share in this tub. Anyway it took three days to get her ready for sea, little Charlie lived 15 mile away, so he decided to stop on board. Chessy gave him £20 a day for watching the job.

Now that is a laugh, as Charlie could not watch himself, it was like giving an Indian Firewater. In the years I knew him I could always tell when he had drank too much, as he used to start singing this song, apparently it came from the men who sailed for a firm in Newcastle. The shore Seville line, the annoying thing about it was that he only knew the one verse. So when he was drunk we knew it was coming. It must have imbedded in my small brain as I can still hear the words, and often sing them, how sad, but maybe not. Here is the ditty.

> The mate's on the foredeck and looking so grim
> Cos somebody threw a tomato at him
> Tomatoes don't hurt when they come in a skin
> But by fu** they do when they come in a tin
> Heave away heave away, from the alehouse to the jailhouse
> Is a fu**ing long way.

It should have been put on his grave stone, but at least he left me the memories, as a lot of my ex shipmates did.

So after the repairs I changed over to the anchor, the same as my last trip in the Bennison, there was very slack fishing on my normal grounds, to be honest it was slack fishing for all of the GY anchor boats. By now at least half of them had been sold or scrapped, the government paid the owner to decommission their boats, and they got more money than the boat was worth as a going concern. Sadly it was the owner who got all the money, but the crews were not even thought of.

So with a lot less boats the deck crews started to get jobs on the oil rig standby boats. (Ex trawlers) and it got harder for the boats still fishing to get decant crews.

Any way I steamed off another 150 mile and was back on the Nameless Bank. (and it is still a stupid name), we were averaging about 3 boxes a haul, then we got hit by a gale, so we laid with the storm gear out for two days. I then heard that the shore radio was trying to contact us, and as I said before, you always think of the worst.

When I got the call, it was from the wife, she told me that we had got the tenancy of the Dolphin pub, which surprised me a bit, as I did not know we had put in for it.

She informed me that we were to move in to the pub in three days, and also it was only £5000. Take my advice guys, never get a joint account.

As the fishing was crap, the lads said that I should be there to do the move, in other words, our skipper has a pub, so let's get in and drink it dry. My life long ambition was to retire to a pub, but I was thinking more on the lines of a nice quiet one, on the Norfolk Broads, not one on a fish quay, but there you go, got to start somewhere. But I never did get my dream pub.

Even though we now had a bar, I still wanted to stay fishing, so I put the Foresome back on the prawns, just until we had got the Dolphin running, at least I would be in every night.

For the first couple of weeks things went ok, Lynn ran the pub, and I went to sea every morning, but one day as we were letting go of the ropes to sail, a guy came up and told me that the alarm was going off, at the Dolphin. I ran straight back to the pub, but all was ok. After that I could not settle while I was at sea, and decided to stay ashore to watch the bar.

I hated it when the lads came in after landing, they stood at the bar, talking about the days fishing, and telling the usual lies about where they had been, or not been, moaning about the prices of prawns, and my drink, but there you go.

I had a new life now, but there was no thrill of the chase, and definatly no fresh air. I am not going to go on about my 5 years in the pub, as it was to me boring and not part of my life at sea, to be honest we did run a lot of fund raising events for the RNLI, and I even ask if I could sign up as a crew member.

They said that as I was over 40, I was not considered for the job, how mad is that, all my working life at sea, plus a skipper's ticket, but at 41, I was too old? But I still praise every crew of every lifeboat in the world.

After two years in the pub, a lad named Paul Dowse, asked me if I would take his boat away for a couple of days, I bit his hand off. The boat the Industry was pair trawling with his brother's boat, Condowan, I knew his brother well, as his wife was one of the barmaids in the Dolphin, John Dowse.

When we got to sea, John shot his net, for the first tow, but while we were shooting the warps trev made a big fu** up, and lost the wire over board. It took John 3 hours to get the net back. I bet he was thinking that he should have had a couple of days off as well. After that every thing went ok, and we did well, after two days fishing, I got £300 so that will do me, thank you John.

Another relief from the pub, was one day a lad told me he was selling his coble, and the price seemed ok, but I wanted to do a couple of days at sea with him to check her out, when I say days, well he sailed at 8AM lifted 4 gill nets, re laid them, and was back in dock by midday. That sounds good to me, one small problem, the nets were rotten and needed replacing, and they do not come cheap.

I took her to sea for a week, and decided that although the boat was decant, the price was not, for once in his life Trev made a sensible move and turned it down.

One last very sad event to finish off. A very good friend of mine, and 99%of the lads in Shields, his name was Eddie Smith, but we only knew him as Jeckles. He was ten years older than me; he had been a fisherman all his life, from the deep water trawlers to the prawn boats. I honestly never heard a bad word said about him. He was living aboard this boat, and every night he came ashore to have a couple of drinks in the Tavern, and then across to the Dolphin for a few more. He was normally drunk on returning to the boat, but either I or the gaffer of the Tavern used to walk back with him, to make sure he got aboard ok.

One particular night he told the barmaid that he was going to see his grand child the next day, so he left the bar SOBER and early. Well Jecks had gone through all that the sea could throw at him, but sadly he lost his life in the Tyne. Shields was notorious for men being lost in the dock. But this time it was a massive hit to all that knew him. It was the biggest funeral I had ever attended. So RIP JECKS.

It just goes to show, that not only can the sea be cruel, but also life, so enjoy what you got.

1995

Well it had to happen, Lynn and I split up in 1995, and it was not a very amiable parting, but there you go, part of life.

The reason I have skipped a few years is that this is my life at sea, not a pub.

When I left the bar Stanton Clay put me up for a while, or do I mean put up with me for a while, well whatever. John Ord came round and said to me "come to sea for a couple of days, it will give you time to calm down, and think, so I did, and that was a great help. Thank you again John.

I never bothered to try to get the marriage back on line, as deep down I knew it was over a year ago. I got a flat in a retired fishermen's home, and decided to get on with it.

The reason I am writing this last year is because I went back to sea for a trip or two, the next boat I sailed on was called the Margit, and the skipper was no other than Nat Herd, a long time friend. But sadly the other crewman was worried about me being reported to the benefits office, so he would not sail with me again. That's a laugh, he was not worried about me getting caught, but he was on the dole himself. To keep the peace I left.

After a couple of weeks ashore, Nat asked me to take the Margit for e week, as he had to go on some stupid training course. If not he would loose his dole money.

So I did, it was not very nice weather that week, but we sailed every day, and did one long tow then hauled the net and steamed back into Shields. We did not break any records but we went ahead.

On my very last day at sea the owner came on board, we were stood in the wheelhouse chatting away, when he asked me why I had three pairs of glasses in the rack, well I told him that I used one for the chart, another for the normal sight, and the other for the sun.

I did say to him that I could see for miles, but up close I needed reading glasses for the chart. Peter then said "pin the chart on the mast and you will be able to see it" do you know what it is? In all my sea life, I could never win.

But I would not change my past life at sea for the world.

Anyway to all my relations and friends, and future generations, I only ask one thing of you.

If you see a seagull taking food off your bird table, please do not scare it away.

As it might be one of my shipmates.
And if it is looking at you it may be
GRAND DAD BOATS.